Overwhelming Victory

Overwhelming Victory

by

Graham Turner

HARPER & ROW, PUBLISHERS
New York, Hagerstown, San Francisco, London

To Roger and Garth,
two of God's troubadours
who helped me find new life

OVERWHELMING VICTORY was originally published in England under the title MORE THAN CONQUERORS.

FIRST UNITED STATES EDITION

ISBN: 0-06-068780-0

LIBRARY OF CONGRESS CATALOG CARD NUMBER: 76-62941

77 78 79 80 81 10 9 8 7 6 5 4 3 2 1

'*Who shall separate us from the love of Christ? Shall tribulation, or distress, or persecution, or famine, or nakedness, or peril, or sword?* ... *Nay, in all these things we are more than conquerors through him that loved us. For I am persuaded, that neither death, nor life, nor angels, nor principalities, nor powers, nor things present, nor things to come, nor height, nor depth, nor any other creature, shall be able to separate us from the love of God, which is in Christ Jesus our Lord.*'

SAINT PAUL
Romans VIII

Contents

Preface

I THINK IT is safe to say that few books have strayed so far from their original design as this one. It began life as a history of money in the dim and distant days of 1968 when, as the BBC's economics correspondent, I was struggling to illumine the mysteries of paper, gold and invisible exports for those who understood even less about them than I did. Since I was also a member of the post-war generation which had pursued money and its fruits with such ardour, I felt at least spiritually well qualified to write such a book!

Then, in 1970, I went through an experience which led to fundamental changes in my own life. Basically, what happened was that I decided to try to live like a Christian again after having forsaken my faith in favour of making a name for myself in the world.

The details of what happened are not of any particular importance, but it is perhaps worth saying that my change of direction involved paying a visit to the tax-man to admit that the way I had been filling in my tax-returns hadn't been all that might be expected of a serious-faced young man who regularly appeared on television indicating that our economic masters were not behaving as they should!

I had, in fact, been falsifying my expense-sheets with an expertise born of long practice. They always included a monthly lunch with a figure I described as 'the senior economic adviser to the Treasury'. I had *never*, in fact, had lunch with any such gentleman! The upshot was a modest gain for the Inland Revenue's income for that year.

I then began to feel that I wanted to write a very different sort of book, and the idea occurred to me of telling the stories of modern disciples, who found what St. Paul calls 'overwhelming victory' over the kind of predicaments which would defeat most of us — drugs, a brutalising childhood, a wrecked career, incurable disease, physical handicap, grinding poverty, the bitter gall of racial discrimination, and so on. Men and women, that is, who had not merely endured or survived those predicaments but triumphed over them and emerged with their spirits enriched.

I did not start out with a circumscribed idea of what I was looking for, apart from that inner radiance which shines out of those who have found real victory, and the total honesty which springs from a penetrating vision of ourselves.

I am myself a convinced Christian and, for that reason, was no doubt heavily predisposed towards stories which were Christian in impulse. Nine of the eleven 'conquerors' are Christians of various denominations and of none, one is a Hindu with Christian inspiration and one is a man whose story echoes the repentant David in the 51st Psalm: 'The sacrifices of God are a broken spirit; a broken and a contrite heart, O God, Thou wilt not despise.' His is one of two stories where I have felt it right to disguise the identity of the subject. The other is the story of Anna in 'The Acid Test'.

The search for stories which covered the widest possible spread of age, environment and predicament proved long and fraught with difficulty. It is one thing to know what you are looking for, quite another to find it. Several times, I almost gave up the search; on each occasion, another of the eleven appeared. It was an arduous but faith-building experience.

The first was a woman who was then dying of cancer. She was an old acquaintance of mine but, although I had spent the previous Christmas close to where she was staying, I had steered clear of going to see her — partly because I was afraid of cancer, partly because I felt the disease might have ravaged her so badly that my distress would show and make her plight worse. I nevertheless had the strongest sense of inner direction to telephone her husband and ask if it would be possible to see her. To my amazement, he seemed delighted to hear from me and pressed me to visit them immediately because, he said, his wife so much wanted to share all she had found while still able to do so. So it was that I spent the last active weekend of her life with Myra Macnicol, whose story is told in the chapter 'And Death shall have no Dominion'. That weekend, I lost my fear of cancer and sensed, for the first time, that the borderline between life and death was far less important than I had previously believed.

This, in itself, was a surprise to me. I had tacitly assumed that my job in writing the book was to find compelling stories and then tell them in such a way that they would help other people. The idea that I would learn something from them myself hadn't crossed my mind!

That lesson was driven home when I met 'Painter B', a young Canadian spastic introduced to me by a friend. 'People talk about "the handicapped",' he said, 'but would you tell me who is more handicapped, a man like me who can't hold his coffee cup steady or a father who loses his temper with his children?' As one who has lost his temper with his children all too often, I found the answer to the question painfully obvious.

I have already said that I often grew discouraged in my search. My lowest point came when I flew to Norway to meet a man who had indicated that he would be willing to tell his story. When I arrived, he told me that he felt he could not, after all, help me. This threw me into the deepest gloom—the cost of the flight and the week in Oslo ... the waste of my precious time ... all this rumbled around inside me, and I was soon venting my displeasure on the Almighty and asking Him bitterly what He meant by leading me up such a costly blind alley?

After four days of moods and savage internal recrimination, one of my long suffering Norwegian friends suggested that there was another man in the country whose story I ought to tell. My immediate reaction was to pour cold water on the idea. I didn't, I said, want a second painful experience in the same week. In any case, the man he had in mind lived five hours by car from Oslo and, since I was only due to stay in the country for another day, it seemed like yet another wild-goose chase.

My friend, however, was not deterred and discovered that the man was not only in Oslo for the day but also had an hour free that evening. That was how I first met Erling Stordahl. He and his wife, Anna, then invited me to spend a week in their home in the Norwegian mountains at the end of our summer holiday that same year, and their story is told in the chapter 'The Dark is Light Enough'.

Another of the stories came out of a meeting with an American diplomat in Geneva. I told him about the book I was writing and asked if he knew anyone who might qualify. 'The face of a man comes into my mind immediately,' he said, 'but unfortunately I can't remember his name.' He introduced me to another man who *could* — the name was John Armore — and, when I finally made contact with Armore by telephone, he said immediately that he had been wanting to tell his story and happened to have three days free in San Francisco at the time when I was passing through the city. His story is told in 'The Man Upstairs'.

In ways like these, the stories were given to me; I say 'given' because, in a curious sort of way, they were more given than found. To me, they make up a marvellous tapestry of God at work in the human heart. They also, collectively, give the lie to many of the prevailing philosophies of our age, which tell us that we shall find our heart's desire through ease, riches or protest. These, by contrast, are the stories of men and women who have found their victory by way of affliction, humiliation, adversity, hardship, sorrow and pain, the very things which our civilisation has tried to edit out of existence but which recur with greater and more disturbing persistence the more we try to banish them. Perhaps, after all, they — and not comfort, higher earnings or greater material security — are what many of us need to help us find God.

I

The Acid Test

HERS, SAID ANNA, had been one of those sheltered, magic childhoods. Everybody had plenty of money, everybody was having plenty of fun, everybody's kids were looked after, everybody's father built them igloos and made them snow-suits in the winter; the background always seemed to be a forest. Only one couple they knew ever got a divorce, and Anna's parents never saw *them* again; among their friends in Oregon, divorce simply wasn't in fashion.

Anna is thirty now, tall, blonde and with a rangy beauty which makes you imagine she would be at home on horseback or the golf-course. Her smile, too, is open and expansive, but tinged with a kind of rueful radiance, which suggests that she has known great unhappiness and also, perhaps, found great joy. The way she deals with her two small children—Joshua, aged five, and Rebecca, aged two—carries the same suggestion. There is in it the tenderness and sense of gratitude of one who is thankful to be alive.

The trouble really started when Anna went away to college in 1963. Until then she was, to all external appearance, a model of staid conformity. She had been moderator of her church youth group and a camp counsellor for the local YWCA; she dressed in a highly conventional way and she did what her parents told her. That autumn, as they proudly waved her goodbye, there was no hint of the tempest to come.

But college, as Anna's mother put it, 'wiped her out'. At first, she was wildly happy. Suddenly, there was nobody to tell her when to go to sleep and when to wake up, and the talk went on and on through the night. Old habits and values began to seem ridiculously antediluvian. While the other girls wore jeans, Anna was still ironing her blouses and pressing her skirts, and a girl who had never heard the word 'damn' spoken at home found herself often walking in on her room-mates, in bed with their boyfriends. As she said with a wry smile, 'I had to learn not to set my hair every night.'

The shock was too sudden and too massive, and Anna caved in. She had already started drinking the previous year on a high-school trip to Europe; now she got drunk regularly. She also began to steal. Her job in the college book-store provided the ideal opportunity, and she took books, money and anything else she thought she needed. At one point, there were 2,000 stolen books in her room. At the time, she saw it as 'stealing love'.

To help cover up her sense of gaucherie and inferiority, Anna also conferred upon herself an imaginary IQ of 165 and frequently lied to her friends about her academic prowess. The lies brought some superficial respect, but Anna hated herself for telling them and felt all the more insecure.

Everything she touched seemed to turn sour. A flirtation with her German teacher blew up in her face when she found him kissing another girl, and she broke off the relationship. The teacher thereupon threw up his job two weeks before graduation and told the Dean of Women that he was leaving because of Anna. Not surprisingly, Anna failed the German course and, at the end of the year, her parents decided it would be better if she didn't go back. 'We just hadn't prepared her for what she found,' said her father remorsefully.

In the wake of humiliation came bitterness; it was then, said Anna, that she really began to hate her parents. One day at church, when a woman asked about college, Anna's mother put her arms round her daughter's shoulders and told the woman that Anna was just 'taking leave of absence'. It was the first time she had ever heard her mother lie, and she despised the subterfuge. At about the same time, she started experimenting with drugs: aspirin, she hoped, might help 'push back the darkness a little'.

Later that year, she went back to college, this time in her own home city, and had soon plunged headlong into her first full-blown affair, with a boy she had known from high school. It was highly romantic. He brought Anna roses, they sang songs and she poured forth a flood of passionate verse. Then, suddenly, the man told her he didn't want to marry her, and, in a twinkling, paradise had become purgatory.

Anna felt spoiled and ruined. Bitterly hurt yet again, she became promiscuous and even made an effort to earn money from sleeping with men. Her career as a prostitute, however, was mercifully brief; her total earnings only five dollars. She also started a sort of one-woman crusade against male heartlessness. If any of her friends was jilted, Anna would try to start an affair with the man involved so that she, in turn, could hurt him by breaking it off.

Desperate for help and attention, Anna turned to the college counselling service. It was not a reassuring experience. Her first counsellor was a minister who was institutionalised as a manic-depressive; the second, a man who seized Anna's hand and insisted 'you've got to let me love you'. She responded by deliberately talking gibberish.

This search for attention was accompanied by carefully orchestrated outbreaks of violence. Once, Anna wrecked her room at home, but, as she said, she only tore up the blouses she didn't want and smashed the records she didn't like. Then she began pretending that she was hearing voices. After all, that was what everybody *said* you did when you were mentally sick. The result was that her parents took her to the local mental health centre. Anna was delighted – at last she was going to see a fully-fledged psychiatrist – and, as she said, she nourished the illusion that 'something external could fix me up on the inside, clean up my life and take the consequences of my actions'.

Anna's psychiatrist recommended that she be given a spell in a country club for the mentally ill – 'candlelight dinners, arts and crafts section, the whole deal'. With her father paying out $250 a week, Anna knew she had his full attention. Part of the elaborate and dangerous game she played while she was in hospital was to pretend to assume a completely different character. Her own surname was – she felt – much too common, so she invented others. Her favourite pseudonym was Leota Sundust. At other times, she assumed an *alter ego*, Carrickael, who was frantically and chaotically disorganised. It was not, said Anna, a manifestation of schizophrenia, but rather an attempt to protect herself from having her feelings hurt still further.

The country club was an expensive and fruitless interlude on a path which led steadily downwards. Anna became the mistress of Johnny, a young archaeologist who was in the city to work for a second degree. That year, she recalled, she was drunk almost every day, she stole systematically — mainly from grocery stores — and she started smoking marijuana.

Then, one day, a band came to town; one of the players was a man known as Buzz. Buzz was the son of rich parents and he had become an alcoholic at the age of fourteen. His wife had recently left him for another man. His life was in tatters; he was so drunk most of the time that he had to be fed.

When Anna met Buzz, she immediately recognised a kindred spirit. They were two deeply wounded people desperately trying to find their bearings in life. Buzz didn't attempt to make love to Anna. He told her that he didn't want to repeat his parent's mistakes; he just wanted to find God and make his women happy. Without love, he said, the whole trip was a waste of time. For the first time, Anna felt she had a real friend with whom she could share things. Buzz, she said, 'understood the crumminess inside me'. Two weeks after Buzz came to town, Anna had dropped out of college again; she began living with the band and, in an effort to try to help Buzz, gave up alcohol herself.

Before long, however, they heard about the drug LSD through a friend, and decided to experiment with it. The impetus came almost entirely from Anna, who by this time felt so desperate about herself that she was ready to try anything to find an alternative to what she called 'all that short-haired stuff'. In a real sense, it was an expression of a deep inner hunger. In the world which her parents inhabited, she felt, all the pressure was for material success. To her, it was a choice between a philosophy which told her to 'keep your hair in pin-curlers every night, wear your skirt the right length, get a job at Bell Telephone, then go have some sharp-faced kids and be miserable' or, somehow, discovering a completely different way.

Religion, as she had seen it practised, did not seem to offer any alternative. To her, it wasn't real religion at all, because it didn't affect people's lives deep down. You couldn't tell whether somebody believed in God or not, and the people who went to church were no different from Joe Blow down the street, who didn't. She herself had been to church a good deal, but nobody there had ever talked to her about what she was going to do with her life on a spiritual basis. As she looked back, all she could remember were church youth conferences where there'd been endless discussions on subjects like immortality. Once, she recalled, they discussed the statement 'I, as a Christian, do not believe in immortality', and they had been told that the word 'immortality' was only used five times in the New Testament, three times in the sense of deathlessness, twice in the sense of freedom from sin . . . It had all been like that; they had never talked about the real things of life, the things which were troubling her. 'Immortality', she remarked with a grin, 'didn't happen to be my problem. I'd been searching all through high school, and it never seemed to touch you where you lived. I found a series of books called *I Believe* and thought, this is it at last, but they were so shallow! We were idealistic kids – if only the grown-ups had come in and said something real, instead of giving us immortality classes and vespers. Even so-called religious people seemed to be saying, "Don't be idealistic." The system just didn't respond to the deep needs, the loneliness in people like me.'

So, she and Buzz turned to LSD. To Anna, its promise was 'an inner journey to the basics', a new perception, a new understanding of what life was really about. It seemed to be 'the only brave road', the only spiritual hope in a world of cover-up. As she said, 'I didn't have any God to tell me what to do.'

The experiment with LSD rapidly led to addiction; Anna 'dropped acid' whenever she could get it. Indeed, if it had not been for Buzz, she would have started taking heroin. That, he resolutely refused to allow.

In the spring of 1967, they were married. Anna was still carrying a child conceived with her previous lover, Johnny. That summer, driving back alone from a trip to Mexico, she took dexedrine tablets to help her keep awake. Despite them, she dozed off, her car overturned and she found herself with blood pouring down her face and copies of her poems blowing up and down the highway. In hospital, she swallowed the rest of the dexedrine and produced a spontaneous abortion of the baby.

By the autumn, she had become another man's mistress (she and Buzz were divorced in November) and she began experimenting with a psychedelic drug called STP. She took a dose every morning as soon as she got up, followed by a Valium tablet at night. The only meal she ate was breakfast, which consisted of a bowl of rice, a soft-boiled egg and a glass of grape juice. Within weeks, she had lost twenty-five pounds.

The effect of the drugs also made nonsense of her effort to go back to college yet again. In class, she would try to look at her notes and find that she couldn't even see her notebook. Nor did the most appalling tragedies among her friends give her second thoughts. A man who had been taking LSD and living with one of her girl-friends blew out his brains. Anna felt sorry for the girl, but still offered her more LSD. The following day, at her own birthday party, she gave away 300 dollars' worth of the drug and was so much under the influence herself that she imagined her mother was the White Rabbit from *Alice in Wonderland*.

These were years of anguish and crushing disappointment for Anna's parents. They lived in constant fear of a telephone call which would tell them that some fresh disaster had befallen their daughter. At about the same time, their only son volunteered for service in Vietnam. Anna's mother was heartbroken; she felt she had lost her son too.

Nevertheless, neither she nor Anna's father ever either rejected her, or entirely lost hope. She remembered so well how her own mother had remained loyal to her father, even though he had often been helplessly drunk and incapable of providing enough money to keep the family going. 'Anyway,' she said, 'I've always believed in excellence, not perfection. If you are a perfectionist, you have to get it right first time round—perfectionists never make mistakes —but excellence you have to grow into.'

Anna's mother also took some comfort from observing the enormity of the world's problems and then reminding herself that her family certainly weren't the only ones in trouble. For the rest, she prayed more often, helped Buzz and Anna where she could and, when the sense of despair became too great, tried to lose herself in voluntary work for the church and community. That, she said, stopped the anguish swamping her altogether. The experience stripped away at least one long-held illusion. Previously she had always thought that she was God's gift to parenthood. Now it was transparently obvious that that wasn't true.

The agony, moreover, had only just begun. The next spring found Anna remarried to Buzz and seeking salvation through the Eastern religions. She began studying books like the Chinese *Book of Changes*, and the Tibetan *Book of the Dead*, which she'd first heard about through Timothy Leary's *Psychedelic Experience*. That summer, after smuggling a consignment of drugs across the Mexican border, she and Buzz headed for the Sierras east of San Francisco. They were determined to transcend, to rise above the pettiness of the world they saw around them and, in particular, to free themselves from the shackles of their own sordid flesh. They ate brown rice from a conch-shell, lived a completely celibate life and spent a good deal of time reading from their religious books. They wanted, said Anna, to be as much like Buddhist monks as possible.

After a few weeks, she began to feel ready for social service, which she whimsically imagined might include playing basketball for her church youth group. Buzz, however, soon brought her back to earth. 'If we're gods,' he remarked drily, 'this god wants a hamburger.' He walked back to San Francisco alone and went on a massive drinking binge. He had not touched alcohol the whole summer.

Anna followed later and lived for a short time in a commune where free love was in vogue and (sex apart) everyone was trying to be his or her own universe. This involved drinking your own urine which, Anna recalled, she found rather difficult.

When she finally arrived home she found Buzz living with a group of heroin addicts. These people, she gathered, had succeeded in transcending, and Anna began to feel that she must be the only stupid person in the universe because, for all her efforts, she had failed to reach the blessed and peaceful state for which she yearned. She longed, she said, to be pure, in every sense. She wanted to be free of jealous thoughts and envy and making judgements on other people, for she felt that one of her biggest faults was criticising other people in her heart.

She had a vision of a vast banquet hall and all the people who had succeeded in transcending—they were all unselfish, they all loved one another—and of herself, in a white dress, slumped at the dining table. Then she heard people chanting 'Come on, baby ... come on, baby', and she knew she had to cross a river, but she didn't know how to go about it. On another trip, she became all the seasons—she was winter, then spring, then summer—and, through it all, she thought she heard her mother's voice calling out, 'Anna, Anna.'

As time went on, the delusions became stronger and stronger.

She imagined she could smell her own flesh burning and, when four friends came to take her out, she thought they were the Four Horsemen of the Apocalypse. That evening, she tried to poke out one of her eyes and open her 'third eye', through which she would be able truly to see. Then she imagined she was walking beside the River Styx and could hear the dogs of Hades barking at her from the further bank. At this point, Buzz and the others wrestled her back into the house, called an ambulance and took her to the Psycho Ward at the County Hospital. There, she was put in a single room and her arms and legs strapped down for a whole week. That was how she spent Christmas 1968.

The doctors asked Anna how often she had taken LSD or STP. Buzz had told her not to answer questions like that, but she was desperate and admitted it was between 300 and 400 times. Then came the 'sanity hearing', when it seemed to Anna that the lawyer and the psychiatrist were fighting over her as if she wasn't there. The lawyer said he didn't think she needed to be committed to a mental institution. The psychiatrist replied that Anna couldn't even find the door to his office. Occasionally, Anna would try to plead with them not to send her away, but they ignored her and she was committed to the State Mental Hospital. Her medical documents described her as a catatonic schizophrenic.

It was a place, said Anna, for broken derelicts, for people with no relatives and no money, a place where nobody cared for you and nobody visited you. It was in this place that her dark night of the soul reached its climax. She could not sleep and found herself ceaselessly beset by delusions, by terrible memories and appalling fears. The car crash and the abortion of Johnny's baby kept coming back to her. At other times, she imagined that the people from the commune in San Francisco were coming in droves to get her. They seemed like scavengers who wanted to own her, to seize her mind and take possession of her soul, and, with the terrible sense she had of being totally alone in the universe, Anna did not know how she could resist them. She felt as if her whole mind was on the point of breaking.

She spent two weeks in solitary confinement. At the beginning of the third week, she was moved into another ward where there were already a dozen or so women. Again, there were no windows and she wasn't allowed out of the building.

At this point, Anna was still suffering from the most bizarre delusions—for a time, she thought she was Carl Jung's ankle, which he had broken on her birthday in 1944—and, as her body reacted to the sudden absence of the addictive drugs she had been taking, she became physically ill with chills and violent fevers. Often, her bed-sheets were soaked with sweat. These withdrawal symptoms were all the more pronounced because, unknown to her doctors, Anna had decided to stop taking the tranquillising drugs with which they were dosing her.

Before long, Anna was eating three good meals a day and, on her own initiative, had begun to help make the beds, clean out the ward and look after the other patients. There was one incontinent old lady, in particular, whom nobody else seemed to want to help, so Anna took on the job of changing her night-dress and sheets. She had a curious sense that angels were helping her, and felt grateful to be alive.

It also began to dawn on Anna for the first time that it was she alone who had to face the consequences of her own actions. Buzz, she reflected, wasn't with her in hospital and neither were her parents; she was the only one who was going through it. Before, someone had always cleaned up behind her. Now, for the first time, she had to clean up for herself.

During her fourth week in hospital, she was allowed to go out into the garden. In the garden was an avenue of orange trees and there Anna walked quietly in the sunlight and fed the sparrows which nested in the hospital roof. And it was in the garden that, unsought and unforeseen, God became real to her for the first time. 'I was walking under the orange trees one day,' she said, 'and I was feeling fresh and clean, and so grateful. What a gift, I thought, to be alive! Then I felt these little songs in my heart, but I knew it wasn't me, it was another force and I just knew it was God. It was as though He was singing to me, telling me that He really loved and cared for me, just me.

'I couldn't believe it at first, it was too good to be true, but He seemed to say it over and over again—and I kept on feeling this sense of overwhelming love.

'Then there was such a peacefulness, a feeling that I was home at last, that He *was* a loving father, that He cared for every little detail of my life. And then I looked at the sparrows, and they, too, seemed to represent to me the peacefulness, the warmth and the humanity of God.

'At that stage, I wasn't even sure whether I was alive or dead, and I'd take out a notebook and write down the reasons why I thought I was alive and the reasons why I was sure I was dead. Then, one day, it occurred to me that, if God had made me in the first place, He could bring me back to life again. So I turned that problem over and I thought, "If I'm alive I can be in Your hands and, if I'm dead, I can be in them too, so I don't need to worry any more."

'As time went on, I'd try to talk to God and I'd ask Him to talk to me. I'd say, "I need You but I can't hear You very well", and I'd take a notebook and a pencil and write down the thoughts which came into my mind. I'd even write in the dark when I couldn't see what I was writing. For a time, I didn't feel I could talk to God without a pencil and paper. My brain was just flapping about somehow—I had a lot of brain damage from drugs and wrong thinking and my thoughts would fly about all over the place.

'Sometimes His sense of humour was terrific, and the humour was very important in the state I was in. He'd say "Coming through your brain is quite a trip, lady", and that made me laugh.'

At other times, Anna felt that God was talking to her in the verse which she loved to write:

> Sleep now, rest
> and keep the day
> God in heart,
> hold fast and pray
> for love and light
> and truth and food.
> The good will come,
> don't worry, child.
>
> He'll keep you safe
> and sound and sure
> and turn you on
> to heaven's store

And then there was the little poem which, she felt, told her how she ought to face up to the difficulties which she knew lay ahead. She called it 'Be joyful, be thankful' and it read, simply:

Often, she admits, she starts to yell at either Joshua or Rebecca, and then has to stop in mid-sentence to ask God for help. One day, she remembers, Rebecca was crying because Joshua wouldn't share a toy with her. Anna put up a silent prayer, 'Father, please help them to be happy and get Josh to play with Rebecca' and, without her saying anything, Joshua came in and made Rebecca laugh. That sort of thing, says Anna, goes on all day.

Another time, she had dropped a box of tumblers on to the floor and Rebecca was sitting crying in the middle of the broken glass. Another silent prayer went up, 'Father, please make Becky quiet while I pick up the glass', and immediately the child was quiet.

But Anna has also made a point of asking Joshua to help her. She told him that she wanted to be really open with him, that she was not a big person who didn't have fear or anger, but just a child of God like him and that she had to ask God's help with her fears and her anger. If she becomes fearful or angry, she tells Joshua, so he can understand her better. The result is that Joshua not only feels needed, he also lends a hand in calling for help. When Anna shouts at him, he sometimes turns up his face and says, 'God, please help Mommy to be a good Mommy and not shout at me.' The first time he did it, it stopped Anna in her tracks and the little boy smiled and said, 'That sure works, Mom!' On other occasions, he will begin to pray silently while Anna is still holding forth, and then say, 'I'm praying to God to make you a better mother.' Anna says she knows now when he's praying, because she feels a change in her heart even before he's said anything.

Joshua is quite sure what *he* thinks about God. 'I like Him and He's a nice fellow,' he said. 'He helps people and He cleans up the world. At my age, you can't hear Him very good, but when you're six, then you can really hear Him.

'Mom talks to God, you know, and it makes her a nicer person. Becky does something or I do something and then she yells at us, but then she prays to God not to yell any more, and then she stops it.'

To Anna's own mother, all this is little short of miraculous. 'She's just a fantastic mother,' she said proudly. 'Watching the other young women around, she's easily the best.'

With only $250 a month from social security payments, Anna has also had to learn a good deal about managing on a tight budget. One unexpected thought which came to her was to pay her bills even when she didn't think she could spare the money.

'When I pay my bills,' she said, 'I feel straight with God, and I have a great sense of inner freedom, far superior to that crummy, indulgent thing of the past. And the fact is that we've always had enough to eat and wear even when we were desperately short of money.'

Looking back over these past harrowing years, still so close, Anna sometimes reflects on the kind of childhood she had, and cannot escape the thought that it played its part in the later tragedy. To begin with, she feels, it was a Peter Pan existence which did nothing to prepare her for the world she eventually had to face. It was idyllic but it was a fantasy, a painless, padded, protected world completely shut off from reality.

'The only things my parents allowed around me,' she said, 'were pretty things, clean things, proper things. They washed my rattle every time I dropped it! I never heard of tragedies, of times when people hadn't enough to eat.'

To her, all this is quite understandable in terms of her parents' own childhood. They had grown up in the depression years and her mother had won a scholarship to the University of Chicago, but had had to turn it down because the family couldn't afford the rail fares. Life, said Anna, had been too difficult for them and they had reacted by taking too much pressure off their children.

When she was young, Anna also felt like a messy and rather inconvenient intruder on a tidy and well-ordered adult world. Mother had run such a neat household and she and Anna's father were so good-looking, so perfect in themselves that they didn't seem to need her. They provided for you, and you weren't expected to do a thing in return. It was all take and no give and you felt you were piling up an enormous debt, which you could never repay, and the burden became too great. That, Anna thinks now, is why she felt so desperate to win her parents' love and approval, and why she was so often ill as a child. It was just a good way to capture her mother's attention.

But the greatest lack, she feels, was the absence of any deep interest in spiritual development. The family went to church, but, so far as she could see, it was purely a social trip. They were raised by the book, but the book was Dr. Spock and not the Bible.

'If we'd seen that what the grown-ups were doing was spiritual development,' said Anna, 'that would have been fine, but the fact

Be joyful—
Then you can consider
all the facts.

It was an experience which Anna could not, and still cannot, explain. She did not feel that she had turned to God. He had simply found her. All she knew was that, slowly and surely, she was being helped to find her bearings. 'Before,' she said, 'I didn't know what was right, because there was no one to tell me. Now, I knew what was right and I had a desire to do the right things. I had a desire to do God's will, though I didn't put it into words at first. It just crept in.

'From then on, I decided, my actions were going to be such that I wouldn't mind the consequences. That's where God's Will came in. It follows as the night the day because, if I'm running my own life, I'm going to make so many mistakes that I won't be able to face the consequences.

'By the time they let me out of hospital I had made three decisions. One, no more drugs. Two, to stick with Buzz. Three, always try to do God's Will in my life. Since that time in the State Hospital, I've never felt alone.'

Anna's nightmare, however, was still far from over. When she arrived home, she found that Buzz was not only drinking heavily and taking drugs daily but also dealing in them. It was like asking a newly-reformed chain-smoker to work in a cigarette factory and Anna found herself physically incapable of holding to her decision to give up drugs. She succumbed and tried to take LSD.

Then, however, she found that she was pregnant, and resolved that what she was not able to do for her own sake, she must do for the sake of her unborn child. She prayed desperately for the strength to hold fast, and the prayer was answered. During the time when she was pregnant, Anna took no drugs whatsoever. After the child was born, she only took them again twice, and each time found it such a 'bonegrinding bummer' that she felt Christ came personally to rescue her. For the last five years, she has taken no drugs of any kind.

While she was pregnant, Anna also decided that, with God's help, she would never again make her mother weep. So often in the past, when she had revealed the depths of her misery and despair, her mother had either burst into tears or else there had been a bitter argument. Anna felt she wanted to live in such a way that it would never happen again.

At about the same time, Buzz came to the conclusion that they ought to get in touch with Alcoholics Anonymous. For the next three years, they attended meetings regularly. There, and in Alanon, its sister organisation for the families of alcoholics, Anna found a reality she had missed in church. AA, she felt, was a real fellowship where you found a sense of what she called 'that vertical connection': the people were sincere searchers, they would share their personal experiences honestly, and many were totally dependent on their relationship with God because they could see no human way to stay sober.

Nor was it a one-way relationship. Despite all their own problems – and they were then living in a condemned house with no toilet – Buzz and Anna tried to give what they could. Together, they paid hundreds of visits to local schools to share their experience and to try to help the youngsters not to fall into the same deadly trap.

Buzz's condition, meanwhile, became steadily more desperate, as drugs and alcohol took their toll. It was not at all unusual for him to drink a quart of Scotch, pass out, wake up, drink another bottle and then pass out again. Soon he was having regular bouts of delirium tremens, vomiting blood and becoming paranoid.

Anna, meanwhile, was trying desperately to cling to her faith and somehow to protect her baby son from the hell through which they were living. She had also enrolled in college yet again. After three years of torment and conflict, however, she felt she could not go on any longer and, for respite, went off to Chicago with Joshua for a three-day religious study course.

Before she left, Buzz told her he was getting ready to die and wanted to go home to God. One night, in total desperation, Anna asked God what on earth she ought to do. The answer was threefold: 'Don't go back to Buzz; keep on loving him; I'm going to take him soon.'

In one way, she felt grateful, because she knew God loved Buzz more than she ever could, but at the same time found the idea of leaving him difficult to accept. She could not understand how separation was going to help him. So she asked God to put the words into someone else's mouth.

On the way home from Chicago, she found herself sitting next to an old man who, she discovered, had been a member of AA for thirty years. She told him her predicament and asked for an honest opinion. He was emphatic: in his view, it was insane for Anna and her son to go on living with someone so hell-bent on self-destruction. That finally convinced Anna. She and Buzz found an institution which they hoped might be able to save him. There, Anna dined with him every night and there, too, despite the desperate straits he himself was in, Buzz would sit up all night with men suffering from delirium tremens, trying to comfort them. Before he died, he helped several to stop drinking.

Then, one day, he came to see Anna. He was at the end of his tether. 'Oh, Pooh,' he said, 'I tried, I gave it everything I've got.' Anna discovered he had already taken three Secabarbitol tablets and she asked him if he wanted her to call an ambulance. 'No, Pooh,' he replied. 'This is it. I want to shuffle the cards.' Then Buzz hugged her, told her he loved her and hoped to see her soon, and went off down the alley by the side of the house. The police didn't find his body for six days.

For a time, Anna felt bitter and angry at the world but, by now, a second child was on the way and, as she prepared for it, she slowly recovered her sense of peace. The house, however, was still full of Buzz's friends, all of them drug addicts, all of them rich, who had decided they wanted to camp out there. Soon, Anna felt she could stand them no longer, and told them they would have to leave. Eventually, they climbed into cars and drove off, taking with them almost everything in the house.

When Rebecca arrived, Anna's parents moved into the house for ten days. They cooked all the meals and, every time Rebecca woke, Anna's mother got up with her to help with the baby.

Now, at last, Anna felt she could start a new life. She had graduated early in 1973, eleven years after she had first gone to college but, with two children to raise, she was entirely dependent on social security and her parents' help.

She decided that the first thing she would need to do if she was going to start afresh was to make a clean cut with old friends and habits. She kept well clear of anyone who took drugs and, without making any moral judgements, decided it would be wisest not to have any beer-drinking friends either. She herself gave up both alcohol and coffee. All of this represented a sharp break with the conformities of the past, and Anna expressed it in a short poem:

The attempt to do God's Will
and not my own
has given me the courage
to go my own way.

Those decisions made her all the more aware how dependent she was on God's help. She began to pray simple prayers like 'Please God, help me not to be scared, I can't do this myself', and more and more to try to find out what God wanted her to do in every situation. 'Every time I have to make a decision,' she said, 'I ask Him what I should do, and the answer immediately floats into my heart. When I'm puzzled about something, I ask myself "Is it good? Is it true? Would Jesus have done it?" That really clears things up.

'Talking to Him is praying—I feel that "thank you" and "I love you" are worship. Too often, the prayer is "I want this" or "I need this", but for me it's not even just "Thy Will be done", it's "This is my free will, Father, to do what you want." I say more "Thank yous" and "I love yous" than "I want" or "I need". I tell God, "I'd die if I couldn't live in Your Presence and become more and more open to You."

'I've tried to lean on a lot of things in my life, but the only thing I've found where the more you lean the stronger you feel, is God. God is the only thing I've leaned on which has never let me down.

'It's just a well-spring of joy for me. As soon as I wake up, I'm conscious of God's presence. I don't like to use these terms—it sounds like what I heard when I was young, when it meant nothing—and it's not what it feels like from the inside.

'It's as though God's reorganising my whole brain—and He's been working on it for five years. Every day, I learn something new. God has always promised to do things quietly for me. No gimmicks, no scary things. Just slow growth.'

Anna found she needed all her faith when it came to bringing up her children. To her, it is the most frustrating activity on the planet—'It drives me bananas every single day'—and she frankly confesses that, without God, she just couldn't do it. 'If I forget God for a moment, it's like I'm in darkness and an animal in a cave,' she said, 'and anything could happen. I could be in Child-Beaters Anonymous tomorrow!'

Often, she admits, she starts to yell at either Joshua or Rebecca, and then has to stop in mid-sentence to ask God for help. One day, she remembers, Rebecca was crying because Joshua wouldn't share a toy with her. Anna put up a silent prayer, 'Father, please help them to be happy and get Josh to play with Rebecca' and, without her saying anything, Joshua came in and made Rebecca laugh. That sort of thing, says Anna, goes on all day.

Another time, she had dropped a box of tumblers on to the floor and Rebecca was sitting crying in the middle of the broken glass. Another silent prayer went up, 'Father, please make Becky quiet while I pick up the glass', and immediately the child was quiet.

But Anna has also made a point of asking Joshua to help her. She told him that she wanted to be really open with him, that she was not a big person who didn't have fear or anger, but just a child of God like him and that she had to ask God's help with her fears and her anger. If she becomes fearful or angry, she tells Joshua, so he can understand her better. The result is that Joshua not only feels needed, he also lends a hand in calling for help. When Anna shouts at him, he sometimes turns up his face and says, 'God, please help Mommy to be a good Mommy and not shout at me.' The first time he did it, it stopped Anna in her tracks and the little boy smiled and said, 'That sure works, Mom!' On other occasions, he will begin to pray silently while Anna is still holding forth, and then say, 'I'm praying to God to make you a better mother.' Anna says she knows now when he's praying, because she feels a change in her heart even before he's said anything.

Joshua is quite sure what *he* thinks about God. 'I like Him and He's a nice fellow,' he said. 'He helps people and He cleans up the world. At my age, you can't hear Him very good, but when you're six, then you can really hear Him.

'Mom talks to God, you know, and it makes her a nicer person. Becky does something or I do something and then she yells at us, but then she prays to God not to yell any more, and then she stops it.'

To Anna's own mother, all this is little short of miraculous. 'She's just a fantastic mother,' she said proudly. 'Watching the other young women around, she's easily the best.'

With only $250 a month from social security payments, Anna has also had to learn a good deal about managing on a tight budget. One unexpected thought which came to her was to pay her bills even when she didn't think she could spare the money.

'When I pay my bills,' she said, 'I feel straight with God, and I have a great sense of inner freedom, far superior to that crummy, indulgent thing of the past. And the fact is that we've always had enough to eat and wear even when we were desperately short of money.'

Looking back over these past harrowing years, still so close, Anna sometimes reflects on the kind of childhood she had, and cannot escape the thought that it played its part in the later tragedy. To begin with, she feels, it was a Peter Pan existence which did nothing to prepare her for the world she eventually had to face. It was idyllic but it was a fantasy, a painless, padded, protected world completely shut off from reality.

'The only things my parents allowed around me,' she said, 'were pretty things, clean things, proper things. They washed my rattle every time I dropped it! I never heard of tragedies, of times when people hadn't enough to eat.'

To her, all this is quite understandable in terms of her parents' own childhood. They had grown up in the depression years and her mother had won a scholarship to the University of Chicago, but had had to turn it down because the family couldn't afford the rail fares. Life, said Anna, had been too difficult for them and they had reacted by taking too much pressure off their children.

When she was young, Anna also felt like a messy and rather inconvenient intruder on a tidy and well-ordered adult world. Mother had run such a neat household and she and Anna's father were so good-looking, so perfect in themselves that they didn't seem to need her. They provided for you, and you weren't expected to do a thing in return. It was all take and no give and you felt you were piling up an enormous debt, which you could never repay, and the burden became too great. That, Anna thinks now, is why she felt so desperate to win her parents' love and approval, and why she was so often ill as a child. It was just a good way to capture her mother's attention.

But the greatest lack, she feels, was the absence of any deep interest in spiritual development. The family went to church, but, so far as she could see, it was purely a social trip. They were raised by the book, but the book was Dr. Spock and not the Bible.

'If we'd seen that what the grown-ups were doing was spiritual development,' said Anna, 'that would have been fine, but the fact that their goals were so much less than I could yearn for somehow made the whole world seem so gross and crass. I could even have stood that fantasy-life upbringing, because spiritual things can pull you over any amount of dross.

'When I looked at the adult world and tried to guess what it was really about, I came to the conclusion that the big pay-off was sex. That's what the grown-ups seemed to be striving for, not spiritual development.

'I want my children to know that my ideals are religious, that my ideal is service, not selfishness or self-satisfaction. People aren't built to be anti-social, they're built to be selfless, that's when they're happy. And I want them to know that my satisfaction comes from my personal relationship with God and that that comes before *all* other things.

'My prayer for my children is that they find God. That's all I ask. Anything else falls short of the mark. If they wanted to take drugs, I'd know I'd failed, because that's just trying to please yourself, not God. I want to make a contribution, if God finds me worthy to do it.'

Anna's mother remembers when, aged eighteen months, Anna was trying to tie her own shoes. After struggling away for a long time without success, she looked up and sighed. 'Truggle, truggle, truggle,' she said. 'I guess I'll have to do it by littles!'

2

Painter B

'MY AFFLICTION IS not what keeps me from having a full life,' wrote Bob Painter from Canada before we had ever met. He added that he was worried about his ability to convince the English immigration authorities that he was going to 'do something' in Britain when he didn't have a work permit. 'If you understand me,' he said, 'how can a Christian claim to be unemployed?' He finally arrived in London via India, where he had been travelling alone for three weeks – quite an achievement for a young man whose mother was once told by a doctor that he would probably never be able to walk or talk or look after himself and was likely to end up in an institution as a human vegetable.

Bob is slight of build, with a lean face, curly dark-brown hair and an expression which alternates between the profoundly th·ughtful and the ecstatic, when his eyes all but disappear in mirth and his entire face seems to be replaced by gleaming white teeth. His spasticity is now comparatively mild, but still apparent in a lurching walk, speech which is slightly slurred and the fact that he cannot hold a cup steady.

He has been an unexpected person from the very beginning. In the later stages of her pregnancy, his mother told the obstetrician that she thought she could feel two heartbeats, but nobody took her very seriously and, when the doctor had delivered Bob's identical twin, Gilbert, he assumed his job was done.

Then Bob's mother, Eileen Painter, remembers him saying, 'My God, there's another one in there. We've got to work fast.' Twenty minutes later, Bob was born, with the umbilical cord caught around his neck. By then, his brain cells had been damaged by lack of oxygen and the doctor had to inject adrenalin into his heart to keep him alive. He weighed only three pounds and ten ounces. His twin brother was five pounds.

To distinguish the two boys, the staff at the Catholic hospital in Toronto where they were born labelled them 'Painter A' and 'Painter B' and their doctor gave them ribbons of different colours. Bert's was red, the colour of the shoulder patches used by the First Division of the First Canadian Army Overseas in World War Two; Bob's was blue, the Second Division colour. When she first saw Bob, Eileen Painter thought he looked 'like a little dead bird'; neither he nor Bert, she felt, would ever look as old again as long as they lived.

When Bob left hospital after a month in an incubator, Mother Vincentia—the matron in charge of the children's ward—stopped the elevator to bless him. 'Painter B is going home today,' she said.

Soon, however, Eileen Painter noticed that Bob didn't sit up or hold up his head despite the fact that she was giving him exercises every day. When he was six months old, she and her husband took him to a neurologist, at their doctor's suggestion. The verdict was simple and crushing; Bob had brain damage, and would eventually be better off in an institution. Nothing much, said the neurologist, could be done till he was eighteen months old.

Eileen Painter comes from pioneer stock. Before she married, she had taught kindergarten in Moose Jaw, Saskatchewan, and, as she says herself, she is not the kind who knuckles under easily. She came out of the consulting room seething with fury, fury that Bob's condition hadn't been diagnosed before, fury that they should suggest consigning him to an institution. She had seen too many children treated like that, put away like unused toys. 'We'll show them,' she said to her husband Gil. 'Wait till he's eighteen months? We're going to start tomorrow.'

She went straight to the library and borrowed every book she could find on cerebral palsy; gave Bob exercises three times a day in addition to keeping an eye on Bert's antics; her husband made a whole series of therapeutic gadgets—a strong but light-weight oak baby-walker, a harness, a pair of specially designed skis and a set of parallel bars made from steel water pipe—to help Bob learn to walk. The little boy was plainly passionately keen to emulate his twin brother; his insistence on doing things precisely right, indeed, led to a good deal of frustration and frequent squalls of temper.

Some months later, holding his mother's hands, Bob walked the entire length of the living-room three times, and repeated the performance when his father came home that evening. Gil and Eileen could scarcely believe it. Neither could the neurologist. When Eileen took their eighteen-months-old baby back again, he was flabbergasted at Bob's progress. There was less spasticity, he noted; the child was moving his arms and legs much more easily; and, he added in a letter to the Painters' family doctor, tests would probably show an intelligence close to normal. 'I feel,' he said, 'that we will all be amazed by the eventual improvement in this child.'

The neurologist was right. In September 1949, when he was thirty-five months old, Bob stood unaided for the first time. Six months later, he astonished his parents by walking without help. Gil and Eileen were eating their supper when Bob suddenly tottered into the dining-room. 'Look,' his smiling face said, 'I can walk! Now I can go to school.' Eileen Painter almost swallowed her jam tart in amazement. This, she felt, was a glorious answer to her prayers. 'It was as though he walked by faith,' she said afterwards.

Eileen did not want Bob to go to a school for the handicapped and, when the family moved to Montreal, she was lucky enough to have the headmaster of the local primary as a near neighbour. He readily agreed to take the boy; both he and Bert were put in the same form. By then, Bob could ride a tricycle and was going to the public swimming-baths three nights a week with his father.

Eileen pulled Bob the half-mile to school in a small play-cart which her husband had made. Before they reached the school yard, she let him climb out so that he could walk in alone. 'So long, Mummy,' he said, on that first day. 'See you at noon.' For the next five years, Eileen Painter made that journey eight times every school day.

Bob, however, did not enjoy school at all. It was not merely that, despite speech therapy, he still had great difficulty in articulating vowels; nor the fact that his father had to build up his pencils to help him write and that he wrote so slowly that he was never able to finish an examination paper on time. It wasn't even that he could never join in PE, or that his uncontrollable laughter in class always started the rest of the children laughing, or that some of the boys called him 'fatso' while others yelled, 'Hey, here's a drunk', when he appeared on the scene. The real trouble was that Bob longed to be accepted as 'normal' (how he came to hate that word), to be like his brother Bert, to be 'in', and, because of that desperate and unassuagable longing, felt that he was constantly on trial in a contest he could not possibly win.

'For me,' he said, 'the classroom was a fight-ring. I felt like I had to control every emotion to keep the atmosphere right; I was terribly afraid of having my vulnerability exposed. It was such a tense moment when I was asked to perform in class. If I didn't speak right, I'd failed. Everything was to prove myself.

'I used to go home and tell my mother how I'd spoken and how I was getting on with the teacher and the other children. Then I'd study the results of my behaviour, go over what I'd done just as you might study a bridge game. I'd say, "Next time I won't do that." I became a tremendously avid perfectionist — and very self-centred.'

The hardest battle, Bob found, was simply to win friends. 'I was always trying to make contact,' he said, 'and to do that you compromise all the time, try to show off, to give the impression that you're a good guy. It always involves selling yourself. And you get very fearful — "If I make a mistake," I used to think, "the whole show is given away." The fear of rejection hangs over you like a hammer all the time.

'I was friendly with one fellow but, when there was a group, he might easily join in a joke about me. That confused me. How was I supposed to play the game, I wondered?

'I felt I always had to be extra to be in. Nobody wanted me to join them, and I couldn't, anyway. I didn't mind not being able to hit the ball, but I couldn't understand why I couldn't converse with people. It presented an awesome problem. I became very self-critical — I wanted to please everybody and that made it worse for me. The effort to please other people always produces tension — and, with the tension, my movements became less smooth and confident. I asked myself why did I have to go through this process all the time. I was humiliated, but it didn't make me humble. It had the opposite effect — it demoralised me.'

The result was that, throughout his time at school, Bob laboured under a tremendous sense of bitterness. Why was he there? It all seemed so senseless. Why did he have this affliction? In one way, the bitterness was compounded by the fact that his twin brother Bert was always, as Bob said, an A1 student and an A1 sportsman whom he couldn't hope to match. The fact that Bert was also his one totally dependable friend, who didn't mind if he couldn't catch the ball and who scarcely ever gave Bob the feeling that he was a burden, didn't change the situation: everything still seemed to be against him.

Nor, so far as Bob was concerned, was there much relief when he got home. There was almost no physical chastisement, but there was a kind of psychological pressure: he had to perform, he felt, to do things right. When visitors came, he must speak properly and he mustn't drop the cranberry sauce or spill the water. If he did, his mother and father might be ashamed of him and next day there might be a rehearsal of what he *ought* to have done. Gil and Eileen were trying to help Bob fight his physical handicap, but it took years before he felt confident that he could pick up a glass of water without spilling it.

'I'd always been taught to do the right thing,' said Bob, 'and it made relationships very complicated. I felt I couldn't really open up to anybody. Relationships with other people were more or less a game, I thought. We are here, I thought, to make sure the ball is passed smoothly from one to the other; there must be no fumbles! So I lived in trepidation.'

Nor were things any easier when the family moved back to Peterborough, ninety miles from Toronto. The school principal there told Eileen Painter that Bob (who was ten by then) would have to go to the school for the mentally retarded, that he would never get through Grade 8 in the normal system. Only after a sharp battle, in which the Toronto neurologist and a psychologist wrote to the local director of the Board of Education, was the principal's ruling reversed.

Not all Bob's new teachers were as sensitive as those he had left in Montreal. When the other children were given their annual reports, Bob was sent home empty-handed. His teacher told him he had failed, and therefore couldn't have one. Eileen struggled to console him. He *hadn't* failed, she kept on telling him as he wept on her knee. Later on, she recalled, that same teacher went to the Gulf Stream School. 'I hope he drowned in it!' she told Gil, with feeling.

Some of the children, too, made fun at Bob's expense. One day he was told to go home because he'd pushed a girl into the snow and sat on her after she had thrown a snowball into his face and 'called him a name'. Again, Eileen Painter refused to knuckle under. She told Bob she was proud of him and gave him a stiff note to take to the teacher who had sent him home. If anybody was handicapped, she told the teacher, it was the girl.

As the years went by, Bob's determination to keep up with the other children grew. He got up at five-thirty to learn how to run, and would often do a mile before breakfast. He did weight-lifting exercises to straighten his bent left wrist. Then, when he found he couldn't get a summer job, he made up his mind that he would learn to ride a bicycle instead. His father fitted a large wire basket to the front of the cycle thinking that it would break a collision or a fall.

Day after day, Bob kept at it. Day after day, he fell off time and time again until his body and legs were covered with cuts and bruises. When his mother gave him a new suit, he put out the knees on the first day and went through more pairs of trousers than she cares to remember.

'He'd come whizzing down the hill past our home,' she recalled. 'All the neighbours used to watch with their hearts in their mouths. Then, at night, he'd say to Gil, "Gee, Dad, I smashed my basket again", and Gil would straighten it out or straighten up the pedals and the forks.'

At the end of three weeks, Bob could ride the bicycle without falling off. Then, he simply put it away. He never even asked his mother whether he could take it out on to the open road. If he had, she said, she wouldn't have known what to say.

By the ordinary measures of success, Bob's efforts paid off handsomely. He could not hope to emulate Bert, who was elected President of the Student Council, but he was nicknamed 'professor' because he worked so hard, always got 'A' for effort, duly graduated from high school and, like his twin brother, went to university. Bob went to Trent University in Peterborough, Bert to Carleton in Ottawa.

There, too, he was quite a success. He kept up a B average and was nominated for the job of secretary to the College Cabinet.

Each nominee had to make a speech before the whole college and, while everyone wished Bob well, nobody thought he could make it. Before the speech, he rehearsed for two hours in the bathroom and then prayed, because he thought it might help. The speech was given a standing ovation, Bob was elected and one of his friends taped to his door the mock headline 'President Lincoln speaks'. In 1969, Bob graduated from Trent.

It was, as he said, a tremendous achievement for someone like him. As soon as he started looking for a job, however, it began to seem a hollow triumph. His applications brought one rejection after another. Soon, he had a drawer full of letters turning him down.

'He travelled to Toronto almost every day,' recalled his mother, 'and came home to Peterborough alone every night. He trod the streets of Toronto from one end to the other, and it's a mighty big place.'

As the months dragged by, Bob began to lose all hope. He felt he would never be able to sell himself; nobody seemed to believe he was capable of doing anything. Then, after almost a year, the Ontario Hydro offered him a job as a computer programmer. To Eileen Painter, it was a blessed relief; to Bob, realisation of his second goal.

Within weeks, however, he found to his dismay that he was still unhappy. 'There's something wrong here,' he told himself, 'this guy isn't fulfilled.' He felt that he had failed after all. The success he had fought and worked for didn't sustain him, didn't after all provide him with more than fleeting satisfaction. He took the only escape route he could see: he began to take a deeper interest in the spiritual life.

As a boy, he had been to church regularly with his parents and had begun to read the Bible in Grade 6 because he liked the teacher, who happened to be a Christian. It meant nothing to him, however – 'It was contrary to what the other world told me, which was to be a success' – and he soon tired of church, which seemed to him 'just a form of Sunday boredom'. By the time he was half-way through high school, he was thoroughly sick of religion.

From that time until his second year in university, Bob thought the Bible 'a very silly book'. This view was confirmed by the fact that his grandmother was always reading it. Since she didn't appear to know anything else, Bob assumed that only people 'not in the know' read the Bible.

When he went to Trent, he began reading what he calls 'success books' – by which he means everything from Norman Vincent Peale to Karl Marx. He also noticed that he was happiest when he was helping other people – opening doors for them, simple things like that. Then, for the first time, he occasionally dated a girl and felt that, if he were going to marry, he ought to have some faith in God. He therefore turned back to the Bible.

'When I started to read it,' he said, 'I thought all my problems would be solved – I'd have better relations with people, I'd be able to control my movements more. I looked on Christianity as a kind of pill and, unless I was getting better physically, it wasn't working so far as I was concerned. I believed it could make me more successful and efficient, not a better person.'

Bob also started to pray frequently, with much the same ends in view. He prayed that he would be able to speak well, walk well – and have a regular girl-friend. The trouble was that he didn't seem to be on the end of the miracle-receiving line.

Then came the discovery that even a good job did not satisfy him. In that moment of profound disillusion, a new idea occurred to him: that 'the big game' in which he felt he had been involved all his life, of trying to persuade other people to like him, was no good. All his life, he realised, he had been shackled by what others thought of him, had tried to conform himself to their image of what he ought to be like, and, in so doing, had become their fawning slave. Now, he decided, he must somehow break those shackles and get free of his concern about other people's opinion.

The method he chose was deliberately aggressive. Presented with an assessment form to fill in at work, he decided he must say bluntly that he didn't care what anyone felt about him. When he told one of his friends what he had in mind, the man warned him that, if he did that sort of thing, he might never be promoted. Bob was not deterred. To him, he wrote, the most important factor was that he should enjoy what he was doing, and that, providing he did the right thing, he couldn't care less what anybody thought of him. Someone found out and put a sticker on his desk saying 'Couldn't care less'.

'It was a show-off, like a gladiator,' said Bob, 'and it gave me an ego-boost, but somehow I had to break with my drive to make a big impression, and that was my way of doing it.'

He also decided that he was going to dare to live what he had read about in the Bible. Before, he had kept his interest in religion strictly to himself. Making it public, he thought, would guarantee that he would be labelled a nut, and finally put paid to any chance he might have had of making friends. Now, he was ready to take that risk.

In some curious way, the decisions seemed to change the whole tenor of his life. One day, as he was crossing a street, he had a flash of thought, a sudden sense that life had become, quite perceptibly, positive instead of negative. From that moment on, he felt inwardly convinced that what it said in the Bible about its being more blessed to give than to receive was not merely a pious platitude but profoundly true.

He began to read avidly – Buber, Bonhoeffer, Kierkegaard and more popular contemporary works like Malcolm Muggeridge's *Jesus Rediscovered*. On one of his vacations, he came to England hoping to see Muggeridge, and walked three miles just to take a photograph of his cottage in Sussex. At that time, he thought Muggeridge was probably 'an old guy on his death-bed' and was pleasantly surprised to find him extremely vigorous.

The encounter meant a good deal to Bob. Muggeridge encouraged him to write and finally convinced him that Christianity was intellectually respectable. He also introduced Bob to the writings of the modern mystic, Simone Weil. Her notion that affliction nails a person to God caused Bob radically to rethink his attitude towards his own handicap. He had the sense that he was beginning to tap a bottomless reservoir of truth which previously he had not even known existed. Drawing on that reservoir slowly transformed his view of life.

He began to question the idea, with which he felt he had been brain-washed, that his basic problem was his physical handicap and that he somehow had either to overcome or disguise it so that he could become like other, 'normal' people. Was his physical handicap, he wondered, really the root of the problem? It was true, he knew, that the nature of his handicap exposed his weakness for all to see: he couldn't cover up like 'normal' people or seek popularity as they did. But, he asked himself, supposing he were physically perfect, would he necessarily be a better person?

The answer, he knew, was that he would not. And, in that case, had he not been completely missing the point?

'The effort to develop yourself is very good,' he said, 'but there's a lot more to life than overcoming my handicap. People would always say the problem with me was that I was handicapped. It wasn't. The problem was that I didn't know how I could be released from myself. What blocks me from a full life is not my handicap, but my ego, the feeling that I am the most important thing, which stops you really giving yourself to others.

'Why did God make me like this? It's not important! It doesn't make me capable of less love, does it? If I weren't like this, I might be a more efficient person so far as society is concerned, but would I be able to love others more? I doubt it. What Christ intends is that we love others. That is our only responsibility.'

Why then, Bob thought, should he seek to deny his affliction, as he had done ever since he was a child? After all, hadn't his affliction proved a blessing? Without it, he knew, he would never have been forced to an understanding of life. It was the nail of affliction which had driven him to choose between God and the Devil. It had been hard to know that nail, which tore the self to shreds and swept away his dignity and his pride, but there had been grace in it, too.

'The afflicted one must not try to deny his affliction,' he said. 'When we deny it, we also deny our imperfection. We should recognise and accept it. Imperfection is not atrocious, but a way of opening yourself to other people.

'Resignation is no answer either. That just means you are cloistered in your wounds. People like that are islands unto themselves.

'I saw that the point for me was to try to become not more like other people but more like Christ. I realised that I only have to behave according to the image of God, not the image people have of me. Whatever that is, it's a bogus image.

'So many people try to live up to the image others have of them. Take a great athlete. People say, "he's fantastic", but *he* knows he's not what they say he is. It's very difficult for him to come down from that pedestal. When they put him up there, he loses his freedom. All idols do.'

Bob also began to look critically and with new clarity at the goals and promises of the world he'd grown up into – 'A-grades, sexual satisfaction and a grand social life—it was all I, I, I'—and reflected on the despair and loneliness which the propaganda machine of advertising caused to people with handicaps like his own.

'You're a sexual animal . . . you *must* be satisfied . . . You *must* have good sexual relations,' it insisted, again and again and again. What a sense of failure that had bred in him, for whom even getting to date a girl was a precarious triumph, for whom rejection was a part of normal experience!

Bob understood more clearly, too, why some people shied away from him as though he carried some contagious disease. It wasn't merely that he was different from them and that they were afraid of being involved. It was also that, in an automotive age when everything was supposed to run smoothly and efficiently, affliction such as his was against the success principle, and being with him a bad mark, an association with the imperfect which some people fled. Such people, Bob came to feel, were preoccupied more with the glory of man than the glory of God.

He was appalled to hear a speaker at a spastics conference in England say that people who suffered from cerebral palsy should not make their disability too obvious, that they should conceal it as much as possible. You couldn't expect people to want to sit near spastics, the speaker went on, so when they went into a restaurant they should sit on the edge of the room, not in the centre. Bob's immediate reaction was that he *wanted* to sit *right* in the middle; if he didn't, it deprived other people of the chance of educating themselves.

To him, that kind of thinking was typical of a world full of 'computerised robots programmed for the twentieth century experience of the candy life'.

Everyone, in any case, was 'handicapped' in one way or another. His handicap, he knew, was clear for all to see. But who was more handicapped, he wondered, a man like himself who couldn't hold a coffee cup steady or a man who regularly lost his temper with his children?

Freed at last from what he called 'the net of perfectionism', Bob felt he no longer wanted to be an expert at the game of putting up a front: only to be himself. It gave him a sense of immense joy that he could be freed from that burden, that there was more to life than what he couldn't do.

'What you have to do,' he said, 'is detach yourself from the values of this society. Otherwise a man like me turns to bitterness. "Why do I have this handicap?" he asks himself. The energy which is generated by that bitterness is not of God and it's not love.

'Love is the most constructive form of behaviour in which you can participate. Love is when you minister to another, and it's a chain reaction—you love, so that that person will love someone else.

'When a person looks at a girl and says, "Gee, that's a sexy girl", that's not love, it just means "There's something there for me". When you really love, the joy comes from abandoning all self-gain. It always seemed pretty screwy to me to say you couldn't love without sex.

'I can see now that leading a full life doesn't necessarily mean having a female companion. I'd marry only if I could in that way give more, become a better person, open myself more to others.'

Not that the world has suddenly become a painless place. Bob still suffers at the hands of people who try to patronise him and ask questions such as 'What d'you do, son?' in tones of sickly sentimentality. They are often considerably put out when he replies that he works with computers. He suffers, too, from the questioning stare and from those who turn away when they meet him.

Such experiences do not trouble him as much as they did, but he constantly has to conquer fear of the unknown and fear of rejection. 'I'm never sure I can talk to that Joe over there,' he said. 'He might be turned off by my speech or the fact that I'm not co-ordinated. When you start thinking like that, you concentrate on yourself and become self-critical in the wrong way. I do feel bitterness occasionally but I know the thing for me to feel is love, not hatred. Once I stop loving, then I'm in trouble.'

After three years with the Ontario Hydro, he gave up his job (much to his mother's dismay) and began to travel with the help of his savings—to India, to Israel and to Europe.

In England, he tried to find social work of some kind. He applied to sixty social-work agencies and each time was turned down. Not one, he said, tried to find out whether he was spiritually fit to do the job or whether he believed in God; all they were interested in were his qualifications and the fact that he was himself handicapped. Several said they never hired the handicapped to look after the handicapped.

Bob bore the rejections not with stoicism but with an undiminished joy which it was difficult at first to credit. In the end, he went back to Canada; that, he concluded, was obviously where he was meant to be.

'Christianity,' he said, 'means dying to yourself. That's more than just thinking that dying to yourself is a good thing – it means actually doing it! That's the difference between a nice philosophy and a faith in action.

'Any victory I've had over affliction has been by trying to surpass its superficial nature. It remains a stumbling-block whenever I cease to desire to grow. Otherwise it is part of the given character which nails me to God. My co-ordination has continued to improve – which it doesn't normally do after thirteen or fourteen – but that is not what really matters. What *is* important is that I live as I should.

'It is the hardest and most difficult way. It demands everything of you, and it means the end of all self-appeasement. Every day I learn. If I didn't, I wouldn't be growing.

'I pray when I feel like it, and that's often. Just like when you want a drink or when you're empty. I go to any church where I find joy. If people ask what church I belong to, I say the Church of God, which means the Body of Christ. Church attendance for its own sake means nothing to me. If it means following Christ seven days a week, fine; if it means just going in for the sake of collective approval, no.'

When I first met Bob Painter, I approached him – I suppose – like many people who have never really talked to a physically handicapped person, who expect to be embarrassed and who hope they will make the right sort of sympathetic noises. I was ready, I think, to pity him, perhaps even to be a little patronising, though I'd never have put it like that.

In the event, Bob taught me that I am a handicapped person, too, and that my handicaps, though not so obvious as his, may well be more destructive. I've never felt patronising towards a physically handicapped person since.

Eileen Painter put it very well. 'The problem of our society,' she said, 'isn't the physically handicapped but the spiritually handicapped.'

3

'This Poor Man Cried'

WHO BUT THOSE who have endured it can know what it is like to be born into a people whose entire culture has been torn apart; whose achievements and way of life over thousands of years have been so derided that you might think it had no history worth the telling, no heroes worth the naming; a people so despised that its pride and self-respect have been all but destroyed?

It is a fate infinitely more painful than that which befalls a nation shattered by war. There, the material destruction can be appalling: ruined cities, pillaged homes, a ravaged landscape. Yet, even amid the rubble, the collective will to restore may survive and from it, fitfully at first, can spring the flame of hope, fed by memories of past glories.

For those, on the other hand, who have been laid waste spiritually, whose roots have been destroyed, whose customs trampled upon, whose ethic shattered, the devastation is far worse. There, even hope may have died. This, in modern times, has been the fate of the Australian aborigines, except in the north.

Since white men first arrived in Australia, less than two hundred years ago, the aborigines have been driven from tribal lands sacred to them for thousands of years, ravaged by European diseases against which they had no immunity, and undermined by the introduction of alcohol, for which they had no tolerance. In Queensland, they were systematically slaughtered. Elsewhere, they were cowed by the rifle and the stock-whip.

Decimated and uprooted, they felt they had lost both their dignity and their reason for living, that they were looked upon as the most miserable people on earth, a poor unfortunate race on the bottom rung of the human ladder. Malnutrition became endemic. So, too, did drunkenness, prostitution and alcoholism. Even the missionaries who worked among them were looked down upon by their fellow-settlers.

This was the world into which Ron Williams was born. He is in his middle thirties, a very tall man, loose-limbed, with an easy stride, but it is the softness of his glance and the gentleness of his voice which is most memorable. It is a gentleness which bears no trace of unctuousness, but seems to spring from some inner music of the spirit. He is, I think, the gentlest man I have ever met, which makes his story all the more remarkable.

Ron was born in the bush, and delivered by an aboriginal midwife. In the part of Western Australia where he lived, aboriginal women were not allowed, at that time, to go into hospital. He has never known who his father was—there were two or three claimants to the position—and, during his childhood, saw little of his mother. Until he was eighteen, he was brought up by his grandfather, Joseph Williams—who had taken his name from the settler for whom he had worked—and his grandmother, whose father was a Welsh convict.

Joseph Williams could neither read nor write; he made his living as a stockman and drover, herding cattle from place to place, from Albany to Cheyne Beach and Gnowangerup and back again to Albany. He and his family lived in tents or bush huts made from old wheat bags sewn together with pieces of stick. Their staple food was bread, sugar and potatoes, supplemented by whatever they could cull from the bush—possum, kangaroo, yabbis (crayfish), wild fruit and bush honey. The white farmers for whom they worked did not allow aborigines into their houses, so they usually ate their meals on the wood-pile outside. Their light in the evenings came from a rag soaked in dripping.

When Ron was five years old, the police came and put him and his grandparents into jail. The jail seemed very much like an animal cage. It had no cover, and Ron remembers the rain pouring in through the open bars. His grandfather was guilty of no crime. The Government had simply decided that he and hundreds of other aborigines from all over Western Australia should be taken to a settlement at Carrolup, one hundred miles west of Albany, and trained to do useful work to stop them being a nuisance to the local farmers. If anyone tried to escape from the camp and was caught, he was given a brutal thrashing by the superintendent and his men.

In the evenings, sitting round the fire, Ron's grandfather would tell stories of aboriginal lore and culture, stories about rivers and mountains, water-holes, animals and birds, and legendary tales about aboriginal heroes who rescued others from the power of evil spirits. Sometimes he would sing a song in the aboriginal language. On other occasions, his grandmother would retell the Bible stories she had learnt from missionaries as a child.

When Ron was nine, the farmer for whom his grandfather had worked before they were taken to the camp asked if Joseph could go back to him, and the family was then free to leave Carrolup. At that time, Ron had never been to school, which was not compulsory for aboriginal children. Now, his grand-mother decided he ought to go.

The things which happened at school made Ron colour-conscious for the first time. Only thirty of the four hundred children were aborigines, and they were mercilessly bullied and abused. The white boys called them 'stinking abos' and 'dirty niggers'. If they accidentally brushed against one of the aborigines, they would blow ostentatiously on their hands as if to remove some contamination. They also sang jingles which carried an obvious menace:

> Nigger, nigger,
> Pull the trigger
> Bang, bang, bang!

Ron found it all very frightening.

The teachers were sometimes little better. One regularly kicked the aboriginal children — something, Ron observed, he never did to the white pupils.

Nor did the history books which they read give Ron much encouragement. They usually referred to the aborigines as lazy savages, and Ron began to feel that the settlers had been more than justified in trying to get rid of them. Soon, he found himself wishing he had been born white.

After all, white men held all the good jobs and owned all the good land, and they could go into hotels and use swimming pools when they wanted to. Aborigines, on the other hand, were surrounded by taboos. In Gnowangerup, for example, they were not allowed to eat a meal in a café, have their hair cut at the barber's shop or use the swimming pool. In Mount Barker, another place where Ron lived for a time, no aborigine could go into town after five in the afternoon unless he had with him his 'citizenship rights', a card which carried his name and photograph.

By the time he was nine, Ron had started to drink. In that, he was little different from other aboriginal children. They drank, he said, because it made them feel good and because it made them feel like white men.

Prostitution, too, was an accepted part of everyday life. White men came regularly to the aboriginal settlements and picked up a woman for a dollar or a bottle of wine. As a result, there were hundreds of children like Ron, who had little idea to whom they belonged.

Ron decided that, when he grew up, he would become a footballer, a boxer, a drunkard or a jail-bird. Being a drunkard seemed a good thing because, whereas aborigines were normally shy and backward, when they got drunk they became lively, sang songs and made friends.

Jail was regarded as a door into the outside world. In jail, aborigines could learn a trade or be taught to read and write better, and they often came out with better clothes and in better health because they had been properly fed. There, they also met people who shared information with them. It was another way of becoming more like the white man.

Surprisingly, perhaps, Ron felt little bitterness towards the whites. All of them, he knew, were not bad. He remembered an old man who had given him picture-books and tried to stop his mother drinking. Then there was a one-legged soldier who had brought him fruit and sweets when he had scalded himself with a billy-can of boiling water.

At the same time, Ron felt afraid of white men. Often they would come and take away aboriginal children like himself, whatever their parents or other relatives said. If it hadn't been for his grandfather, Ron knew he would have several times been taken into government care.

Ron was also terrified of the devil-men who were supposed to inhabit caves in the bush and of the *kadicha*, or featherfoot men, professional killers from rival tribes who lived by settling scores in inter-tribal feuds. They came mainly from a tribe which lived in the goldfields area to the east and were the traditional enemies of Ron's people. They wore shoes made out of cotton wool or emu feathers, so that they would leave no tracks, and they were trained to kill people in ways which puzzled the doctors. They might take a man's tongue and break the ligaments with copper wire so that he would choke from internal bleeding, or poke steel wire down his throat until it pricked his heart. They had often threatened to kill Ron's grandfather who was the son of one of his tribe's most famous chiefs and so, when the *kadicha* were in the area, the entire family would leave their shanties during the night and huddle together in the bush in terror.

When he was fourteen, Ron left school and began to wander from place to place with his grandfather. Sometimes there was a job which paid well (he joined a sheep-shearing gang at Meeka-tharra, six hundred miles north-east of Perth) but for the most part there was little work and not much to eat.

When they came back from Meekatharra, the family lived in a sort of open-air aboriginal commune outside Perth. They camped under the trees and, when it rained, dragged a piece of canvas over them to keep dry. For food, the children stole veget-ables and chickens from the local farms (once, Ron was almost shot by an angry farmer), or else 'fossicked' on rubbish-dumps for food and scrap metal. They sold metal to dealers, and with the proceeds bought either dog meat or 'grog' — cheap wine at twenty cents a bottle. It was cheaper to get drunk, said Ron, because when you were drunk, you didn't need so much to eat.

There was a good deal of fighting in the commune, and the police were regular visitors. Often, one or other of Ron's relatives was taken to jail. At that time, jail was even more popular than usual. The aborigines were starving and jail was a passport to good, free meals.

For a time, the family's luck seemed to change. Grandfather found a farm job which paid six dollars a day. Then, the farmer accused him of taking a clock — it had, in fact, been stolen by someone who didn't even work on the farm but, nevertheless, he began to lock all his doors. That hurt Joseph Williams's pride and he told the farmer that, if he didn't trust him, there was no point in working there. So it was back to the rubbish heaps.

One day, grandfather asked Ron to go with him on their usual tour of the dumps. By this time, Ron had joined a gang of young aborigines who reckoned they could make an easy living by stealing money left outside by housewives to pay the milkman. Ron told his grandfather he wasn't going to come that day. Instead, the gang went off to the local baker's shop and asked for stale bread. When the baker refused, they stole a bagful and had their best meal for weeks, as much stale bread as they could eat washed down with mugs of hot tea.

Joseph Williams, however, never came home again. He had been killed by men from another camp, and his body had been hidden in a bush. One of his sins, so far as they were concerned, was that he had seen their fellow-tribesmen robbing a white man, and testified against them to the police. For Ron, this was a shattering blow. His grandfather meant more to him than anyone else in the world. Now, he felt, he had nothing to live for. For the first time in his life, he really prayed. 'God, if you're there,' he said, 'send my grandfather back alive and I'll believe you're real.'

Soon, he had begun to drink more and more heavily. A relative told him he would end up like his mother, 'the biggest boozer under the sun'. Ron didn't care. The one whom he loved most was dead and, if this was all there was to life, he didn't want to go on living anyway. Often, he contemplated suicide. Back at Meekatharra again, he would go out into the bush and stand on the edge of a disused mine-shaft weeping and trying to screw up enough courage to throw himself into the abyss. The only thing which deterred him was the thought of getting stuck half-way down among the broken timbers.

One of Ron's uncles, seeing his misery, lent him a tattered old Bible with no cover; that, he said, might help him. Ron took the book with him when he went out hunting kangaroos and often read it under a tree or in a cave.

Out in the bush he discovered the 34th Psalm:

This poor man cried and the Lord heard him, and saved him out of all his troubles.

O taste and see that the Lord is good; blessed is the man that trusteth in Him.

The Lord redeemeth the soul of his servants; and none of them that trust in Him shall be desolate.

The words stirred a hope in Ron's heart, though he did not feel he fully understood them. When the winds of adversity blew, he asked himself, did a man have to go under, or could he somehow rise above them?

In Gnowangerup again for the sheep-shearing, he stayed with his grandfather's relatives. His Uncle Fred had just come back from a six-months' spell in Fremantle jail for stealing a motor-bike. There, he had learnt to read and write, and he had also been to church. He told Ron that he ought to go if he had the chance, because it made you feel good. Ron knew that Uncle Fred had had family problems while he was in jail and realised that attending church must have been a real help to him. At the same time, he didn't like the idea, because he felt that church was something for women and children. There didn't seem anything manly about it. In any case, so far as he could see, Christianity was only a white man's religion.

Gnowangerup was known for its fighters and sportsmen, for gambling and a liberal supply of prostitutes. It was also a mission station, with a handful of missionaries who worked from an old, galvanised-iron church which had previously been a schoolhouse. One of the young men at the United Aboriginal Mission, a white Tasmanian called Frank, befriended Ron and often called on him. Ron noticed that Frank wasn't ashamed to come and squat by the camp-fire and talk, even though the aborigines dressed in rags and lived in squalor. They were not even allowed to draw their water from the rain tanks but instead had to take muddy water from a nearby dam. As a result, there was a good deal of sickness.

Then, one day, Ron noticed a little aboriginal girl called Terese crying because nobody would take her to church. All her family were busy gambling. This, thought Ron, gave him a perfect excuse to go to church himself. If people laughed at him, he could tell them he'd only gone to help the little girl.

After that first visit, he knew he had found what he was looking for. He was filthy and in rags—he'd worn the same clothes for three weeks without changing, and had no money for soap or a razor—his trousers were torn, he had no shoes and, as he said with a grin, 'You could smell me before you saw me.' But neither the torn clothes nor the smell seemed to make any difference to the missionaries.

'Despite all the rags and tatters, nobody turned their nose up,' said Ron. 'They told me it was good to see me, and that I'd be welcome any time. When I went up to see them again, they weren't like the other white people; they took me into their houses and I sat at the same table as them and used the same plates, the same towel and the same sink. At last, I felt wanted.'

Ron began to wonder what it was that made these people so different from most of the other whites he had met and one day, at the County Agricultural Show, Frank told him how God had changed his life. If God could do that for Frank, Ron thought, I'd like Him to do the same for me, because I'm at the end of the line.

So, that Show Day, he and Frank sat together under a gum tree away from the milling crowds and Ron asked God to take his life and change him.

His first thoughts were for his mother. He felt that, as a boy, he had treated her very cruelly — often killing little birds and hanging them round his belt like scalps, though he knew she disliked it — and that he wanted to make amends. By this time she had remarried but, although Ron had always hated his stepfather, he decided he would live with them for a time. To his surprise, he found that he could feel a genuine love for his stepfather.

Both his mother and stepfather then drank a good deal, but Ron read to them from the New Testament he carried with him. They asked Ron what had happened to his taste for wine and liquor and he told them that he had finished with it. That Christmas, he sang carols to the prisoners in Gnowangerup jail. Before his mother died, of cancer, at the age of thirty-eight, he felt he had been able to do something to heal the deep wounds of the years.

In 1960, Ron became one of the first students at the Gnowangerup Bible College. While he was there, a missionary told him he had just come back from the goldfields and that he had seen a man die in another missionary's arms after being speared. There was, he said, a great need for someone to go to that area. Ron immediately felt that was where God wanted him to work, among the men who had killed his grandfather and had been his people's enemies for centuries.

When he first arrived in the goldfields in 1962, he was terrified of the reception he would get. He also knew that, if he was going to help people, he would have to be free not only of his fear, but also of the hatred he had felt after his grandfather's murder. He asked God to take both away so that he might represent Him better.

He immediately went to see the man mainly responsible for his grandfather's death. The man had become a drunkard and, in any case, did not know who Ron was. He begged for twenty cents so that he could buy another drink. Ron explained why he had come, and told the man that Christ loved him and could offer him a better life. The man hung his head and walked away.

Ron then began working among the aboriginals in the gold-fields area. He would sing to them with his guitar, and tell them what had happened to him. Soon, however, he was facing a personal crisis of a different kind. He fell in love with a white girl who worked with the mission, but ran into fierce opposition from her father, who declared flatly that there were already enough half-caste children. This summary rejection made Ron bitter against the white man. The aborigines, he thought, were like the Jews—a despised people for ever condemned to travel an uphill road. He remembered that a white Christian worker had once said to him that aborigines could never take any leadership, that they were descendants of Cain and needed white men to guide them. For a time, he thought of leaving the mission and joining the army.

While he was still in turmoil, he had a serious accident. One morning while he was rounding up cattle, his horse bolted and threw him into a tree. His skull was fractured and he lay there unconscious till late in the afternoon out in the bush, thirty miles from the mission station. As he recovered consciousness, he was found and taken to the nearest house.

That night, the pain was agonising and Ron felt sure he was going to die. Why not end it all quickly by his own hand? He looked for the strychnine which farmers used to kill the wild dogs which Australians call dingoes, but he could find only iodine. As he considered whether to take it, the thought occurred to him that the aborigines had very few leaders and that he would be a coward if he, too, opted out by taking his own life.

In his agony, he told God that he didn't want to die and asked

Him what he ought to do. Some words from the 118th Psalm came into his mind:

I shall not die, but live, and declare the works of the Lord.
The Lord hath chastened me sore: but he hath not given me over unto death.

Then, said Ron, he felt sure he would live and, although his doctor in the Perth Royal Hospital told him he ought to have been dead, after a major operation and several weeks' rest, he was able to go back to the goldfields.

One night, alone in the little house in the candlelight, it seemed to Ron that Christ spoke to him in an audible voice. The words were those spoken to the woman taken in adultery: 'Neither do I condemn thee.' That night, for the first time in months, Ron slept like a baby and woke up with the conviction that there were many others with needs far greater than his own.

He broke off his relationship with the white girl by letter and became a missionary in the bush, camping and working with the wild aborigines. At first, he was afraid that he would be killed. Not only did he come from another tribe, but he was also a half-blood, and full-bloods, he knew, hated half-bloods. Murders were not at all uncommon. He had seen several, and had often intervened in fights by jumping between the men and telling them to ask God to help them forgive each other. When he was alone in the bush at night and gripped by fear, Ron would pray or sing hymns until the fear left him.

Working for a 'faith mission', as he was, he had no salary and depended entirely on what people gave him, so he usually either hitch-hiked or travelled on foot, carrying only a blanket, a change of clothes and a little food. He lived off the bush and often slept on the ground.

Ron camped with one group of aborigines, helping them to sink wells and set up windmills. He remembers digging a well with a hundred other aborigines and then having to walk ten miles in a heat of 120 degrees for a drink. When they arrived, there was a dead snake in the water but Ron still drank copiously.

That night, with his leg covered in boils and freezing with cold because he had no blanket, Ron asked God why he had to be a missionary. Then, suddenly, one of the aborigines who had initially been most suspicious of him began singing a song thanking God for Ron's coming. After eighteen months, the men in the tribe called him *koorda*, which means 'brother', and the children *kamaroo lampatju* or 'uncle of us all'.

When he had been in the goldfields for six years, Ron set off on a 12,000-mile tour of Australia, visiting churches, schools and hospitals. On the way, to make sure that he had lost his bitterness, he called on the white girl's father. Before he went, he asked God to make him really friendly and, much to his relief, the man received him warmly. Afterwards, Ron felt that a burden had been taken from him.

He still felt a need to get married, partly because he was working so much with families, and he prayed that God would send him the right partner.

An unlikely possibility occurred to him: a girl called Marjorie who had been at Gnowangerup Bible College but had told him she would never like him because he was too untidy. Like Ron, Marjorie had known great unhappiness. When she was fourteen, she had been raped by a white station manager and the child born to her had died. After leaving Gnowangerup, she had a heart-valve transplant and the doctors told her she had only two or three years to live. Ron nevertheless proposed to her and was accepted.

Since he had no money to buy an engagement ring, Ron set out to earn it by collecting scrap metal from rubbish heaps or picking wool off the backs of dead sheep and selling it for three cents a pound. It proved to be a hopelessly slow process, and in despair he and Marjorie asked God to help them. Their prayer was answered. Not only did friends send enough money for a ring, they also offered to pay for the wedding.

Ron then became pastor of an inter-denominational church at Derby in the remote Australian north-west. Derby is a port of perhaps 3,000 people which serves as an outlet for the cattle stations in the surrounding area. Once described as a town of sand, sin and sore eyes, Derby's conditions are so bad that wives often refuse to accompany husbands posted there. The humidity is very high in summer; the temperature often climbs to 115 degrees; and the area is prone to the kind of cyclone which devastated the city of Darwin in 1975. 'Definitely not the sort of place you'd want to stay in,' as one West Australian politician put it.

The People's Church, to which Ron and Marjorie had been sent, did not look any more promising. The building itself was a converted dormitory which had been condemned by the public health authority but, far worse from Ron's point of view, it was regarded mainly as a church for aborigines and even as a kind of Black Power centre.

Ron took a job as a part-time hospital orderly, Marjorie became a domestic science teacher and they set out to make friends in the white community. It was discouraging work. There was a good deal of suspicion, and many of the whites treated Ron in a highly patronising way. He felt they had built little fences around themselves as well as their houses.

One place where he always found a warm welcome was the Derby leprosarium, which had about one hundred patients, all of them aborigines. One was an old man, known as Boxer, who had been there fifteen years and acted as a kind of unofficial chaplain to the others. His 'assistant', Isaac, who spent most of his day praying at patients' bedsides, had been in the leprosarium for eighteen years.

Boxer was often in great pain, but the fact that Christ had suffered so much pain on the Cross gave him great comfort. He felt Christ understood his pain. He told Ron that he had once complained to God for keeping him so long in the leprosarium. God's reply, Boxer said, had been quite simple – 'And who's going to look after all these people if *you* go?' – and he had thanked God that that was his job.

What a difference, Ron thought, between the leprosarium and the homes of affluence where people were too proud to admit their need of God. 'When folks have got everything,' he said, 'the Gospel is often just a convenience, a pep pill when you're feeling down. For people like Boxer, it's the Bread of Life, the one hope.'

The more Ron saw of the prosperous white families, the more he realised they were often in greater spiritual need than the inmates of the leprosarium, or even the aborigines who lived in appalling conditions on the edge of the town. When he was rebuffed and inclined to be bitter, he told himself that there were many faults in his own life if God cared to point the finger.

Slowly, his bridge-building work bore fruit. More and more of the white community – teachers, nurses, a doctor and his wife—began to come to the People's Church. Soon, instead of the thirty aborigines who had attended evening service when Ron and Marjorie first arrived, there was a congregation of 140, half-black, half-white. Before Ron left, the foundations of a new church building had been laid.

In Derby, too, they adopted a child. Marjorie was unable to have children of her own and, when one of her relatives who was a patient in the leprosarium asked if Marjorie would look after her baby girl, Carol, she was delighted.

One day, Ron heard that his much-loved Uncle Fred had committed suicide. Even though he had ten children to raise, Uncle Fred had always sent money to support Ron's work. When Ron went to his funeral, he discovered why he had killed himself. For fourteen years, Uncle Fred had worked for the same white man and, in the process, had become one of the most respected members of the community. His great hope was that he would eventually be rewarded for his devotion by being made foreman. When the position became vacant, a white man turned up and was given the job. Uncle Fred came to the conclusion that he was just a no-good aborigine after all, a 'no-hoper'; and he went out and shot himself.

Ron had seen so many deaths like Uncle Fred's, where an aborigine had wanted to take responsibility but been denied it. It made him more determined than ever to try, with others, to give the leadership he felt his people so badly needed.

He had already taken part, in 1970, in the creation of the Australia-wide Aboriginal Evangelical Fellowship. There were 70 at the first meeting and, by 1974, the number had grown to 800, including 200 whites. In the same year, Ron went to the Bible College in Victor Harbour, South Australia, to get more training and to learn how to write in such a way that he could reach aborigines all over the country.

Victor Harbour, the college principal told him, had once been inhabited by aborigines who kept the first white settlers alive until supplies arrived from England. When, later, the town developed into a holiday resort, it was feared that the aborigines might scare off tourists and they were shipped forty miles across the bay.

'We've a real lack of leadership,' said Ron. 'So many of our fellows have just drifted along as they pleased. Many of them didn't want to think, they just lived for the day. What we need now is a moral and spiritual revolution for both aborigines and white men, in which both are willing to re-think the situation and accept change rather than say the problem is too great.

'To start with, we aborigines need to change in our attitude to ourselves. We've let ourselves be brainwashed with the idea that we can't make the grade and we've believed it. And our attitude to God needs to be changed so that we can rise above our feelings. We've got to get up and work.

'So often people have said our folks cannot do this or that. That doesn't help, but I do believe these very winds of adversity can be the things to help us. Just as it takes a wind to fly a kite, so the winds of adversity can help our lives soar up to God. The cord of the kite I liken to the love of God, which is unbreakable. The cord has to be held, and the one who holds it is Jesus, who will never let us go.

'I'm glad I'm an aborigine now, because we do have a contribution to make. I think of those humble men of Galilee who were trained by Christ to give something to the world.

'As for the white people who want to work with the aborigines, I'd like to be sure they have the right thing to give. If they're not free of bitterness themselves, then I'd say they've really nothing to offer. With bitterness and hatred in your heart, you can only stir up more bitterness and hatred in others, and the wounds will never heal.

'There is a right kind of militancy, but if the motive is bitterness, living in the past, it's not going to be healing or constructive. Revenge has never worked — we've seen that among the aborigines. We've had killings for centuries, but they've only caused bigger wounds and more fear.

'We don't want better laws, we want better men and for that you need a change in the human heart and only God can do that.

'There are a lot of things our white friends can do without making a loud noise. They can help at mission stations and they can teach and nurse and serve, things which are more obscure than sit-ins but which may be more to the point. People are too good at using the aborigines like a political football, but they're not so good at laying down their lives and meeting simple human needs. I'd say to those people, "Roll up your sleeves and stop shouting."

'When an aborigine is looking for a certain kind of spear, he breaks the branch of a tree and it tells him whether the root is good. Then he shapes it and carves it and straightens it and balances it in a fire. That is what my people and the white people need, to be straightened out in that kind of purifying fire.'

I am a white man and, as such, descendant of a race which has for centuries mercilessly exploited black, brown and yellow men. We do not deserve people like Ron Williams. They are God's gift, against all logic and expectation. If we cannot or will not learn from them that it is character which counts and not colour, then God help us.

4

The Man Upstairs

JOHN ARMORE WAS a diligent prosecuting attorney. To him, the courtroom was an arena of combat between himself and counsel for the defence. The outcome had nothing to do with the individual who stood accused and everything to do with preventing what he called 'the criminal element' from disturbing that nice suburban society of which he was a part and, in the process, enhancing his own status and reputation. Whether the charge was petty larceny, armed robbery or rape, the pursuit of justice was his theme: the law was society's instrument for taking revenge on those who flouted its edicts and his task was to make sure that that revenge was exacted in full.

How ironic, he thinks now, looking back, that he who was so thirsty for vengeance, so ardent in pursuit of justice, should himself become its prey, and—irony of ironies—that he should find in its bitter clutches a freedom he had never known before.

Armore looks exactly like what he is, a second-generation Italian-American. He is short and square-shouldered, with a swarthy complexion, dark, greying hair and an alert intensity of manner which suggests that he has lived either on his nerves or his wits, or both.

His father came from Sicily, his mother from Rome and, since his Roman grandmother didn't speak any English, John had to learn Italian. Grandmother was also a devout Catholic, so John was despatched to Mass every Sunday. Since his devotion to Mother Church was not so intense as his grandmother's, he usually contrived to end up reading comics in the boiler-room.

At home, his mother preached the virtue of thrift and impressed on him the merit of sharing in the household chores. Every Friday night, he became the floor-scrubber, an operation performed not at arms-length with a Johnny-mop, but on his knees.

In due course, John did what every good Catholic boy should do: he married a good, devout Catholic girl, Rosemary. He'd known Ro since he was small (though he hadn't been very interested until she started dating somebody else) and his father and her mother were both members of the same fraternity.

After two months of marriage, Rosemary saw her doctor to find out why she still wasn't pregnant. In their first five years together, she gave birth to three children and had two miscarriages.

By that time, John had joined his father in the successful family law practice and become president of a Young Democratic Club, the first step, he thought, to becoming a State legislator.

On the surface, it all seemed very promising if what you had in mind was a career which was a judicious mixture of politics and the law. Beneath the surface, the omens were a good deal less favourable. Only six months after his wedding day, John slept with another woman for the first time. He felt bad about it, but then a lot of people he knew in politics were leading double or even triple lives, and soon he'd embarked on a whole series of affairs, many of them with prominent female members of the Young Democratic Club. John tried to make sure that none of the girls knew he was having an affair with the others, and his life took on a somewhat baroque complexity.

He also discovered a passion for gambling. It began with occasional visits to race-tracks in and around New York— Roosevelt, Yonkers and Belmont, Long Island—and soon became a compulsive urge. The bets were small at first, but before long John was getting through $300 a meeting. That, however, was still well within the means of a man with a law practice which was developing very nicely.

The practice, like the Club, provided admirable cover for John's extra-marital enterprises. Rosemary had always said she wanted to live out in the country, so they bought a house forty-five miles from the city. It gave John a perfect excuse for coming home even less frequently. He took an apartment in the city and soon was home only at the weekends.

Rosemary resigned herself to what she thought was the inevitable. This, she assumed, was the way life was. She had never felt very close to John; there had always seemed to be a barrier, something between them that she couldn't identify. What that something might be she didn't know. Her upbringing had been very sheltered. All she knew was that there were certain topics she couldn't broach, because John would always block her and, after a while, she thought 'Why bother?' Communication between them became restricted to small-talk about the things which had to be done. 'How's young Tony? Did you take him to the doctor?' Looking back, their relationship *had* been kind of empty . . .

John, meanwhile, was savouring the sweet smell of success. His friends in the political game had begun patting him on the back, telling him that he was going places, promising him support. He sensed that they were buying his soul, that he was the locomotive while they were the cars and the caboose, but the price had to be paid. In many cases, the price was a slice of the political patronage which was available. There were, for example, a lot of jobs which were simply 'no show', men listed as county auto-mechanics who scarcely set foot in the place. They just signed the time-sheet and took the cheque. John knew people who held two or three jobs like that at the same time. It was a relatively easy matter to buy these sinecures by doing favours for the men in whose gift they lay. He would take care of their traffic tickets, or do legal work without charge or provide them with women. He had several girl-friends who would sleep with anyone he nominated. Then the man concerned could be pressured, if necessary.

The place where John was living in those days was fertile soil for the racketeer. Although betting was prohibited, gambling flourished. Many candy-stores were book-making operations, waitresses were running numbers and a lot of politicians were taking a lot of money to allow this to continue.

Occasionally, there would be so much public pressure that one of the operators would have to take the rap. There would be a raid on a particular establishment, but everybody would be notified in advance, and when the operator had been fined, he would move to another location and start up again with the full knowledge of the authorities.

Virtually everyone, said John, was in on the act. So many people, from the top down, were playing the game and sharing in the emoluments. His part in the racket was to defend people charged with being in possession of betting slips or having illegal telephones hooked up for taking bets. The entire procedure was cut and dried before the case went into court. Both sides knew exactly how much the fine would be. It was John's first view of the criminal justice system. It seemed to him a colossal charade, but a charade he was glad to take part in because it was both profitable and undemanding.

By this time, he was attending Mass only once in every three or four months, partly to pacify Rosemary, partly because the monsignor had a certain amount of political clout in the community. On the increasingly rare occasions when he went to confession, he would admit a variety of minor peccadillos but never the real truth about himself and his activities. He also insisted that his children should be taken out of the Catholic school system. He didn't need religion, so why should his children?

In 1959, John—who was already assistant city attorney—was appointed municipal prosecutor. Now he had become the very bulwark of justice with, as he saw it, a priceless opportunity to establish himself in the eyes of the public as Mr. Clean.

The ardour of his efforts in the courts, however, depended almost entirely on the likely benefit to his career. Sometimes, he simply looked the other way and let people he knew were guilty go scot-free. On other occasions when he had nothing to lose, he would prosecute with great vigour. On these occasions, he felt no compassion. The person in the box was a case, not an individual; all John Armore was interested in was the information on the file. When the judge had passed sentence, he felt no regret. Justice had been done and he had won a victory.

Soon, however, his marriage reached breaking-point. Rosemary had always hated his involvement in politics and, when he brought local politicians home, she often said afterwards that she wished he would get out of the whole rotten business. Now, she said, she couldn't tolerate any longer the way in which he was neglecting the children. They *had* to make a new start somewhere else.

This implied ultimatum gave John a nasty shock. He could suddenly see his marriage disintegrating, and found the prospect intolerable. He could justify to himself the way he had deceived Rosemary over the years, but could not face the thought that *she* did not want *him*. It was the same double standard which he had practised in the courts.

In the end, he took a job in Arizona, setting up a state-wide operation for an insurance company which wanted to move into the area. It meant a 40 per cent drop in salary, and an end of John's political ambition, but there seemed no alternative.

For two years he became, if not a model husband, at least a dutiful one. He genuinely tried to get closer to Ro and the children (every weekend, he turned out to watch his two boys play in Little League baseball); he went to confession regularly for a whole year; and he steered clear of other women for two years. His only indulgence was gambling which, in a very real sense, took the place of extra-marital sex. He started by exploring the local horse and dog tracks but soon tired of them because of the twenty- or thirty-minute gap between races. Then he discovered Las Vegas, which was only three hundred miles away. There, at the tables, he felt for the first time the exhilaration of a game where you could win or lose everything in a split second and go on playing with mounting intensity until you 'bust out'. There was, he found, a strange satisfaction in knowing that you'd lost all you could possibly lose.

The monthly trip to Vegas became part of his life. Often, Rosemary would go with him. John would take several hundred dollars and invariably lose it all within fifteen minutes of arriving at the gaming tables. He always made sure Ro had enough money to see them through the rest of the weekend. On one occasion, when she wasn't with him, he ran through $2,000 and they had to cash in some of their savings to meet the IOUs.

The insurance business, however, flourished and in 1965 the company asked John to open up for them in California. The salary was good, they had all the luxuries which went with the middle-class dream and John worked hard to build up the operation. In the evenings he taught law and insurance at a local junior college – partly to keep his mind off the gaming tables of Reno, which was just one hundred miles up the road, and partly to curb his wandering eyes.

For a time, it was effective. Eventually, however, the almost ceaseless activity caught up with him, and he ended up in hospital.

The doctors told John the trouble was over-work; he had to take life easier. With time on his hands in the evenings, the magnet of Reno became irresistible.

The trips were modest enough to begin with. John would drive up on Thursday night with perhaps $300 in his pockets and spend the entire night at Harold's or Harraha's. He played conservatively and usually didn't 'bust out' till five or six the following morning. The next Thursday, the routine would be much the same. The only difference was that John had $400, then $500, then $600 in his wallet.

As he sees it in retrospect, the urge which took him to the gaming tables was in reality a desire for self-destruction which happened to be channelled into gambling. 'I sought out the avenue of escape which was most palatable to me,' he said. 'If I'd had a propensity for alcohol, I'd have been an alcoholic; if it had been drugs, I'd have been an addict. For me, gambling was the vehicle I used to enter a comfortable but unrealistic world where I wouldn't have to face the frustrations and problems going on inside me.'

His life increasingly took on a Jekyll-and-Hyde quality. There was John the gambler, who had a complete disregard for money and its value, to whom dollars had no relevance once they had been turned into chips; and there was John the prudent family man, who would scan the telephone bill critically and, when he saw that someone had made a $3.85 call, would deliver a stern lecture to his wife and children.

By now, he had begun to spend money at a rate which bore no relation to his income. First to disappear was the $20,000 which he and Rosemary had laboriously accumulated in their savings account. John would go through the motions of studying the *Wall Street Journal* and then tell Rosemary they ought to get hold of some Bank of America stock, though he hadn't the slightest intention of buying any. Then he wheedled $15,000 out of a woman by hinting that he might be romantically inclined. Finally, he began stealing systematically from his employers.

The technique was simple enough. He drew up fraudulent policies insuring either a car or a home, and issued them to fictitious people. Then he bought four Cadillacs for their serial numbers — because repair bills for Cadillacs can run into thousands of dollars. Four, he judged, was adequate because he could always insure the same car under someone else's name and simply have the licence plates changed. Then the car concerned would be involved in an 'accident' and a claim supported by a collection of documents, all of them fraudulent, was sent to the company's head office. There would be police forms, bought from a highway patrolman; hospital bills purchased from members of the staff; forged letters from employers alleging loss of working time; doctors' bills bought from doctors' offices; repair estimates bought from local garages. When the insurance cheque duly arrived, the 'injured parties' cashed them, subtracted 20 or 25 per cent for themselves and gave the balance to John.

What surprised him most was how easy it was to persuade people to come in with him. Nobody turned him down, even though some of those he approached were regular churchgoers earning a comfortable living. Everyone seemed to have a price, whether it was money or a woman. Altogether, there were about twenty-five people in the ring of deception which he built up.

Even so, it was an apparatus which could scarcely support the demands John made on it. Every Thursday he would leave home for Reno and often did not arrive back until Sunday night. Sometimes he would sit at the tables for seventy-two hours without a break and with only an occasional orange juice to keep him going. He didn't want to sleep and he had no appetite for food and drink. As his adrenalin began to flow, he lost all count of time. There were no clocks in the casino and he didn't know whether it was day or night.

When he had used up his line of credit in the Reno casinos, he would take a cab to Lake Tahoe, where he had another line of credit and, when that was used up, catch the next plane to Vegas. Soon, he was gambling away $25,000 of the company's money every week.

Back at work on Monday morning, he would frantically begin drawing-up bogus policies so that the insurance company's cheques would reach the 'injured parties' before the cheques he'd given in the casinos came home to roost on Wednesday.

Rosemary, meanwhile, was becoming more and more desperate. She wasn't sure exactly what was going on—and John cut her off whenever she tried to find out—but she was shattered by the way he took off every Thursday and by their growing estrangement. Soon she began getting blinding headaches, and worried how she would be able to look after the children if any-thing happened. A woman she taught school with had been left with three small children, and Rosemary always had the feeling that the same thing would happen to her.

Then, in November 1967, the company began to get worried. A woman John had become involved with committed suicide and one of her friends wrote to the company, saying that John was responsible and that he was misappropriating company funds. The executive vice-president and an accountant turned up to investigate, but John knew exactly what they would be looking for and had prepared everything to put them off the scent. He emerged with a clean bill of health. Indeed, the president was so apologetic that he gave John a $2,500 bonus.

For a month, John stayed away from the gaming tables. He had looked into the abyss and didn't like what he saw. Then, in mid-February, he went back to Reno and, through the spring and early summer, gambled like a man gone mad. Altogether, in the eighteen months to 4th July, 1968, he went through at least $500,000 of the company's money.

At last, he felt he could go on no longer. On that 4th July, he flew to Chicago, telling his wife it was an urgent business trip. Rosemary remembers the day well. That morning, she had put up the Stars and Stripes on the garage. The following Sunday, a special delivery letter arrived from John. She opened it and started to read. It began, 'What I'm going to tell you is terrible. I have to let you know what I've been doing and if, when you've finished, you still want anything more to do with me, call me at this number.'

When she'd finished the first paragraph, Ro felt she just couldn't go on. Her eyes were scanning the words and her heart was pounding. She gave the letter to her sixteen-year-old son Tony, and asked him to read it for her.

Tony's reaction was simple. 'Momma, he's got to face up to it. That's what Dad has always told us—if you do anything wrong, don't be afraid to admit it.' Rosemary, however, was numb with shock. She was already taking tranquillisers. Now she lost her appetite and when, eventually, she did force herself to take food again, found it had texture but no taste. All she could think of at first was to follow the instructions which John had given her at the end of the letter: to transfer ownership of the house to herself, so that the authorities could not take it if he were caught.

The idea of leaving John simply never occurred to her. The furthest thought from her mind was to tell him that he was no good and that she didn't want ever to see him again. She had been searching for some way in which she could get close to him again and, when she recovered from the initial shock, realised that this, perhaps, was an opportunity for her to say, 'Here I am, let's start again.' God, she thought, sometimes works in strange ways and she wondered if perhaps this was His way of forcing John to see that he could not turn his back on what he knew to be true.

When she called John in Chicago, he told her that a ticket would be waiting at the airport. It turned out to be first-class: he had remembered that she suffered from claustrophobia. It was the first time Rosemary had ever flown first-class.

On the plane, she decided she would try to put down her thoughts in the form of a letter to John. It was the fruit of a lifetime's faith. She told John that sometimes disasters happen to help people become better human beings. A lot of people took the wrong road and it needed a crisis to bring them to their senses. Anyone, she said, could make a mistake, but it took a great person to face up to it. She added that someone who had slipped to the depths could still climb to the heights.

When she arrived, she gave him the letter together with a note which Tony had hurriedly scribbled on the pages of a diary. 'You've always told me never to lie and always to face up to the truth,' he wrote. 'You've also told me that there's no problem that can't be worked out if you just give it the good ole college try. Take your own advice and come back for my sake, for Mother's sake and especially for your own. We have never been really close but, if you come back, I think we could be.'

Rosemary spent two days with John in Chicago, and he told her everything. Of all the things which happened in the next months, John found being honest with his wife, owning up to the lies and hypocrisy of the years, the most difficult. He wept and asked for her forgiveness and understanding, and she did understand and forgive. There was, he remembers, not a word of reproach. All Rosemary said was that she wished he had told her before, because she could have helped him.

It was the first time, John said, that he had ever been completely honest with Rosemary, the first time they had sat down and *really* communicated. They had been married for seventeen years, and now he faced the fact that the whole business was quite literally based on a fraud.

Then he told Rosemary the alternatives as he saw them. There were three: disappearing off the face of the earth, doing away with himself, or being honest. He had already arranged another identity for himself in Dallas, Texas. He had left some clothes there, together with a driver's licence, social security card and credit cards in a fictitious name.

Rosemary told him that he couldn't go on running for ever, that the police would catch up with him at some time. Her advice was simple: go back and face the music. Before she left, John had already decided to take that advice. Once he had been honest with Ro, he said, he felt he had to start doing things right. When he had seen her off, he flew to Dallas, destroyed his new identification papers and took a plane back to California.

He went straight to the district attorney's office and made a full statement admitting what he had done and explaining how he had done it. Then he told the others involved in the fraud what he had decided to do, so that they would have the choice of either giving themselves up or making a run for it. Later, he spent an entire day with the DA's men taking them through his office files one by one, pointing out which were fraudulent.

At his trial, John pleaded guilty to larceny, forgery and violation of the insurance code, and spoke not a word in his own defence. His sense of guilt was acute and he wanted to be punished; he was a penitent who had chosen the penitentiary. The court sentenced him to an indeterminate term of between two and twenty-eight years, which meant that the date of his release rested on his prison record and the decision of a parole board.

In the days before he went to jail, John felt closer to Rosemary than ever before. 'I could look at her and not feel guilty,' he said. 'It was so refreshing to be a totally honest human being.'

Soon, however, he felt the full cost of repentance. He was driven to Vacaville Prison in chains and shackles; there were irons on his legs and handcuffs wrapped around his wrist. Then, for the first time, he was overwhelmed by despair. He began to think of the stories he had heard about prisons, the killings which went on, how inhuman they were. He wondered how he would ever survive in that jungle. As he heard the steel doors slam behind him, he thought, 'My God, what *have* I done—I'll never get out of here alive.'

In the prison reception centre, John was given a crew-cut, ordered to take off his clothes, deloused with a chemical spray and given a green uniform to mark him out as a 'fish', a novice in the prison system. His rings and his wrist-watch were taken away. Even a book of stamps was confiscated.

Then he was given a number—B17228—which was stamped on his shoes and photograph; issued with a mattress and a pillow, a sheet and a blanket, a razor and one blade, a toothbrush and pocket comb, and taken to his cell. It was five feet by eight and had solid steel doors with a small glass panel. The furniture consisted of a concrete bunk, a metal desk, a stool, a toilet and a sink.

The first night, said John, was 'like seeing hell for the first time'. He felt like a fish out of water, gasping for air which wasn't there. That night he prayed, prayed fervently on his knees for the first time in his life, asking God to give him the strength to endure what he had to undergo. He didn't think God had heard him. Then he wrote to Rosemary, trying to comfort her.

In the next days, John felt he had become an object, a human part of a mechanical process. The door of his cell opened at fixed times. When he lined up for meals with the other prisoners, he was told when to sit down and when to get up. And at seven-thirty every evening he was back again in the solitude of his cell.

There was no telephone; the only 'money' was prison scrip, pieces of cardboard issued in five-cent denominations, and cigarettes were both a luxury and a medium of exchange. You paid in cigarettes for illegal items like chewing-gum—which the prison authorities were afraid might be used to jam locks—for magazines like *Playboy*, for heroin, or for having someone killed. The price of that was three boxes of cigarettes: that was the value of a human life in prison, said John, about $10.

As far as possible, he steered clear of the other prisoners. He didn't want to become part of them, he thought he was somehow different from the rest of the prison population—and he was afraid. Before he went to prison, he'd pictured them as a group of ogres like the men played in movies by Humphrey Bogart or Jimmy Cagney—vicious, mean, and talking out of the sides of their mouths.

First impressions suggested that he wasn't too far wrong. He was given the job of co-ordinating prisoners' intelligence-test results for the prison's vocational psychologist. The man John replaced had been imprisoned for incest and the prisoner who put together the test scores for each inmate's 'profile sheet' was inside for sexual perversion.

John then discovered that another of the men working in the unit, an old 'con' who had been found guilty of armed robbery, was selling test scores. For an appropriate fee, he would 'adjust' an IQ from 80 to 120 and even a personality profile could be doctored if the price was right. John felt that he had to make a stand on the issue and told the old 'con' that the tests had to be run honestly. The response was brutal. If he didn't toe the line, he'd have his knee-caps smashed. John was terrified, but the 'con' eventually backed down.

Soon, however, he began to see his fellow-prisoners through different eyes. There were two cheque-forgers (known in the prison jargon as 'paperhangers') who seemed to him fine young men. Whatever had prompted them to do what they had done, John wondered. And there was a former police officer who had arrived home drunk one night, twirled his gun round his finger and accidentally shot his wife through the head. This man lived in constant anguish: he couldn't forgive himself for what he had done, and the only time John ever saw him happy was when he knew he had cancer of the liver and was going to die.

The more prisoners John came to know, the more he saw that imagination was his worst enemy and that the other inmates, far from being ogres, were human beings just like himself, except that the majority had little or no education, bad work records and came from ghetto areas. Very few, he thought, were pro-fessional criminals. Most wanted to do their time, get out and start afresh.

This change in John's attitude to his fellow-prisoners was part of a fundamental shift in his entire way of life. One external sign of the shift was that he began to attend church as soon as he arrived in prison. While he was still on bail, he had been ashamed to enter a church. When he had been punished, he felt

able to go at last, and say honestly that he was seeking for understanding and guidance.

John attended Mass regularly and went to confession when he
thought he had something he ought to confess. During the week,
he often sat quietly at the back of the prison chapel and meditated.
He also spent a lot of time praying. 'I don't think it's necessary
to be on your knees all the time,' he said. 'I prayed lying on my
bed or meditating or even when I was writing a letter to Ro.'

He knew from weekly visits and from her letters that Rosemary
was having a difficult time with her health and pleaded with God
to give him the chance of eventually going home and helping
hold his family together. He promised God that, if he was given
that opportunity, he would try to be the kind of man he knew
he ought to have been all along, concerned with his fellow-men
and not just himself.

'I realised,' said John, 'that what He'd been trying to tell me
all those years, but I was too thick to hear, was that He had
given me my talents to help my fellow-men, not to bastardise
them as I had done. I didn't pray for things like "let me out,
please". I prayed "Please help me to be a more efficient vessel
for You".'

While he was in prison, John's relationship with Rosemary
blossomed. After the first weeks, when they had to speak by
telephone across a glass partition, John was allowed to go to the
visiting-room and embrace Rosemary when she arrived and
before she left, and although he was brought back to earth by
being stripped and searched after his wife had gone, he appreciated
her as never before. 'We became closer than in all the seventeen
years we'd been married,' he said. 'We had an absolute honesty
and a pure love we'd never had before. For the first time in all
those years, I wasn't thinking only of me, saying, "Hey, look at
me, feel sorry for me." I was trying the best I knew to emulate
and live Christ's teachings.'

'We were certainly closer than we'd ever been in our entire
marriage,' added Rosemary. 'John became a very patient person,
much more open to anything I said. One day to my amazement,
he gave me a holy picture, with a picture of Christ on it. He
could never have done that before! Something I had lost faith in
had finally happened.'

John also began to sense the birth of a new purpose for his

life. 'For my first eighteen months in prison,' he said, 'I was doing time, asking for forgiveness and seeking a better understanding of myself. Then, during a conversation with another inmate, it came to me, just a feeling and a warmth and an understanding that I was going to be given a new purpose and that it would in some way involve working with these men.

'I just knew at that moment beyond reasonable doubt that this was my mission, that I was going to help my fellow-humans and that my incarceration was a preparation for that mission. It wasn't a Voice which thundered, "John, you're going to do that," but there's no doubt it came from The Man Upstairs.

'I told Ro, I shall have to work with these people, some way, somehow. I was deeply moved by them. If two hundred out of the two thousand ever had visitors, that was tops. There were at least 80 per cent nobody cared about—either they'd been shunned by their families, or they had no one, or they were too far away to visit.

'There were men constantly kept under heavy medication to control their behaviour. They were the ones with a propensity to violence and they were given a drug called Prolixin. The result was that they looked like robots; they just stared and they couldn't sit still; their hands and feet were on the move all the time. We've progressed such a long way!

'But I guess the ones who moved me most were the youngsters. I remember one young man on LSD who'd been sentenced to Reception Guidance for ninety days, and then perhaps probation on parole. Apparently he hallucinated and started to climb the fence. I saw them shoot him off it. I thought, there's *got* to be a better way.'

Rosemary told John she was 100 per cent with him and herself started giving lifts to wives who had no cars in which to visit their husbands. John took correspondence courses in vocational rehabilitation counselling and began working with some of his fellow-prisoners on a voluntary basis. He tried to help men who were having trouble holding their marriages together and befriended those who had lost all hope, like an ex-World War Two and Korean veteran who was an alcoholic.

After he had been in jail for eighteen months, John went before the parole board for the first time. He told them that he had made peace with himself, his wife, his employer (to whom he had written, offering to make restitution) and his God, but the board turned him down and ordered him to come back in a year's time.

John found the next year intensely frustrating. He knew there were problems at home, but he was helpless to do anything about them. He was moved from Vacaville to San Quentin and then to a half-way house in Oakland. There, he was asked to look after the cash register in the staff canteen, which made him feel that at last he was trusted.

At the half-way house the idea was that if he could find a job, he was allowed to work outside during the day, though he had to go back to the house at night. He was given three weeks in which to find that job.

Some clothes were provided, but no money and John even had to borrow a dime to call Rosemary to ask if she could let him have a few dollars. At that moment, he felt profoundly frustrated. Would his debt ever be paid? Would society ever forgive? Or was he really doing a life sentence on the instalment plan?

The feeling became stronger as the days went by. He went first to the local Legal Aid Society and asked whether he could help in the preparation of litigation. They'd like to have taken him on, they said, but couldn't run that risk. Then he tried the Employment Service and told them that he'd already qualified as a vocational rehabilitation counsellor and wanted to take the State examination. They were sympathetic but said he wouldn't be able to do that until he'd finished his parole.

In the next days, John learnt what rejection meant. He applied for everything from service-station operator to dishwasher — 'I wasn't proud, I just wanted to stay out' — and each time he was turned down. 'We'll let you know,' they'd say, but they never did. Altogether, he was turned down thirty times. By now, two weeks had gone by and he was desperate.

Finally, someone suggested that he go to the Community Action Council at Placerville, between Sacramento and Tahoe. The Council was being run by a former Catholic priest, Dave Pollard. John told Pollard his qualifications and how much he wanted to help people, and Pollard gave him a job as the Council's legal services specialist.

John found himself giving advice to the poor and needy of all kinds, anyone who needed food, clothing or shelter. After six months, Pollard asked him to take over the Pla-Neva Corporation, a non-profit organisation with a contract from the National Alliance of Businessmen to find jobs for disadvantaged people. In reality, the Corporation was all but defunct: local employers had pledged 138 jobs but Pla-Neva hadn't been able to persuade them to honour their commitment or provide the back-up services which the NAB contract required.

John rapidly put the Corporation back on its feet again. He got the companies moving by explaining the benefits of the scheme (the government paid up to forty-five weeks' salary to cover the cost of training) and did so well that he collected forty new job pledges. Soon, Pla-Neva was given two additional NAB contracts, one of them — to John's delight — specifically for forty ex-offenders.

He worked a fourteen-hour day, fighting to find the former prisoners not merely jobs, but jobs he knew would satisfy them, and he gave them most of his $500-a-month expense allowance. He knew from experience they needed the money much more than he did. At his suggestion, the Council bought a small apartment where ex-offenders could live until their first pay-check arrived and he persuaded local car dealers to give the Council used models which they had taken as trade-ins.

There were problems — one man ran up a $200 telephone bill in the apartment — but plenty of successes too. There was the fork-lift truck driver who had become a burglar: John spent two or three evenings a week talking to him, and eventually found him a job. Soon, he had become a foreman. Then there was the man convicted of armed robbery who had had his teaching credential withdrawn as a result. John found him a job as head of a drug-abuse programme.

After four months in the half-way house, John was put on parole. After three long years, he was free to go home. Curiously, the prospect filled him with apprehension. Would the children accept him? What would Ro feel about having him around again? John knew that they had built up a deep relationship while he was in prison, but he was desperately afraid it would fall apart now.

Re-adjustment was indeed a difficult and painful process. The children had been deeply hurt, and communication with them was far from easy, while Rosemary, who had had to fend for the family alone for three years, had naturally become much more independent.

One thing they had learnt in the years of separation, however, and that was to talk problems through, even when they seemed to be at loggerheads. 'It was difficult,' said John, 'but at least we had the sense to sit down and be totally honest with one another – and that's the basis of any real relationship.'

Freedom also brought the return of old temptations. Once, John took a trip to Reno and spent $60 at the tables, but Rosemary gave him such a roasting that since that time he has not gambled, taken a bet, nor been anywhere near a race-track. 'The propensity is still there,' he said, 'and I just have to keep well away from the sources of temptation. For the same reason, I have a checking account to deal with current bills, but Ro is the only one who can draw on our savings account.

'It's the same with women. Sometimes I look, but then I tell myself, "Now you're going to your room," and I can honestly say that the only woman I want to be with is my wife.'

After John had been with Pla-Neva for fifteen months, the president of the NAB, John Delorean, came to Sacramento to speak at a lunch which was part of a campaign to collect more job pledges for the disadvantaged. John Armore spoke at the same lunch. Afterwards, Delorean asked John to drive him to the airport and, on the way, asked if he would be interested in coming to Washington to direct the NAB's entire national ex-offender programme. The job, said Delorean, was basically to wake up the business community to the failure of the prison system and to the vital importance of their own part in helping ensure that ex-offenders didn't find their way back into prison.

Ever since he had left prison, John had felt that his path was somehow predetermined, but this was the crowning glory, an opportunity he had never expected in his wildest dreams.

There was only one problem, he told Delorean; he was still on parole. Two weeks later, his parole agent rang to say he had great news: John was discharged from parole, with effect from midnight the following day. In the autumn of 1973, he was on his way to Washington. He threw himself into his new work with tremendous intensity. In 1974, he spoke on 150 occasions in no less than eighty different cities. Always he told something of his own story, always he spoke of the men and women in prison as his own brothers and sisters.

He also visited between forty and fifty prisons all over the United States, to see what the conditions were like and to speak alone with prisoners so that they would know there was someone who cared. He went despite the fact that each time he hears the iron doors clang behind him, he experiences the same sense of overwhelming despair that he felt when he arrived at Vacaville. He has never lost the fear of going into prison, the fear that he may never be allowed out. That, at least, he says, reminds him that he has walked in the prisoners' shoes.

Talking to businessmen, John often asks his audience a blunt and disturbing question: what would they do if 70 per cent of their product were sent back to them? That, he points out, is exactly what happens in the prison system, where 70 per cent of the 100,000 men and women released every year are back behind bars within five years, mainly—he argues—because of the way they are screened out of jobs and discriminated against after their release. The average offender, he goes on, is disproportionately black, under twenty-five, from a background of ghetto and broken home and with no vocational skills; yet all the system does for men like that is put them behind bars and expect them somehow to become better people, instead of helping them help themselves. The vast majority, he claims, are not professional criminals. Only one in a hundred is imprisoned for murder or rape. The average burglary yields only $226. What then, he asks, is the point of a system which returns such people to society older, more bitter, more frustrated, more volatile and actually *less* able to take their place in society again? What is the point of a system based on 'doing time' when the 'time' does nothing to fit the individual to resume a normal life but actually renders him incapable of doing so?

Far from arguing against law and order, John says, he firmly believes that, without a proper framework of law, any society will fall apart. Nor is he suggesting to employers that they should hire ex-offenders at the prison gate. The whole point of the NAB programme is to give the best possible guarantee that the ex-offender concerned really does want to make a fresh start.

No, what he wants is for America to open its eyes to the plain message of the figures—that it has a prison system which, far from solving any problems, merely perpetuates itself. The future prospect, he declares, is equally plain—more Atticas unless

America will face the fact that it has a problem and that that problem is 'stinking thinking'. An alternative, says John, has to be found to putting people back into breeding-grounds for crime rather than correctional establishments.

He recalls his own experience of what was, in many ways, a sick society. He observed, for example, that there were a good many homosexuals in the prison population. They were known as 'the cuties' or 'the sweeties' and men were constantly fighting for their attention, condoned by the custodial staff. John often saw them walking down the corridors holding hands and kissing. On Saturday mornings, they were allowed to go into the shower-room undisturbed. He came to the conclusion that about a third of all the prisoners took part in active homosexual practices and that the danger of young men being seduced while they were in prison was very considerable.

Similarly, he has noticed that in some prisons there is not even professional counselling for men convicted of rape. The 'counselling' sessions which do exist are sometimes conducted by prison officers with, at best, a high-school education who merely want to collect some extra money. At one session John sat in on, they simply discussed football and basketball, but that appeared in the Corrections Department Manual statistics under 'group counselling'.

The same kind of public-relations version of the system, he says, disguises the fact that very little rehabilitation is currently taking place in America's prisons. He recalls a recent visit to a women's institution with 176 inmates which had no vocational training except sewing, hair-styling and make-up (and in that State, cosmetology is a restricted occupation from which ex-prisoners are precluded). The NAB persuaded a local employer to provide a computer key-punch training programme entirely free, but the institution, which already has a staff of 132, said it couldn't afford the extra security such a programme would demand.

He had met the same illogical nonsense in other States – most prisons, for example, train their inmates to become barbers, despite the fact that ex-offenders are barred from becoming barbers in half the States in the Union – and the same reluctance to do anything constructive. 'The general line,' he said, 'is "we're providing all these services", but the truth often is that they're not. Far too much correction is just a matter of pre-serving the status quo.' He estimates that only 10 per cent of the prison population get any meaningful vocational training.

He also believes that, if you want to help offenders prepare themselves to return to the community, it is self-evident that they ought to be kept as close as possible to the community, not isolated from it. He wants to see offenders who are not a physical threat allowed to work in factories during the day, and then go back to prison at night—on the lines of what happens at the Federal Correctional establishment between Fort Worth and Dallas. There, he said, 300 passes were given to prisoners at Christmas 1973; only two did not come back.

John, however, is not inclined to lay all the blame for the failure of the prison system at the door of reactionary custodians. To him, it represents a failure of society and its attitudes. 'Penitentiary,' he said, 'comes from the word penitence, mean-ing to give an individual time to reflect and repent, but we've twisted that into a system of revenge.

'The truth is that America is a very self-righteous and judge-mental country. We're revengeful, we're the first to condemn. I know I was. Boy, if I read a story in the paper about someone who'd been punished, he deserved all he got and then some. I didn't even understand, but I was always ready to pass judgement.

'What we've done is build a wall around ourselves, a wall which is higher than any prison wall—and it's a wall of self-righteousness. We're good, we're righteous, we seldom err and those who do deserve all they get.

'The trouble is that so many of us are not honest about our-selves. If we were, we wouldn't ever be self-righteous. We see ourselves as good and law-abiding. It's all right for us to steal—time from our employers, towels from motels, items from the office, money from the tax-man. The people who do these things aren't offenders, you know, but everyday citizens. The truth is that those who talk loudest about upholding the standards of justice are often its greatest violators.

'If we practised our religion 168 hours a week, we'd break out of that wall of self-righteousness for ever and then we'd be able to understand and forgive and reach out and help. Each of us has to look first and foremost to Him and, in doing so, we may be able to find both our true selves and a moral rebirth.

'What I've been able to do so far is just a drop in the bucket. In the last two years we placed only 20,000 people in jobs through the NAB. I feel we're just crawling. When you're bucking a system that's been stagnant for years, you often feel as if you're beating your head against a wall.

'We have so much to do and such a long way to go and I don't ever want to stop. I want to go on more than I want to breathe. I feel such a yearning within to do it.

'You may wonder why. I know I could still be concerned first and foremost with me but, if I did that, I'd be right back where I was. Through the experience I had, I found myself—but, as a condition of so doing, I was given an obligation to help these fellow human beings. I was given a second chance and I want the same for all the others.

'What have I learnt through it all? Not to live for myself, but to try to pattern my life after Christ's image. I'm not that way naturally, but I'm never going to give up trying.

'What happened to me, I felt was meant to be; it was His Will. I had to be brought to that point and shaken up. Has it left a mark? Yes, a Cross—not a Cross that I'm carrying on my shoulders but a Cross over my heart.

'The things that have happened have made me a better person. Before I went to prison, I never noticed things. Now, I see beauty in everything. I talk to people on the plane or the train just because they're them. It's a feeling of "Hey, I'm your brother and we shouldn't ignore one another and get hung up in this world of got-to-get-ahead".

'Before prison, I had great difficulty in sleeping. I used to get up in the middle of the night and take a drive, because there were all these things I was hiding. That stopped the day I got to prison because I was at peace with myself and, to this day, I can take a fifteen-minute nap anywhere. I've also lost all fear of death. I'd hate not to finish what I've started here, but I'm sure there'd be somebody else.

'Before, I had to keep going because I was afraid I might look into the mirror and see what I was really like. Now I can relax at home, and I spend a lot of time communicating with The Man Upstairs. Mostly, I'll be asking, "How can I handle this situation? How can I do things better?" When I need help, there's always a thought there. At night, I ask His concurrence in the way I've lived and what I did wrong. If I've been sharp with Rosemary, I say I'm sorry. I have an acute feeling that He is taking me by the hand and leading me. With one hand, He guides; with the other, He provides comfort and serenity. He's there all the time, it's not something that comes or goes.'

'Even today,' said Rosemary, 'I don't know how it's all happened. Our marriage has been reborn. We don't agree on everything, but we know how to talk to each other. I feel so much part of John now. I guess in a way I'm glad we went through it. If not, we might have been married for fifty years and never known each other.

'It's strengthened my faith so much. Life is very short and we don't see things the way God does, in the light of eternity. It's like a parent with a child. God knows what's best for us even when we don't.'

5

The Trivial Round

IF A SOCIAL scientist were able to measure and rank the
characteristic emotions of our age, gratitude would not be
prominent among them. The more we have, the less grateful
we are. Each improvement in our material condition is greeted
by louder complaint, each extension of human rights or freedom by yet more strident protest. The refrain for an anthem of
our times would surely include the words 'not enough'.

By the same token, gratitude for what you have is regarded by
many of our luminaries as both a sign of feebleness of spirit and
a passive surrender to the forces of reaction. If any conclusion
can be drawn from the way they act, it is that human happiness
springs from ceaseless complaint.

Yet the truth is that gratitude is to happiness what flour and
yeast are to bread. It is a difficult lesson for the twentieth century
to accept and certainly not one which can be learnt from our
contemporary oracles, whose endless dissatisfaction so often
produces furrowed faces and devastated lives. It is a wisdom best
seen in the lives of the poor and the humble, lives like that of
Bessie Johnson King.

Bessie was born somewhere in Florida. Exactly where, she is
not just sure, nor just exactly when either, since she has no birth
certificate. She *had* to have a birthday for social security purposes,
so she negotiated one on the basis of her own best guess. According to that, she is now seventy-three.

If you saw Bessie in a crowd, you'd probably pass her by
without a second glance. She is amply built, plainly dressed, unremarkable in appearance, just an elderly black woman of very

modest means who takes care of herself, you might think—if you thought anything at all.

In a crowd, though, you might miss her eyes, which still have the mischievous twinkle of a child's, eyes in which laughter flows as freely as tears; and you would certainly miss her chuckle, which rolls around inside her like underground thunder.

Bessie lives in a simple wooden house in one of the less fashionable parts of Alexandria, Virginia. It has a small white screened porch with a rocking chair. In back is a vegetable garden where Bessie still raises some of her own vegetables—tomatoes, peppers, sweet potatoes, corn and squash—mostly because she loves to see things grow. Inside the house is another rocking-chair, where Bessie sits when she isn't doing anything else, which isn't often.

Her maternal grandmother, she said, was born a slave. During the Civil War, Grandmother once told Bessie, some white soldiers from the North had threatened her and ordered her to throw down a white child she was nursing. Grandmother refused and ran off with the child still in her arms. Grandfather, he'd worked in a cotton mill. One day, it was so hot he drank half a gallon of iced water and had a stroke.

Bessie's father ran away from home before her memory could capture his face, and he never came back. Mother raised Bessie and her three brothers by taking in laundry. She did Mayor Chappell's shirts, said Bessie proudly; that brought in $9 a week. Soon, however, Mother was stricken with pleurisy and, on the days when she was laid low, Bessie did 'jus' about everythin'.

She'd wash and she'd iron with a small board and small irons, heated by charcoal, which Momma had bought especially for her. 'I started with pocket handkerchiefs,' she recalled, 'then I went on to towels and underclothes. Hate it? No, *sir*, I used to love it. I *still* love it.

'You wet 'em, an' then you let 'em grow. The big thing is don't leave any cat tracks, those little wrinkles where the iron don't touch. I sure enjoyed it and I sure did feel pride.

'What Momma taught us was to work and to try to save a little in case you have to have somethin'—and don't ever wish for what the other feller got. And she made us mind tryin' to do things right. She was hard on me, but I'm kinda glad she was, otherwise I'd be jus' like the rest of 'em.'

Helping Momma to pay the doctors' bills meant that Bessie didn't have much schooling. 'Education?' she said, eyes gleaming. 'Why, I got very little of that! Only till sixth grade, and then jus' some days. I couldn't truthfully say *how* many, but it wasn't *too* many. If you want to know the truth I never did like school.'

When she was twelve, Bessie went to work in a cotton mill, sweeping up the waste and separating it out into its various colours. 'I had to put up my age to get in,' she said with a twinkle. 'I tole 'em I was sixteen. But I knew brown from white, green from blue, and that's all I had to do, split 'em up. A chile can do that.'

She worked from six in the morning until six at night, Saturdays until noon. If she was a minute late in the morning, her pay packet was docked twenty-five cents, maybe more. At night, she was tired when she got home and did nothing for a while, then she'd go and help Momma with the ironing. She'd iron till dark, sometimes after it was dark, an hour, two hours, till it was finished. Sunday, she said, you had to go to church, then you'd go to the picture show, over in Locust Hill.

They lived in what Bessie calls 'a shotgun house – it just went clean on through'. They ate simply – corn or corn meal, beans, potatoes, greens and sometimes fifteen cents' worth of meat – and almost all her clothes were given to her by Mrs. Ray, over at the tin shop. Mrs. Ray had two daughters just about the same size as Bessie and she handed down their dresses. 'I ain't *never* seen hard times,' said Bessie, with emphasis.

Often, she recalled, tramps would knock at the door in the middle of the night. Then Momma would get up and cook for them. A lot of people said not to do that, but call the police instead, but Momma had never thought of that. She had just said, 'What if they's one of my own?' Some of the tramps were nasty-smelling and needed a change of clothes, so Momma would get them to take off their clothes and wash them, and then make them have a bath in the iron tub.

Other times, said Bessie, you would see old people stirring around in garbage bins to try to find food . . . and Momma would feed them too; she'd give them all *something* to eat.

Momma used to tell Bessie a story about the time a smart lady was expecting Jesus to call, for company. First, a little raggedy boy had knocked at the door, and the smart lady had run him away. Then an old man came and she ran him away too. 'I'm expecting company,' she said. Then, at last, Jesus came and she said, 'I've been waiting for you all afternoon,' and He said, 'I've been here twice already.'

When you turn people from your door, Momma had said, you don't know who you're turning away, so she never did.

As the years went by and she became older, Bessie did the same, even when there was very little food in the house. 'If you have anything, divide it,' she said. 'That's what He said, wasn't it — divide? Sure, Mister, I did — *every* time. When I started cookin', I didn't know where I'd get the next food at, but when I got ready to cook again, there'd be something there. I helped folks with their rent, too, I'd jus' pay it for 'em. It don't take big things to help people, jus' little things.'

Bessie worked in the cotton mill as a sweeper for fifteen years. 'Sweepin',' she said, 'that's all they allowed you to do, because you was dark. Black people did nothin' but clean and sweep and some drove trucks outside. White people done the other jobs. I didn't feel nothin' about it — a lot of us didn't want that dangerous work anyhow. You see more one-arm people on those machines . . . it sure is dangerous.' After fifteen years, Bessie was earning $39 a week.

She had married when she was seventeen, but her husband turned out to be mentally unstable and they never had children. Instead, she brought up her brother's family, three boys and a girl. 'I cooked for 'em,' Bessie said, 'and I cleaned for 'em in a morning, I talked to 'em and I whipped 'em some. If they needed it, I'd sure get to 'em! There's not one been in any trouble. People say, don't whip 'em, you'll make 'em crazy, but they're going crazy anyhow and now the chillun are whippin' *them*.'

From the factory, Bessie went into service. She worked first for a family with a little boy who was diabetic. Bessie, as she puts it, 'attended to him' and eventually he went to West Point. Then she moved to Alexandria, where she became maid to Dick and Betsy Thomsen. Dick was headmaster of a well-known Episcopal school and they had two young children, Rip and Randy.

Bessie stayed with the Thomsens for twenty-three years, cleaning and ironing, looking after the children and talking to Betsy's old father in between times. 'I always was crazy about old people,' said Bessie, shaking her head. 'I don't know why, they just looked like they needed help.' On Saturdays, she often went out to clean and iron for other families. 'You'd tell 'em it was your day off, but they'd just keep on at you and I like to work anyway.' Bessie still works five or six days a week.

'She takes pains, *real* pains,' said Betsy Thomsen. 'Pride is the right word. Her ironing is *superb*. To this day, she still does it with the same interest; it's never seemed to be a drudgery to her, and the last thing Bessie ever wants to do is sit around.'

'She's absolutely unconscious of time,' added Dick. 'Even now, we have to get her to sit down to take lunch, otherwise she'd go right on working. Sometimes I really have to drag her away from the work, and tell her to sit down and talk to Betsy. She'd iron all day.

'She's never complained about work — and she's never asked for a salary raise, never.

'She's so frugal — she lives on about $150 a month — and she never seems to buy clothes for herself. Once, Betsy gave me an apron with "galley slave" embroidered along the bottom, and Bessie borrowed it and used it for herself. One day the parents of some students came to the door, and Bessie answered it in the apron. The visitors didn't know what to think, but it didn't bother Bessie a bit.'

'She always seems to be in good spirits,' said Betsy Thomsen. 'Even when her health is bad, she'll be trying to get back on the job, and she has such a wonderful sense of humour. She can always laugh at herself and her fears.

'She doesn't care for doctors and needles, and she's absolutely terrified of snakes. Some friends of ours asked her to go down to their farm in West Virginia, but she'd heard they'd had a snake in the cellar and she wouldn't go near the place.' ('Snakes,' said Bessie with a shudder. 'I'se scared of where they was at last year!')

'I have the greatest admiration for her,' said Dick Thomsen. 'If she can do what she does, at this age and with her infirmities, it makes my problems seem relatively unimportant. She has always overcome whatever came her way, without complaining and without bitterness. I just feel she's been one of the great gifts of our life. We'd do anything for her.'

'When I was a child,' said Randy, who is now married and in

her late twenties, 'I took Bessie a bit for granted. I loved her, but I didn't reflect on her values. Then, when I went away to high school and college, I appreciated her care and her heart of gold, but now I begin to see more.

'I grew up in a society in which education and accomplishment and the way you dressed were *quite* important! When I began to find a faith and to try to live a life regardless of those things' (Randy is now working full-time with a Christian group without salary), 'I found it very difficult, but Bessie has made me see that, if I accept myself as I am, others will too.

'She doesn't think of material things and she's got a really satisfying life because she doesn't want anything for herself apart from a place to lie down, food and a roof over her head. All she wants is an opportunity to go on being of service. You never feel she's just doing a job. She comes to help and she'll do whatever needs to be done.

'Her lack of interest in material things is a deep challenge to me and so is the fact that she's never trying to be something she isn't. She never puts on the dog and she has no pretensions whatsoever — and that gives her such a dignity.

'Her life is infinitely worthwhile because of what she gives to people and the spirit in which she gives it. Plus, she's delightful!'

Bessie is still an early riser: she is usually up by five. 'When the sun comes up, I hit that floor,' she said with a chuckle. 'I jus' can't stay in that bed, I wish I could!

'I always did like work. When you don't see me workin', I'm sick enough to die. When I stir around, I feel better. Even if there's only one or two dirty things, I'll wash 'em. I like to do, do, do. Mister, ain't we suppose to live by the sweat of our brow? He said that, didn't He? — and that means work. I hope I can work all my life, I hope I never quit.'

If anything, Bessie's interest in material things seems to have grown less with the years. 'I like things,' she said, 'but I don't go overboard for 'em. Too many people's gone overboard for 'em. I want enough to go clean, but I never did want a heap of somethin'.

'Some people do love things. That's the Devil workin'. I know I ain't able, so I ain't sittin' and wishin'. People with more than me? I'd be glad for 'em. They got it, and that's all. I jus' don't stay in the store.

'It's the same with aeroplanes. When I get in an aeroplane, you know I'm on my way to Heaven. What need is there to go up in an aeroplane, to be up high and then fall? I prefer to stay down, and just go right along. You don't have to fall, because you're down already. It don't hurt near as bad.

'Fed up? I ain't been so far. I ain't never miserable unless I fall sick. A heap of people always seem to feel low. I tell 'em, be grateful, you're living, it could be worse. You're just thankful, and I got somethin' to be thankful for, living so long without being sick. I done pretty well.

'What's wrong with people is they need more religion. They go to church, but often they got no religion. What does it mean? Well, love each other more and help each other more. It's not what you says, it's your ways. Like if I see a person and I say, "I know you're sick, but you're white, so I don't care." That's not religion, that's hatred and hatred kills everything.

'Race? — why, I think this. There's some people I don't associate with, jus' like there's some you don't associate with. There's some black people I don't like because they're nasty and dirty and have crazy ways, and there's some white people like that, too. It's not their colour, it's their ways.

'Sure, I say my prayers every night. God? In the Bible, it says He'll be a father of the fatherless and all you have to do is trust Him. Well, I feel like He's been a father to me.

'I sure want to go to Heaven when I die, if there's any place like it. Ironin' in Heaven? No, *sir* — He don't want this 'ere old body, He just wants the soul.'

Bessie need have no fear. It was surely to such as her that Peter held out that great promise of 'an inheritance incorruptible and undefiled, and that fadeth not away, reserved in heaven for you'. It is also the grateful who inherit the earth.

6

'The Dark is Light Enough'

ERLING STORDAHL COMES into the room, snapping his fingers softly to announce his arrival. An ecstatic smile creases his face and illumines his sightless eyes. His face is ruddy, his hair curly and reddish-gold; he wears an open-necked shirt and carries himself stiffly, like a prize fighter of the old school.

'So glad to see you,' I say. Never, surely, a more inept beginning to a friendship.

Stordahl does not appear to notice the gaffe, and we sit down in this homeliest of homes. His wife, Anna, serves the coffee. She has the face of a madonna, grave and slender with eyes of the utmost tenderness. The house is called Bamseli, which means a place where bears roam, and it is on the outskirts of Beitolstølen, a village in the Norwegian mountains four hours north of Oslo.

Stordahl speaks English to help me. His difficulty with the language often makes his meaning all the more pointed. His favourite word is 'concrete', which he pronounces 'concrate'.

In one sense, the most concrete achievement of Stordahl's life is the health sports centre which is just up the hill from Bamseli. Even at first sight, there is plainly something unusual about the Helsesportsenter. Outside is parked a collection of wheelchairs; their owners are on horseback, learning to ride under the supervision of two of the centre's staff. One of the newer buildings is a riding-hall, so that the clients (nobody ever uses the word 'patients') can ride throughout the winter.

On the track up to the new sports stadium we meet a blind man striding off towards the forest with a helper in tow.

The idea behind the centre, Stordahl explains, is what he calls 'active health', bringing physically and socially handicapped people to the liberating atmosphere of the mountains and then, instead of smothering them with help, encouraging them by their own efforts to break out of the boxes into which their predicaments have often driven them. 'Self-activity,' says one of the staff. 'Not what we can do for them, but what they can do for themselves.'

As a result, the clients spend very little time on a depressing comparison of ailments: they talk instead of what they have achieved. 'I rode for an hour today,' says a girl in a wheelchair . . . 'I walked eight kilometres,' replies a blind man.

But perhaps the most surprising thing about our first meeting was that Stordahl said little or nothing about the successes of the Helsesportsenter; none of the rigmarole of well-memorised, well-publicised statistics which the founders of institutions normally retail to convey the splendour of their own creations. Instead, with a foreigner he did not know and could not see, he spoke of his problems and his failures.

How could they meet the *spiritual* needs of the thousand or so people who come to live at the Helsesportsenter every year? Why had they not done better in that respect? What were they doing wrong? Many people believed in God, said Stordahl, but had no concrete experience of Him in their daily lives.

Then, as we sipped our coffee, Stordahl spoke of his own blindness in a way which amazed me. What he wanted from life, he said, were 'possibilities for experience' and God had provided so many *through* his blindness. If he were to list the three things he wanted most, being given back his sight would not be among them. He was not, he added, advocating blindness, because, for many, it meant the closing of doors. His blindness, too, had created difficulties but it had led him to God and it had *opened* so many doors.

In any case, when you could see, you saw too much, like pictures on a movie screen, so that the gift easily became devalued. The most important thing was not to look *upon* but to look *into*. The ability to feel, Stordahl added, was also more important; a bird in the hand was better than ten on the roof.

He had spent that day discussing sewers at a series of committee meetings and spoke of the heaviness he felt at the end of it. 'Where is God when you don't have the spirit?' he asked, rhetorically. 'But then I believe He is always near when the situation is extreme.' Most people were grey, between darkness and light. This was because they had 'disturbed their spirit through materialism' and become shackled to it in a negative way. 'In greyness,' he said, 'you go round and round, but when you know dark and light, black and white, then you can find your bearings, you know where you are.

'I found this truth in my childhood, when I first became blind. I was isolated. That was darkness. Then I understood light.'

When he had finished talking, Stordahl came to the door. It had been an overcast day. He turned his face towards the evening sky. 'It is clearing up,' he said confidently. 'It'll be warmer tomorrow.' The next morning, the sun was blazing through my window and the weather remained fine for the rest of the week.

Stordahl's childhood was a very happy one. He was a wild boy, a dare-devil who liked to experiment with everything. Once, when he was seven, he backed the family Chevrolet down a steep hill, and his father only stopped it from careering over a precipice by flinging himself against the bonnet. Astonishingly, the only thing he said to his son was, 'Well, now you have the experience!'

He seems to have been a remarkably cheerful and courageous man who was fascinated by his son's daring and enterprise — and endowed with an enviable sense of proportion. He was also the despair of Erling's mother because, during the Depression years of the 1930s, he 'sold' food and paraffin from their little grocery store to people who, he knew, wouldn't be able to pay for them.

In the same year as the Chevrolet incident, another of Erling's experiments brought disaster: a paint scraper fell into one of his eyes, and the eye had to be removed. This, of itself, didn't worry him at all. Because he only had one eye, he was unique, and the fact that he could take out his glass eye and polish it in front of his friends gave him a competitive edge which none of them could hope to match.

The trouble was that, largely because of the additional strain put upon it, the sight of his remaining eye gradually deteriorated. He was terrified that he would be sent to blind school but, although he often rode his bicycle into cattle gates, in class he managed to escape detection by learning his lessons off by heart.

Erling compensated for his increasing blindness by initiating ever more audacious pranks. On one occasion, dressed in a brand-new green velvet suit and white shoes, he led an attempt to ride one of the pigs from the local piggery—with disastrous results for the suit and shoes. On another, he devised a competition to see who could run farthest into a lake backwards and would have drowned if onlookers had not hauled him out.

Then, when he was twelve, a teacher noticed that he was holding his book upside down. He would *have* to go to blind school, she said. Erling protested passionately. He looked upon the blind as people foreign to him. For him, everything was associated with a colour, and to be blind was dirty green. Eventually, his parents decided it would be better if he stayed at home for a while.

The year at home proved to be a seed-time. At first, the boy felt more and more isolated. He was oppressed by the way in which people stared at him. Their pity and their prying curiosity gave him the impression that seeing must be more important than living. Soon, he became so afraid of their staring eyes that he bumped into trees, even though he could still see a little. He felt that he was becoming the prisoner of their attitudes, that he was turning into the kind of person they expected him to be.

He sought solace by going out into the garden of his home in the middle of the night. There, he discovered a new world full of richness and beauty he had never known before. He touched the grass, the flowers and the trees, became aware for the first time of their beguiling scents, listened to the night calls of the birds. All these became the persons of his new universe, new friends to replace the old, and in this torrent of discovery and joy, his scarred soul found healing.

'The smells were fantastic, the trees were so living, the birds were so near and all these things spoke to me. After many nights in the garden, I began to build up a kind of mental surplus and then, suddenly, I felt I could forgive those staring people everything. I thought, "Tomorrow I can meet them and forgive them because I am so happy for nature and the new riches I have found." There, in the garden, I gained a deep joy and happiness and was liberated from the opinion of others.

'Then, too, God was a near thing, a close friend, someone I could speak to as a flower. He had a shape. He was a human being like a man; He was concrete for me. In this way, I gradually developed my own method of discussing problems with Him.

'At New Year, I would say to myself, "Now this year you have to live without sin", but [and he laughed] it was impossible — and I was so very sorry for that!'

Erling's parents knew about his nocturnal excursions, but never questioned him about them. Nor did they allow their own grief to burden him. Once, he heard his mother praying in the kitchen that he would die when she did, but he didn't understand and his father, in any case, always seemed more interested in his possibilities than his limitations. Neither ever tried to treat him protectively.

Erling, indeed, discovered that by taking the initiative in talking about his own problems, he was able to help his parents solve theirs. They had sharply contrasting personalities. His mother was very correct and loved cleanliness — 'She would feel the floor with her finger': father was gayer and much less interested in the floor. When there were financial difficulties father would always take the view that they would find an answer somehow. 'Yes,' his mother would say, 'but HOW?' When there was a quarrel, he simply left the room.

To his surprise, Erling's willingness to talk about his fears and needs encouraged his parents to speak of their own more openly. As a result, they discovered a much deeper life together. It occurred to Erling then that perhaps he had a task in life: to help people speak about their problems by being honest about his own.

During the daytime, his mother would read to him from the Norwegian classics, Ibsen, Bjørnson and Hamsun — he felt ready to die just to meet Victoria, one of Hamsun's heroines — but it soon became painfully apparent that he would have to go to blind school. His parents found him a place at an institution outside Trondheim. He was thirteen.

When Erling arrived, he could still glimpse the occasional animal or tree. Soon, even that was taken away from him. The generally accepted leader of the boys in the school was an enormous youth of fifteen who weighed 195 pounds. He evidently felt that Erling represented something of a threat, and on the third day after his arrival they had a fight before breakfast. One of the punches landed squarely on Erling's remaining eye and so much blood poured out from the wound that his trousers were soaked. He was rushed to a doctor in Trondheim but, when the eye was opened, it fell down in three pieces on to the doctor's knees. Nothing could be done, he said. Couldn't he just glue it together, asked Erling. No, said the doctor, there would have to be an operation.

Erling's first thought was for his parents, whom he had only just left. He telephoned them to say that he was fine and that the eye didn't matter. The next day, when he came round from the anaesthetic, his first thought was that his favourite team was playing in a football match on the radio. They won 3–2 and there were meatballs for lunch; so everything was fine.

During the next few days, Erling felt he could still see everything which he observed through his ears. When he heard a car, he believed he could still see it. Back at school, the boys tested him by asking him when the electric light was on and off. Now, there was no doubt. He was blind.

Oddly, perhaps, the young Stordahl was neither bitter nor angry. Before, he had been between two worlds, neither blind, nor seeing. Now, he felt, he was whole; being blind was fine, because it was something concrete. In the garden, he had learnt to regard obstacles as something positive and soon he came to think that, through this escape from opaqueness and the half-light, he had actually gained something.

Erling's years in blind school proved to be both fruitful and happy. One day, the headmaster caught him in the kitchen eating cakes which some of the girls had been baking. With commendable speed of thought, Erling forestalled criticism by suggesting that the boys ought to be given their own kitchen. The result was that his became the first school in Scandinavia to teach domestic science to boys.

He also became an increasingly accomplished musician. He had first learnt to play the accordion when he was ten; in 1939, at the age of eighteen, he won the national accordion championships. By then, he had written a tune called 'The Melody of Memory' which remained the most popular song in the country until long after the Second World War was over.

When he left the blind school near Trondheim, Stordahl decided that he ought to go to Oslo to continue his musical training. His parents, however, were very doubtful. By this time, the war had begun, Oslo was swarming with Germans, and Erling had never been alone in a city. He pleaded, and finally they gave way.

Having arrived in Oslo, Stordahl decided he would get up in the early hours of the morning and try to find his way to school when there were no cars on the roads. This he managed to do successfully, and repeated the journey later in the day despite the frightening noise of cars, lorries and tanks and the silent menace of bicycles and baby carriages. On the way home to his lodgings, however, he found himself trapped in the middle of a main road and, when he heard cars rushing towards him from both directions at the same time, leapt in panic for the pavement and was lucky not to be killed. As he stood there trembling, he thought his parents must never hear of what had happened. At that moment, a car drew up beside him and he heard his father's voice. He had driven to Oslo and followed Erling to and from school just to make sure that he could cope with the journey. Despite his anxiety, he did not utter a critical word. He just told Erling to stand still if he found himself in the same predicament, wished him luck and drove off.

During the war years, Erling found his blindness deeply frustrating. Particularly when he heard that a hundred Germans had occupied the family's farm at Storedal in southern Norway, he longed to join the Resistance — but there was no place in the Resistance for the blind. The most he could do was engage in what the Germans might reasonably have thought were provocative acts.

One night, for example, he and two friends (one of whom was so strong he could bend an iron bar round his neck) decided to walk through the streets of Oslo singing 'It's a long way to Tipperary'. Two drunken German soldiers drew their guns and threatened to shoot. Erling assured them that he didn't want to fight, only sing and pointed out that, in any case, two of them were blind. He then waited for the strong man to take some decisive action but, when this was not forthcoming, assumed that their last hour was at hand. The three of them began to move slowly away, expecting to be shot in the back at any moment.

The soldiers followed close behind but, when Erling and his friends turned off the main street, the Germans let them go.

The war years also brought moral crises of other kinds. Like most Norwegian families, the Stordahls were often short of food. Nevertheless, when Erling came home late at night, he used to raid the pantry regularly. His favourite was a dish made with whipped eggs and, although his mother put a lock on the pantry and hid the key, he always managed to find it. When this had been going on for some time, it occurred to Erling that he was doing something which was both selfish and anti-social and that he had within himself exactly the same instincts as a criminal.

Stordahl's blindness was also a distinct handicap when it came to pursuing girls. On his first date, he rushed up to the young lady just to show how fast he could move. Unfortunately, there was a low fence in the way and he finished flat on his face in a flower-bed. From somewhere above him came a woman's voice saying, 'Hello!' He also found it mildly ridiculous that girl friends should have to escort *him* home.

In this field as in others, he had a deep longing to be accepted by the world of the sighted. He could see no purpose in self-pity, so he tried hard to be as like them as possible. The result was that, in pursuit of cheap popularity, he swallowed the view, fashionable then as now, that faith in high ideals is naïve, and suppressed the memory of his mother's constant warning always to be on guard against following the attitude of the majority. Soon, he was embarrassed to admit to a belief in values which he was no longer living.

Early in the war, Stordahl had begun touring to raise funds for the Norwegian Society for the Blind. He teamed up with another blind musician, Gunnar Engedahl and, as they travelled, they often discussed religion and philosophy right through the night. Engedahl used to say that, if people only knew what it was like to die, there would be a colossal queue. At the same time, like Stordahl, he was sceptical of the genuineness of many of the priests they met, and they became involved in a good many arguments. The priests would tell them that it was not good to smoke or drink, to which Stordahl and Engedahl replied that it was also not good to take coffee with women or to eat so much. 'We met a lot of big food priests,' said Stordahl with a chuckle.

In the early days after the war was over, there was a good deal of bitterness about Norwegians who had collaborated with the Germans and, on one of their tours, the two blind musicians passed close to a prison where a good many of these Quislings were detained. Engedahl said he thought it would be a good idea to give a concert there and asked the local priest if they could borrow his piano. The priest refused. The Quislings had done too much wrong, he said, and it would not be popular to help them. The two men talked over the problem and decided that, even if the Quislings had done evil things, this was the time to forgive. Otherwise, they thought, they would simply be creating a new enemy and, having won the war, would be in danger of losing the peace.

'Like so many people today,' said Stordahl, 'the priest was afraid of doing right for fear of the consequences. They fail to cross imaginary borders because of what others will say.'

So he and Engedahl borrowed a car and eventually succeeded in prising the piano out of the priest. The concert turned out to be an outstanding success; they collected 100 kroner for the blind and many of the prisoners were weeping as they gave.

For Stordahl, the concert marked the beginning of a lifelong desire to seek out those whom he regards as prodigal sons.

He often remembers one of his friends who went to Borstal and turned to a life of crime because he found no understanding at home. His mother would tell him he could not play first in this room, and then in that one, and punished him for being a few minutes late for supper. Finally he didn't come to supper at all and, after he had become a criminal, told Stordahl that he had decided it was better to be a top expert in a bad milieu than nothing in a good one. That, said Stordahl, seemed a very intelligent decision to him, because everyone needed to feel important.

When he is in Oslo, he usually goes down to the railway station to spend time with the alcoholics and down-and-outs who gather there. He tells them simply that he has weaknesses very much like their own and that he could easily have gone their way.

As the years went by, he and Engedahl became phenomenally popular all over Norway. They raised two million kroner for various organisations for the blind, and also made a good deal of money themselves. By the early 1950s, they were giving 250 concerts a year and earning as much as 5,000 kroner a day in fees.

It was at a concert for the blind at Valdres in 1944 that Stordahl first met his wife Anna, the daughter of a journalist. Anna had found a deep faith through her parents – 'I never saw my father angry or depressed,' she remarked. 'He always faced difficulties in a conquering spirit' – and Erling fell in love with her immediately. 'I knew at once that I had met my ideal of a lady,' he said. Their rapport was so obvious that, afterwards, a local clergyman said he would marry them that night. They began to correspond in Braille – 'My letters were like parcels,' recalled Anna with a smile – but the courtship was a long one and they did not marry until 1953.

Their first idea was to build a *pension* for sixty guests at Beitolstølen, which Anna would then run while Erling was on tour. The venture failed miserably. The house was always full of guests but since, as Erling said, 'We just couldn't write a bill', they gave up the experiment after a year.

By this time, finding they were unable to have children of their own, they had decided to adopt Gunnar, the spastic son of one of Anna's relatives. This boy of twelve, unable to walk and needing constant attention, breathed a new spirit into their home.

'We started to stay here in this new building,' said Erling, 'and soon we were tied up with material things. Everything was new and, we felt, ought to get nicer and nicer. New chairs, new carpets, everything was fine. I could feel a little blemish in the wood which must be put right. Very dangerous. If you start that way, you soon become totally absorbed by it.

'The house was very big and we were not able to fill it with the right spirit. Then came Gunnar, and he filled it because he was in need of us. In his helplessness, he created something in our lives. His joy and gratitude over the smallest things forced us to reassess all our values.

'His way of life is still an inspiration. Imagine, to be very happy to be carried from the second to the first floor. Every night, he asks, "May I be allowed to get up tomorrow?" It is true there have been many difficulties, and that has driven us to pray often, but when he asks, "Can I come down tomorrow?", I forget all that.'

'Erling says that Gunnar means more to us than we do to him,' said Anna. 'When he says his prayers each night, his thoughts are so fine, so mellow, they touch us very much.' Before he left the home where he had been staying, Gunnar bowed his head and said the Lord's Prayer; and once, when Anna had a very bad attack of migraine, she found Gunnar gazing at a picture of Jesus and praying fervently for her.

Stordahl's tours continued to be successful but, as time went by, he gradually lost interest and increasingly felt the need of a change. In the meantime, he had turned to sport as a way of breaking out of the box to which he felt his blindness might have consigned him. He believed it was unnatural that a blind man should be physically weak and so, in 1957, he started to ski alone in the mountains. He knew the area well and, when he could, used the sun's position as his compass.

If such an activity might have seemed hazardous to some, the thought never seems to have crossed Erling's mind. 'I've never been afraid of excursions,' he said with a grin. He was aware only of a sense of massive physical and mental liberation, of hearing the woodcock calling and feeling the wind shrieking across the fells.

Even when he was at blind school, he had wanted to help other blind people, but could see no way to do so apart from raising money. Now he wanted to share with them the sense of freedom he had discovered.

He talked to some of Norway's Olympic ski-ing champions about the idea of training the blind to ski. Some of his friends told him he was mad, but he ignored them. 'When you are engaged in an idea,' he said, 'criticism cannot have influence on you; it doesn't matter at all.'

In 1962, he ran his first international ski-ing course for the blind at Beitolstølen. Thirty-four people came; they stayed either at Bamseli or in local hotels and skied round a ten-kilometre course under the supervision of some of the finest sportsmen in the country. There were no accidents; the course was a great success and Anna wept for joy. 'It will never happen again,' she said.

On the contrary, it was only a beginning. The following year, while Erling was wondering how he could develop his idea, a taxi-driver in Oslo gave him a Bible text which said, 'Put your

trust in God and He will do it.' That same year, he went with a
friend to visit his mother's grave on her birthday. When at last
they found it, Stordahl traced his mother's name on the stone
with his finger and, at that very moment, a bird came and perched
on his hand. 'Look,' said his friend, 'your mother has come to
visit you.' The incident also gave Stordahl an inner sense that
God, too, was with him.

He asked to see the Norwegian king to tell him about a scheme
which had taken shape in his mind for a twenty-five-kilometre
cross-country ski-ing race for the blind. With the help of machines,
they would cut deep tracks in the snow so that it would be
virtually impossible for the blind skiers to stray out of them;
each competitor would be accompanied by a sighted guide;
and the race would be called Ridderrennet (Knight's Leap)
from an incident in an old folk-story where a Valdres knight
had abducted a girl from her family and then escaped by leaping
a great chasm high in the clouds.

All this he explained to King Olav – and asked if he himself
would like to take part. 'How can it be done?' asked the king.
'The weather in the mountains may be stormy, and then everything will be finished.' 'It will be completely successful,' replied
Stordahl. There was a pause, and the king looked at Stordahl
thoughtfully. Then he said, 'Well, if you are optimistic, I will
take the chance.' A few days later, he telephoned to say that
Crown Prince Harald also wanted to take part.

Now, Stordahl faced more severe criticism. What he was
attempting was crazy, it was said, quite impossible. As the race
came nearer, he became so nervous that he had severe stomach
pains, but he was determined to carry it through.

The day before the Ridderrennet, there was sun during the
morning and afternoon but, in the evening, storms began to
blow up and the forecast for the next day was bad. King Olav
became worried and asked Stordahl what he thought they ought
to do. Then Stordahl remembered the words of the text and
replied, 'Tomorrow, everything will be a fantastic success.'

The storm went on throughout the night and the army had
to turn out to keep the tracks clear. Next morning, however, the
sun was shining and the competitors, forty blind and forty
sighted set off. Stordahl had told the blind ones among them
to go so fast that it would be impossible for the guides to follow

them and they followed his instructions to the letter. Many of the guides had soon fallen well behind their charges (a dozen did not finish the course at all) and reserve guides posted along the route had to take over. The time-keepers barely had time to scramble into position before the first blind man to complete the course arrived. There were no accidents and, as the race ended, the storm descended again. Then, said Stordahl, he was convinced that the Ridderrennet was important.

'It opened up a new world for those blind,' he said. 'When I am in the house, I have to listen very carefully all the time and observe—here is the table, there is a chair, there are people. I have to use my ears to walk, and I can't walk as fast as I want, I have to put the brake on. Blind people always have the brake on. When you take the brake off, the spirit soars.

'In this deep track, from which you can't come out, you can use all your strength for running flat out and you can stop in the mountains, ten kilometres from here, and feel the sun and listen to the wind. It puts you back in your natural element. You can feel the sweat again, you are clear in your brain, quiet in your nerves and sharp in your senses.

'In the garden, I was able to forgive all. The same thing happens when you are ski-ing in the mountains.'

The 1964 Ridderrennet was the first of many. In 1968, the course was extended to fifty kilometres. 'We really felt we wanted to break down the barriers,' said Stordahl. 'We wanted to demolish for ever the sentimental view of the blind; we wanted to be acknowledged as full human beings.' He expected the fastest blind finisher to complete the course in about $5\frac{1}{2}$ hours; in fact, the winner crossed the line in 3 hours 45 minutes.

Each year, the numbers who took part increased. By 1969, there were 500 competitors. Nor has the Ridderrennet ever justified the fears of its critics. Among the three thousand or so blind skiers who have so far taken part, there has not been one serious accident. Instead, the contests have proved to be rich in their own kind of salty humour.

In one of the early races, a blind skier went over another who had fallen on the track. 'My,' said the first man, 'this is bumpy terrain!' On another occasion, Crown Prince Harald—who had finished the course and was busy massaging his feet—was knocked flying by a blind competitor who had overshot the finishing line.

It turned out to be a man whom Stordahl had wanted to seat next to the Crown Prince at the previous night's dinner, but who had refused because he was too shy. 'Well,' Stordahl said to Harald, 'now at least you have made concrete contact!'

The same year, King Olav fell and one of the guides, thinking it was a blind man in difficulties, rushed to help. 'Oh!' he said to the king with some surprise. 'It's you.' 'Yes,' replied King Olav dryly. 'It's me.'

Some of Stordahl's anecdotes also show how effectively the race breaks down barriers between the blind and the sighted. As he was coming down the course one year, a man shouted to him as he went by, 'Do you remember me?' 'No,' Stordahl shouted back, 'I don't.' 'Why,' the man replied, 'I'm the man who followed you into the toilet at Toten two years ago!' Later, Stordahl found himself talking to a teacher in a nearby town and told him the story. Had he ever heard such a stupid thing? 'That man,' replied the teacher, 'was me.'

Until 1970, the Stordahls paid most of the expenses from their own savings. They gave well over 200,000 kroner, although neither likes to talk about it. 'It didn't matter at all,' said Erling. 'It's not important to mention it, it was easy for us.

'It wasn't a question of giving or not giving, it was a question of necessity. When you are gripped by an idea, you are not thinking of your own situation, you do not stop to consider the money. In any case, we have never believed money could make you happy and, when I toured, I could make it so easily, I lost my respect for it. If you have to struggle for your daily income, it must be harder.'

Stordahl, however, did not want to limit his work to the blind. He had a passionate desire to help all kinds of handicapped people find release. When his father died in 1957, he had inherited a number of horses along with the family farm. How marvellous, he thought, if men and women who had previously been confined to wheelchairs could somehow be freed by learning to ride the horses.

Then he thought of the socially handicapped, the drop-outs, the misfits, the rejected, many of them habitual drug-takers. Somehow, he felt, they must be given a bridge back to humanity. Could the horses be that bridge also? The misfits could feed and care for the horses without fear of criticism or reproach and perhaps feel again that they were needed. Once that bridge was crossed, they could take the next step and begin to care for a physically handicapped person.

All this, of course, required money and it soon became apparent both that the Stordahls could not pay for everything out of their own pockets and also that a centre was needed to house the work which was going on. Stordahl could not imagine how they would raise the millions of kroner which were needed but, in the event, the money came pouring in. The government gave a million kroner to buy the land and the Lions Club ran a fund-raising campaign which brought in another eight million. 'Fortunately,' said Stordahl, 'it did not depend on one human brain, but on the fantastic resources of God.'

The centre is splendidly equipped with a swimming-pool and a gymnasium, a sports field and special running-tracks for the handicapped, a lake for rowing and canoeing, and trained dog teams for dog-sleigh riding, but it is the atmosphere of the place which is most impressive.

One day while I was there, everyone set out for a picnic on the shores of a nearby lake. Nine of the clients had left their wheel-chairs behind and travelled by horse; the more severely handicapped rode in dog-carts, while many of the blind walked with the help of guides or guide-dogs.

The means of transport were certainly enterprising, but the most remarkable feature of the occasion was the complete absence of any feeling that these were poor handicapped folk being given a day out by kindly patrons. There were no busy helpers ensuring that nobody tripped over a rock or lost his hat; no do-gooders with sugary voices to make the clients feel like invalids; no sense that they were being set down in the mountains, to be collected in due course and put back into their boxes.

On the contrary, the handicapped were largely left to their own devices, unencumbered by help. In short, they were treated like equal human beings and not pitiable and imperfect flesh; and, as a result, there was such a sense of freedom and happiness and joy and such an absence of patronage and oppressive ministration that, as I looked at the crowd of people and the water shining in the sun, I thought instinctively of another lake long ago and far away, and of the way the thousands were fed with fish and with bread. This, too, I sensed was divine food.

The next day, a Danish teacher working at the centre said he had seen two blind men with guide-dogs struggling down the rocky path from the lake. At first, he had been tempted to interfere, but had resisted the temptation. The two men, he realised, wanted to see how far they could go alone. Why should he be the one to say what their limit was? In so many institutions, he said, people were followed everywhere, with the result that they were never liberated. 'It is hard for my parents to let me take part here at all,' added a blind singer, 'because they think my difficulties are greater than they actually are.'

'The people who run places like this so often feel superior to us,' said Egil Wolf, a spastic in his mid-twenties whose arms are virtually useless. 'We depend on them, they are being kind to us, "poor fellow!" Soon, it becomes a prison mentality. Even doctors patronise and do not understand. In one place in England where I was treated, they made me feel like a broken machine, not a human being. We have ourselves to blame, too. Many handicapped people give up and do what they are told. I'm appalled at how protected they are. I've got a friend, a nineteen-year-old girl, who has never struck a match in her whole life. We have to break out of our boxes and then help others break out too. The most important thing here is that they allow themselves to listen to us. Stordahl wants to be approached like any other person – and he really understands, because he's handicapped like us.'

Later, Stordahl sent a message asking if I would like to hear a man play the piano with his feet. He and Egil then played 'Frère Jacques'. They made an extraordinary duet, the one blind, the other picking out the tune with his toes. At the end, both collapsed with laughter.

Stordahl has a remarkable talent for persuading everyone to give the best of themselves. 'You must talk to these people about what you have found,' he said to a businessman, who in reality was still deeply depressed by the thought that he was slowly going blind.

'But my state is so low,' said the businessman sadly.

'That's just the point, that's wonderful,' replied Stordahl. 'In that state you have such a lot to give.'

His presence also helps to ensure that the staff do not set themselves apart from the clients. Ingmar Kleive, the resident chief physician, said that he thought the centre was much more democratic than any other place in which he had worked. 'Previously, I was chief of a rehabilitation centre,' he recalled, 'and there I told everyone what to do. Here, I often have to give up my plans because someone from the kitchen suggests a better idea.'

Now that Beitolstølen is well under way, a second idea has begun to develop in Stordahl's mind. He wants his family farm at Storedal to become an integrated youth leadership centre, bringing together the physically handicapped, social misfits from the surrounding schools, and potential leaders from the developing countries of the world.

There would be academic courses in the morning, open-air activity in the afternoon. The 'losers' from the local schools would begin by taking care of plants and animals, then perhaps build canoes for the physically handicapped. 'I want to make something whole,' said Stordahl, 'something which combines art, nature, physical and mental health, what it is to live, our relationship to God – and I want to show that treatment and education are not separate things.'

I had been much struck by Stordahl's lack of self-importance as we walked around the Beitolstølen centre and I talked to him about it. 'I know it so good I could have been puffed up,' he replied, 'but, when I am honest, I know I am helpless. In spite of such success, I honestly feel I am completely insufficient.

'It is very important to be honest with others, but equally important to be honest with yourself. Then you will at least be conscious of your own helplessness. Otherwise, you cannot call on God for help. You must feel honestly helpless. It is not enough to understand it. You must really *feel* it. You meet God when you are enthusiastic to do so.

'I am praying so often every day – in an office, a car or on a train. I say to God, "You must know I can't do it without You. Please give me what is necessary, and most of all free me from myself, so I can give my life to many persons."

'I am so thankful for my difficulties because it makes it necessary for me to pray, just like taking food. The only reason I pray is because I'm in need. If I didn't need God so desperately, I wouldn't have to pray.

'All of us ask God to give us so many things. It must be a great problem to Him to listen to all those requests! What is He to do about it? But I think "Thy Will be done" is a very safe prayer!'

Stordahl also feels a great need for times of silent contemplation. That morning, he had woken at four and gone downstairs to be alone. 'I'm very much in need of being quiet,' he said, 'because, working so much with others, I feel I must speak, so then I need time to seek out the thoughts deep inside. Then I have a much better chance of listening to God speaking.

'When you are alone and going deep, then you find you have great depths, and also confirmation that you are in relation to God. We are both much more than we believe, and much less. The potential is because we can be in touch with God. The limitations come because we are people. You find both in the quiet.

'Sometimes, I cannot understand God. I protest—"Why is this happening?" I find it very difficult to wait—"It goes so slowly, God; I'd like it to happen now." Sometimes I just have to take a rest. Then the way opens up.

'I have just had to accept that one step is enough for me. God has to lead the way, otherwise we would think we did it. If I go too fast, very often I create a wrong picture of the future, speculating on things which God does not want. We should live in the expectation of miracles, but not be bitter if they don't come.

'You cannot expect the Holy Spirit to come if you are totally preoccupied with materialism, because the two are mutually exclusive. How do you steer clear of this materialism? To work in a way where everything is linked to it, that is sin, that has a depressing effect. It gives you a kind of indifference and you get empty.

'Sin is much more than the Ten Commandments. It is a very big sin not to do anything, but the greatest sin is not to be interested in other people. When you live for others, that reduces your sins. Sin is also to place other people in a situation where they are not able to experience light, and this situation you put them in is not darkness, but what I could call twilight. Twilight leads nowhere, it is a half-life, a dead end. It is a safety life, no big problems, a circle life, round and round and round.

'These twilight people don't want to take a risk. Economic progress, that is enough for a happy life. That way, they can manage easily and they don't need outside help. The important thing with those people is to help them break out of that self-centred universe. All people have possibilities, but they will never realise them while they hide themselves and while they are not honest with themselves.'

'There is so much falseness in each of us,' said Anna. 'We do not want to be false, but we are. It is like being on the stage, we like to play our part well. Now, if God were to be the producer and the prompter, then we would play our parts properly, but the Devil wants those jobs too!'

'We must find new ways of talking about God,' Stordahl went on. 'We put everything in a box, God in a box, the poor in a box, the blind in a box, we have developed a box mentality. We put other people in boxes too. We see this man every day and we think he is just so—we almost demand he remain just so. That is wrong. We should try to treat each other freshly, to try for and expect a liberation. We should not expect other people to be the same, but give them the chance to be different. God is in the people you don't like.

'If you put your hand in the hand of God, there are fantastic possibilities. You don't need to be brilliant. There is no limit to what you can do with God. The ordinary man can do extraordinary things. Isn't the point to make God great? He makes us small not to go into a box, but so we are able to receive Him.'

Nobody will ever box Erling Stordahl in. A few years ago, at the age of fifty-one, he began ski-jumping. Even those who have seen that semi-vertical descent followed by the terrifying leap into space can scarcely imagine what it must mean for a blind man. Stordahl arranges a series of bells down the slope which brush against his legs and help him judge when to jump: one at seven metres from take-off, when he gets into a semi-crouching position, a second at four metres (full crouch), and a third at one metre, which is his signal to jump.

All this, he said, was fine. The difficulty came with the landing. 'The big question,' he said, laughing, 'is what happens when you come down. I've tried it several times, but I keep falling like a sack of potatoes. But, with exercise and instruction, I am sure it will be possible for a blind person to jump twenty metres without danger—and it will be very good for helping blind children to get their balance.'

A thousand years ago, a Norwegian king, Magnus the Blind, was born at Storedal, on the site where Stordahl's family farm now stands. Stordahl is a worthy successor. In an age when leadership so often goes to the compromiser, the manipulator and the self-seeker, he embodies the finest qualities of that older style of Viking leadership: unflinching courage, uncompromising honesty and an unconquerable spirit.

'Concrete, concrete, concrete,' he said with emphasis, roared with laughter and went off to bed.

7

The Thoughts of
Brother Dennison

THE PHOTOGRAPH SAYS it all. Taken in the 1950s, when Les Dennison was organiser of the Communist cell in the Coventry plant of Standard Motors, then one of Britain's leading car manufacturers, it is the face of a man consumed by bitterness and anger. The eyes are hard, the line of the mouth grim and unyielding; the furrows in his cheeks are like scars in a landscape ravaged by man's exploitation and the fury of nature. Like most photographs, the only thing it doesn't tell you is why.

All Les can remember of his childhood is unhappiness and grief. He was born in London, the illegitimate son of a servant woman who refused to marry the boy's father because he came from a background of wealth and privilege whereas she could neither read nor write. The child was christened Leslie Willett Brannen; the middle name, which he carries to this day, was the only sign of his paternity.

When he was six months old, his mother took him back to the industrial North-East, from which she had come; and soon she met and married a miner, Bill Dennison, an eighteen-stone giant of a man, well known as a bare-fist fighter. Bill Dennison was a fugitive of a different kind. He had been victimised for reporting faulty ventilation in a pit at Stanley in County Durham. As a result, a section of the pit was closed by the government inspector, and Dennison was fired. He moved across the River Tyne into

Northumberland to escape the mine-owners' blacklist and eventually found a job at the Rising Sun pit in Wallsend.

There, in a grimy little terraced house near the shipyards, Les grew up. Before long, he had two half-brothers and three half-sisters and, as the eldest in the family and the one who personified the shame of the past, he became both its drudge and its whipping-boy.

In those early years, he cannot remember his mother ever getting up before midday and, since his father went off to work at two-thirty in the morning, he was left with the job of washing and feeding the five younger children and making sure that they were sent off to the Buddle Board School on time. He himself was allowed to go to school on only two or, at most, three days a week, although he loved reading. On the other days he cleaned the house, did the shopping, placed bets for his mother (who was an inveterate gambler), peeled the potatoes for lunch and cleaned every pair of shoes in the house. He can still remember the stairs, fourteen of them, each one with a pair of shoes on it.

His mother's gambling often put considerable strain on the family income. Every Monday, Les was sent to the pawnshop to hock whatever was available: suits, shirts, shoes, even bed-sheets. Every Friday, when his stepfather had been paid, he would redeem them all so that his parents could go off smartly dressed for their regular outings 'up the town' on Friday and Saturday night.

Les himself always wore second-hand trousers which were too large and hung below his knees, and his boots and jerseys were often bought with the help of public assistance.

He dreaded night-time as much as he hated rousing and feeding five grubby youngsters every morning. Since his mother made a habit of going to the cinema three nights a week, he also had the job of putting the other five to bed. All six slept in the same bed, which had no sheets and often reeked of stale urine. Not surprisingly, Les had a horror of going to bed.

Nor did all his drudgery bring him any thanks. His mother was an extremely violent woman, quite capable of flinging a pan of hot fat and Yorkshire pudding across the room at her husband; and when Les did something to annoy her, she would tear up one of the wooden stair-rods (the bottom one, he remembers, was always loose) and thrash him until he could no longer feel the pain. If he tried to escape into another room, she would tear open the door, often wrenching the latch from its hinges in the process. In that way, she broke the latch on almost every door in the house.

Almost more painful than the beatings was Les's instinctive sense of being, in some mysterious way, an unwanted interloper who had no right to be a member of the family. His 'brothers' and 'sisters', for some reason he could not understand, were always strangely aloof. Only after an aunt chased him from his grandmother's house with the words, 'Get out, you little bastard', and he investigated what the word 'bastard' meant, did the truth dawn upon him. Thereafter, he felt even more of an outsider. Little wonder that, as time went by, he began to hate both his mother and his half brothers and sisters.

It was during the General Strike of 1926, called to back the miners in their battle against lower wages, that Les felt the first stirrings of class-consciousness. His father took him to mass rallies to hear miners' leaders like Sam Cook, and the young boy had a sense, not merely that he was with his own people, but that solidarity with a whole class might somehow give him and others like him power to free themselves from the degradation and misery he saw around him.

As the strike dragged on, and he—like thousands of other youngsters—helped his parents by collecting scraps of coal from the pit-heaps, his feeling of injustice grew; and when, after standing in a queue for soup, he was told by the middle-class volunteers who dispensed it that they disapproved of what the miners were doing, he reacted violently to what seemed to him patronage from people who assumed they were superior to him and his kind.

When Les was thirteen, his stepfather at last felt it was safe to move back nearer his old home. The family went to live in a little village called No Place on the estate of the Edens, a great mine-owning family whose most famous scion was Sir Anthony Eden. No Place had three streets and one pub, the 'Robin Hood'. Nearby, in West Stanley, was a mine known as 'Jackie's Pit', and it was there that Les first started work. Before he could do that, however, he had to produce his birth certificate and, to avoid embarrassing questions about his origins, changed his name by deed-poll to Dennison.

He was told to join the early shift, which began at four in the morning. Since the pit was a mile and a half away along the railway tracks, that meant getting out of bed at three and putting up his own 'bait' of bread and jam. Then off he went through the pitch-dark village in terror of the ghosts which the older miners told him haunted the place: he was still in short trousers.

When he arrived at the pit, he went down the shaft, picked up one of his two ponies, Loppy and Ginger, and walked a mile to the pit-face. His only light was the flickering beam which came from his miner's lamp and, since the miners threw down a white powder to stop coal dust from rising, the lamp cast long shadows along the walls of the tunnel. To begin with, Les found the journey terrifying. Soon, however, he knew every inch of the way, as he and the ponies ferried the tubs of coal from the face to the pit-bottom.

He arrived home from the pit at noon, utterly exhausted. He would wash in a zinc bath in front of the fire, eat his meal, and go straight to bed. Once he fell asleep while he was still eating, and remembered nothing more until his mother wakened him in time to go to work again. For this, he was paid 7s 3d (36p) a week. His parents did not allow him to open his wage-packet, but his mother gave him 1s (5p) or 2s (10p) a week for pocket money.

After the week of exhausting labour, Saturday night seemed like a release from prison. Les soon began visiting the local pubs and, by the time he was sixteen, had become a hardened drinker. Every Saturday night, he would deck himself out in broad-bottomed trousers and pointed patent leather shoes, tie a white silk scarf round his neck and tour the pubs. Afterwards, he either slept rough in the fields or else caught the last bus home, roaring drunk. Home, to him, was nothing more than a place to sleep in.

In 1936, when he was nineteen, Les decided that he had had enough of the North-East, with its unemployment and its grinding poverty, and, together with an uncle, he set off for the Midlands, where there was said to be plenty of steady, well-paid work.

After a night on a bench in the bus station at Coventry, they found beds in a doss-house. There, to his astonishment, Les saw a man lift up his bed and put his boots under two of its legs so that they wouldn't be stolen during the night; there, too, he met men who were earning a living by picking up cigarette ends in the streets, re-rolling them and selling them at five a penny. Each night, a policeman came into the doss-house and shone his torch on to the faces of the sleeping men.

It was a policeman who told Les and his uncle that there was a pit 'just down the road'. 'Just down the road' turned out to be seven miles, but they found work at Keresley pit at 25 shillings a week (£1·25) and were soon urging the rest of their families to join them.

The two of them hired an open lorry and a tarpaulin, drove north and piled it high with furniture and people, thirteen in all, including eight children. Then they dragged the tarpaulin over themselves and, clinging grimly to the more stable pieces of furniture, set off again for the Midlands through the bitter winter night. Les had never been so cold in all his life. When they arrived, they crept out one by one, to the astonishment of the onlookers, and eventually managed to find an abandoned house where they could camp out temporarily. Later, they were able to rent it.

It was at the Keresley pit that Les first began to take a serious interest in Communism. He met a Scotsman from Fife who painted a picture of the inevitable advance of world communism, of the great struggle being waged in China and of his own vision for the world, a world where all men could live in dignity and decency. First, however, the exploiters must be destroyed. There were only two classes, he told Les, the exploiters and the exploited; he must never forget that. It was a logic which instantly appealed to Les.

He went to the local Communist Party headquarters, met some of the officials, and read all the Marxist literature he could lay his hands on. Soon he was selling the Communist newspaper, the *Daily Worker* on the city's main street and going to the Co-operative Hall every week for a long training session.

The dozen or so men who met there were almost all trade unionists, and most were Welsh or Scottish by origin. To Les, they seemed a workers' élite who knew where they were going. He also accepted the discipline of the Party as a necessary part of their struggle to overturn a corrupt society, and often took part in public demonstrations which led to pitched battles with Oswald Mosley's Blackshirts. Several times he was beaten up by fascists while the police stood and watched.

He also began to enjoy himself with the local girls. He had left the pit for better-paid work in the motor industry and it was in a car component factory that he first met Vera. She was just sixteen, extremely pretty and the best dressed girl he had ever seen.

Vera had started work in a textile mill when she was fourteen and then moved to the component factory where, she remembers, the workers were expected to wash their hands in buckets of cold water and there was seldom any heating even in the winter. Vera's family, too, had had its share of unemployment. Her father, who was a spinner, had been on the dole for seven months, and an uncle had walked the streets for two whole years looking for work. Finally, he found a job, but was so weak after the long months of searching that he died two months later.

Vera herself was, by her own admission, 'rather spoilt'. Her parents had always given her everything she wanted and, at one point she and her closest friend decided they would like to be chorus girls. When she started work, she gave her mother none of her wage, but spent it all on clothes and brightly coloured make-up. 'I've never seen any bugger with orange cheeks before,' her father remarked in disgust.

Les Dennison was scarcely an ideal boy-friend as far as Vera was concerned. He told her that she could either come to the Communist Party training sessions or 'get lost' and so there she would sit through the ideological verbiage, bored to tears. Soon, to her horror, she found she was pregnant. Her mother told her she didn't want her in the house and Les was even less sympathetic. It was just too bad, he told her as she wept hysterically; the best thing she could do was get rid of the baby.

Les, indeed, was appalled at what had happened. After the life he had led, to get stuck like this just when he was enjoying himself! In any case, he was far more interested in the Party girls: Vera had been little more than an attractive side-line, and now he was faced with the prospect of being shackled to her for ever. He decided to leave home, take a job as a barman and move from pub to pub so that Vera could not find him.

Vera's father did succeed in tracking him down once, but Les made it clear he had no intention of marrying Vera. Only when some of his old mates from the car factory told him they would knock hell out of him if he didn't 'do right' by the girl did he relent.

The wedding took place in what was scarcely a festival atmosphere. Vera was several months pregnant, Les turned up in plusfours and, after they had been married at the local Registry Office, Vera went home alone on a tram while Les walked back to the pub where he had 'digs'. They lived with Les's mother until the baby arrived.

A son was born to them on Christmas Eve and Vera, still only seventeen, felt very proud of her baby which was dark, just like his father. Les was less enthusiastic. When he arrived at the hospital that night, he made it plain that he did not like the baby. One thing he *had* decided: the boy would be called Karl, in homage to Marx.

For a time they were reasonably happy. They found a little house of their own, and Vera began to save to buy furniture, although Les never gave her more than three-quarters of his pay-packet and often as little as half. Soon, however, he had begun to come home in the early hours of the morning, and her mother said that he was going around with other women.

He also began to repeat the pattern of violence which he had seen in his own home. Often he would sit reading and throw cigarette ends into the hearth one after the other. Vera would shout that it was meant to be a home and Les would hit her across the face. There was one particularly violent row after Les had been carpeted for not attending a Communist demonstration. The local officials had insisted that they had sent him a note about it and Les eventually realised that Vera was burning his letters before he saw them.

When war was declared against Germany in 1939, it did not at first have the Communist Party's blessing because it was not a 'workers' war' (that is to say, the Russians were not involved), but soon the line was changed and Les was told to join up.

He became a special fitter in the Army Service Corps and, after a brief interlude in Northern Ireland, where his efforts at political activity brought him into conflict with extreme Orangemen and he finished up by being thrown through the window of an ice-cream parlour, he sailed with his unit for Malaya. By this time, Vera was pregnant with their second son, Alan.

When Les arrived in Kuala Lumpur, life appeared to be proceeding much as usual; nobody seemed to realise there was a war on. The Japanese, however, made landings further and further down the Malayan coast and the British and Australians were eventually forced to beat a rapid retreat. Les, who had never handled a truck outside the workshop, was ordered to drive a 15-tonner down the precipitous road to Singapore. Some of the other drivers were equally inexperienced, and some never arrived at all.

In Singapore, he found morale was at rock-bottom; everybody seemed to be in a complete panic and the red tape was appalling. When it was announced that a Red Cross ship would carry away some of the remaining women and children from the island, a number of men managed to get aboard and had to be physically dragged from the ship. Everything he saw confirmed Les's belief in the rottenness of the system, and made nonsense of all the pious talk of fighting to the last man. So far as he could see, it was every man for himself.

He also saw for the first time, and shared in, the mindless brutality of war. One of his mates deliberately ran the back-wheels of his truck over an injured man to make sure he was dead, and Les himself gunned down a Malay boy who was crossing the Singapore *padang*, although he knew perfectly well he was not Japanese.

When the British commander on the island surrendered, Les remembers, there were men who sobbed right through the night. They had heard of the atrocities which the Japanese had committed against the Chinese at Nanking, and were terrified lest they should be given the same treatment. The next day, a tiny man less than five feet tall, wearing jack-boots, white gloves and a sword which trailed along the ground, ordered Les's unit to line up and told them all to bow to him. Those who did not bow low enough were hit across the ears with a cane.

The Japanese then marched all their prisoners to Changi on the north-eastern corner of the island and put them behind a wire fence. All the available food was brought together into one place and Les remembers General Percival, the British commander, coming round to allocate it. One of the items was between thirty and forty cases of tinned fruit. Percival directed that it should all be taken to the officers' mess. 'All of it?' asked a sergeant incredulously.

'The men would expect their officers to have that, wouldn't they?' replied Percival, slapping his cane against his leg.

Next day, said Les, there wasn't a tin of fruit left in the place: the men had looted it all. Nor did his opinion of the other officers improve in the months ahead. Most, he said, would see the Japanese kick soldiers and just turn their backs. There was one major who took thrashings on behalf of the men but, for the most part, so far as he could see, they were out to save their own skins.

By way of reprisal, Les and some of his friends stole shirts and shorts from the officers' laundry lines, slipped under the boundary fence and traded them with the Chinese for food. The Japanese eventually caught him and three others red-handed; they were sentenced to be beheaded, and were imprisoned in a tennis court. There they were kept for four days and nights without food in almost continuous rain. Then, mysteriously, Les was released, but his punishment was not finished. When he rejoined his unit, he was charged with being absent for four days, and spent the next fourteen chopping wood for the officers' mess.

In Changi, Les and the others slept six to a room in cells originally intended for one. His bed was a concrete slab, his only covering a rice sack. At first, he was continually disturbed during the night by bugs which crawled out of holes in the concrete and into the sack. The only way to fight them off, he discovered, was to put brown ants into the sack before he went to sleep. Being bitten by the ants, he found, was marginally less unpleasant than being chewed by the bugs.

Some prisoners refused to co-operate with the Japanese and were brutally punished. When Les's unit was ordered to repair a fleet of Bren-gun carriers and sabotaged them instead, the sergeant in charge had his head crushed in a vice. When Les himself dropped a starter motor, he was slashed across the neck with the steel shaft of a golf club.

One day, a soldier from Portsmouth who couldn't fit two pieces of pipe together, called one of the Japanese guards known as 'The Screamer', a 'slant-eyed bastard'. He and the other guards ordered the soldier to kiss 'The Screamer's' boots. When he refused, they beat him almost unconscious and threw him on to a nest of red ants. Before long the ants covered him from head to toe. Each time he tried to drag himself clear, the guards threw him back to the ants. They never did succeed in breaking him.

On another occasion, the Japanese orderly officer insisted that the daily parade should number off in Japanese. They managed the numbers up to ten easily enough, but thereafter subsided into noises which, they hoped, sounded vaguely oriental. The officer stopped them angrily and ordered them to begin again, but again the numbers tailed away into grunts. Beside himself with rage, the officer put on his white gloves and struck the sergeant in charge across the face. The sergeant thereupon hit the Japanese so hard that he fell backwards into an open drain, and disappeared from sight. While the parade looked on in mingled horror and delight, the orderly officer climbed out of the drain covered in mud, wiped himself off as best he could, looked the sergeant up and down and walked away.

The next day, everyone assumed that the sergeant would be publicly executed, so they put him in the rear rank in the hope that he might somehow escape notice. Nevertheless, he was spotted immediately and ordered to come forward. Then, to everyone's astonishment, the officer pulled from his pocket a packet of Player's cigarettes and handed them to the sergeant with a bow. 'British Iti very brave,' he said stiffly, 'Churchill . . . this present.'

During the months at Changi, Les managed to keep up his Communist training. He found comrades not only among his fellow-prisoners but also among the Japanese guards and the Chinese on the other side of the wire. It was from them that he got hold of copies of one part of Stalin's *History of the USSR*, and five or six of the prisoners met regularly every Sunday to study it.

One day the Japanese announced that a Red Cross consignment had arrived in Thailand and that men would be needed to handle and transport it. In fact, they were being drafted to work on the Burma–Siam railroad, later known as Death Railway.

Hundreds of men were crowded into closed steel goods trucks at the Singapore railway station. There were forty-seven in Les's truck alone, and they spent four days and nights there; by day, it was like an oven, by night, an ice-box.

Then began a nineteen-day forced march through jungle and waist-high swamps infested with leeches. After the first few days, men began to fall out. Some crawled off into the jungle, others were left to die along the way. Once, when they stopped to rest in the middle of a torrential downpour, Les sank to his knees and, despite the rain, fell asleep in that position.

As soon as they arrived, the exhausted and emaciated prisoners had to begin building the *atap* huts in which they were to live. Each one housed two hundred. Before long, cholera and dysentery were sweeping through the camp. Men screamed in agony with terrible stomach pains and cramp; some even vomited their stomachs up. Within two days, they had lost almost all the flesh they still had; within three, they were dead. Their bodies were placed on tiers of brushwood, five bodies to a tier, and burnt.

In an effort to stop the epidemic, an Australian major threatened to flog to death men who did not use the latrines provided. Three were flogged to death before the order was obeyed.

All Les's friends died in the epidemic. The only reason he himself survived, according to the Japanese, was that he was a carrier of the disease and therefore immune. He became a member of the burial-party.

Almost all the survivors suffered from huge jungle-ulcers which writhed with maggots and had to be cleaned out with a spoon. Some of the men had to have their legs amputated without anaesthetic.

Each day the prisoners walked five miles through the jungle to the railway track, which ran close to the fast-flowing River Kwai; they lived on whatever the jungle yielded: lizards, maggots, snails and the occasional snake fried in a tin.

Les felt the Japanese engineers in charge of the project were the most formidable bunch of men he had ever met. At the same time, he grew to hate many of the guards. Once, when they were sawing down trees, a hornets' nest fell on to a guard and, as a punishment, Les was made to kneel on a piece of rough timber. Each time he lifted his knees to ease the cramp and pain, the guard hit him across the back of the neck with a cane while the other guards stood around laughing.

One night, Les took his revenge. He saw another of the guards standing near the edge of the river, crept up behind him, and threw him into the rocks and water below.

When the work was complete, the survivors were marched out and loaded into trucks again. At the start of the journey, there were fifty men in Les's truck but, by the time it reached Bangkok five days later, seven were dead. Another five died on the way to Singapore. Les arrived back at Changi semi-conscious and covered in jungle sores. Liberation, however, was not far away. To Les's amazement, the first literature dropped by air to the British troops after the news of the Japanese capitulation was the Young Communist newspaper *Challenge*. When he was finally freed, he weighed five stone four pounds, less than half his normal weight.

Vera, meanwhile, had had an unhappy war, much of it spent with Les's mother. She had decided early on that she wasn't going to throw away her youth for a man who had treated her badly, so she went dancing regularly. She also gave away Les's Marxist books: in that way, she thought, she might also get rid of his ideas.

When she was informed by the War Office that Les was 'missing, presumed killed', she was not heart-broken. After all, she was still only twenty-two and attractive enough to know that she could easily find another husband. Indeed, she promised one of her men-friends that, if she didn't hear from Les, she would marry him. When she heard, through the Red Cross, that Les was still alive, she was not overjoyed.

That was one reason, no doubt, why his homecoming was so unhappy. The returning troops had been given their first mail at Gibraltar and some had discovered, to their horror, that their wives, believing them dead, had married Americans. Several went berserk. As a result, when Les saw Vera standing on the quay-side at Liverpool with his stepfather and their two sons, he thought, 'I wonder what you've been up to?' Vera seemed disappointed and aloof and he could see that the children were not at all happy to see him.

He soon realised, too, that he had come back to the same old England. Nothing had changed. Despite all the sacrifice, everybody still seemed to be out for what they could get. Within a week, he was at the local Communist Party headquarters offering them a good slice of his gratuity.

Because of his war record, Les was offered a council prefab, but life at home soon deteriorated into a series of rows and fights. He was jealous of the children's relationship with Vera, and the children, on their side, felt he always wanted to monopolise their mother. One day, young Alan clutched hold of Les's trouser leg and said bluntly; 'I don't like you. Why don't you go back into the army?' Les knocked him across the room. From then on, they were at daggers drawn. To Vera, Les always seemed to be shouting at the boy, and Alan would wake screaming in the night.

Often, however, it was Vera who took the brunt of Les's anger. He would hold her by the neck and slap her across the face. She found herself wishing that he had never come back. If it hadn't been for the children, she would certainly have left him.

Les, meanwhile, had decided to become a plumber. He passed the final of the City and Guilds examination within eighteen months and went into the building industry. He also became more and more deeply involved in the activities of the Communist Party. He was asked to go to special weekend schools and rapidly became one of the local Party élite. Eventually, he was ordered to move into the Standard Motor Company to organise the cell there. He took a job as a maintenance man to give himself maximum freedom in moving round the plant.

His dedication was as intense as that of any missionary. He was up before six, and his first job was to collect bundles of the *Daily Worker* from the early morning train and drop them at various places round the city. Then he might brief fellow-travellers within the plant on a current industrial dispute or attend a cell meeting to decide what the Party line was going to be. As a matter of tactics, the Communists preferred those who put forward motions on their behalf not to be members of the Party.

When Les arrived at the factory at seven-thirty, he did no work until he had distributed 150 copies of the *Daily Worker*. One of them was for Sir John Black, the company chairman. Each day, Les personally put a copy on Black's desk. He soon became known as a troublemaker and a thoroughly 'bolshie' character. 'We need a fitter,' a foreman would say to the maintenance superintendent, 'but for God's sake don't send Dennison.'

It was the kind of reputation Les was delighted to have. His whole purpose in going to work was to involve men in the class war, and creating industrial disputes was the quickest way of doing that. If he and his comrades could get them to stop work for a day, or even an hour, that would give them a chance to feel their strength as a class, to show them what they could achieve by united action.

In 1956, the Party managed to engineer a major strike at Standard on the issue of 'no redundancy'. Thirteen thousand men came out and, although they went back after three weeks having accepted redundancy, Les was not concerned. Nor was he much more concerned when he was fired as soon as he reported for work. He simply went on holiday and organised a series of factory-gate meetings.

After seven months on the dole, he found a job at Jaguar but it was a difficult plant to organise and so he moved back into the building industry, where he had a succession of jobs. Invariably, he became a shop steward and, equally invariably, the management took the first opportunity to get rid of him.

'I was pretty bloody-minded,' he recalled, 'and it was always easy to find something to pick on—no place to wash your hands, no decent facilities for eating, no toilet. Then there was demarcation. If the mortar wasn't mixed and the labourers hadn't shown up, the brickies would say, "Let's start", but I'd say, "No, mate, that's labourer's work." I've had eighteen bricklayers on a scaffold not doing a tap, and none of my plumbers were ever allowed to drill a hole. Building was my trade, but demolition was my philosophy.'

Soon Les had become so notorious that no private employer in the area would hire him. The only job he could find was with Coventry Corporation.

At home, meanwhile, the situation became worse and worse. By this time, Vera had had three more children, a daughter and twin sons, and was terrified of having any more. Her weight was down to six stones and she couldn't bear Les to go near her. 'For ten years,' she said, 'it must have been like sleeping with a cold fish on a slab.'

Their fights, too, became more and more violent. 'I threw everything at Vera,' said Les, 'including two new chairs we'd been saving up for for twelve months.' Then Karl announced that he intended to marry a major's daughter. Les exploded. His son, Karl, named after Marx, getting married to an officer's daughter, an enemy of their class! It seemed to him a piece of deliberate provocation. And what would the comrades say? He raged at Karl, telling him that if he did marry the girl, he need never darken the door again. So Karl left home, Alan wanted to follow suit, and Vera, too, felt she had had all she could take.

The first turning-point in Les's life came in 1959. One of the shop-stewards on his building site was a plasterer named Stan Peachey. Peachey was a religious man who annoyed Les by his talk of 'finding the right way'; he was regularly ridiculed by the other workers for quoting Biblical texts. Les used to taunt him by telling him he was 'a proper gaffer's man'.

One day, Peachey lost his temper with Les. The argument started when he told Peachey he wouldn't finish a job because the bricklayers hadn't made a hole for a pipe to go through a wall. 'Come off it,' said Peachey, 'anybody can make a hole.'

'And do another man's work?' retorted Les. 'Where's your bloody solidarity?'

'And what about the people who need these houses?' shouted

Peachey. 'You're sabotaging them. And, let me tell you this, the workers here don't like you. You're the biggest bloody reactionary I've ever known—and you'll never do anything unless you begin with yourself first! For a start, just tell me how you hope to go about uniting the labour movement when you've got a divided home yourself.'

That was too much for Les. 'What the hell is my private life to you?' he bellowed, and pushed Peachey off the scaffold plank.

The barb, however, had gone home. Deep inside, Les knew that if his ideas didn't work out in his own family, all his talk about changing the world was just so much hot air; and it was only too obvious that they didn't. When Peachey asked him to meet some of his friends, he was sufficiently needled to accept.

The 'friends' turned out to be a local Anglican parson and a draughtsman from an aircraft factory. Les went in 'tense as hell' but within twenty minutes felt completely relaxed. He had plenty of experience of the sacrifice and discipline of the Party, but this was something different: these men, he felt, genuinely cared for him as an individual.

The Anglican priest spoke about a revolution which went beyond Marxism and included all classes. He also talked about living by absolute standards of honesty, purity, unselfishness and love. 'You *do* mean absolute?' asked Les. 'That's the key,' replied the parson. Impossible, thought Les, reflecting that it somehow made Marxism seem very narrow and sectional.

Then the draughtsman said that, when individuals changed, situations changed with them. That, too, was an entirely new thought to Les. He had always believed that the individual was the victim of his environment. It was only when the draughtsman talked about 'listening to God' that Les jibbed. That, he said, was going a lot too far. 'Well then,' said the draughtsman, 'try listening to the deepest thing in your heart.' Grudgingly Les agreed to give it a go.

When he arrived home, Vera remembers, he seemed to be 'all smiles', but the experiment proved to be more than he had bargained for.

'When I got home,' he said, 'I went up to my bedroom and, for a start, thought about my life in the light of absolute honesty. Floods of thoughts poured into my mind—the wrong things I'd done, the other women I'd messed around with, the way I'd used men, the stuff I'd knocked off from work, the money I'd fiddled in the shop-stewards' committee.

'I felt angry and worried. The whole thing was impossible. The idea of going to a gaffer and saying, "I'm sorry for knocking this off!" It would be reported to the police and I'd be back where I started from. But I also had the feeling that this was socialism in practice, and that it was questioning and undermining the things I'd believed for years.

'The rebellion and the pain I felt! That it should have to begin with yourself! I was always pointing the finger at "them", "it", "those", but how could I go on talking about the dishonesty of the management and the exploitation of the system, when I was doing the same things myself?' There was no doubt in Les's mind that the experiment had worked—it had, in fact, shaken him to the core, but he shrank from putting it into practice.

Shortly afterwards, Les went to a union meeting in Peterborough. After the meeting, he sat on the railway station deep in thought. His train came, but he had no sense that he ought to get in: he felt rooted to the spot.

Instead, he took the next train and shared a compartment with an elderly Anglican parson. Haltingly, he told the parson about the struggle that was going on inside, that he was looking for God but couldn't find him, that he couldn't understand what this idea of faith was all about. From Les's point of view, faith didn't make any sense because he could not relate it to things in which he was involved. 'When you tell your son something,' said the parson, 'he believes you, doesn't he? And when he talks to other people, he boasts, "My daddy can do this or do that." Now why do you think your son does that?'

'It's because he has got faith in his dad,' Les replied spontaneously.

'Exactly,' said the parson, 'and that's the kind of faith I'm talking about.' For Les it was a massive piece of illumination.

Next morning, he announced to Vera that he was going to church. When he arrived, it was empty and he hurried out again. What on earth would the lads think if they saw him? The following Sunday, he went back and this time knelt at the back and tried to pray. When the rest of the congregation had gone, the vicar came across and asked him what his trouble was. 'I'm looking for God, but I think I'm wasting my time,' Les replied.

Thinking he might be an awkward customer, the vicar walked with him to the church door but then remembered a letter he had had that week from a parson friend, telling him about a man he had met on a train who was looking for God and who came from his own parish in Coventry. This, he realised, was that man. He asked Les whether he would like to pray.

They prayed for more than half an hour. The vicar began by asking Les his name. 'Dennison,' he replied.

'But Christ knows you by your Christian name,' smiled the priest. 'At one point, he said, "Behold I stand at the gate and knock",' and Les was filled with an overwhelming sense of the evil within him. 'God, help me,' he asked. The vicar went on praying and Les felt the things which were tying him up inside begin to melt. 'When I came out of that church,' he said, 'I felt so different I thought everyone was looking at me. I had talked about peace all my life, but I'd never known what inner peace was till then.'

Peachey's friends invited him to spend another evening with them, and suggested a time of quiet together. In the silence, Les had the thought that he should go and see his son Karl, ask for his forgiveness and beg him to come back into the family. He told the others what he had thought and added that it didn't make sense. 'It can't work,' he said. 'It'll only lead to a punch-up!'

Les had already told Vera about his new friends. 'He said they lived by some standards or other,' she remembers. 'I thought, "You can live by them if you want, but don't include me." ' At the same time, she had to admit there was *something* different about Les. She told Karl that he had met some new people and that it made him smile. 'Don't worry,' said Karl. 'It'll soon wear off. The old man will never be any different.'

When Les mentioned the idea of apologising to Karl, Vera encouraged him, but pride held him back. *He* should come and apologise to *me*, he told himself angrily, but the thought persisted and Vera kept on pressing him to go. Karl was twenty-one on Christmas Eve, she said, and it would be a lovely surprise for him. Les wasn't so sure. That day, Vera and the draughtsman forced his hand by picking him up from work and depositing him firmly outside Karl's door.

'I walked up that path,' said Les. 'I remember every step. I could feel Vera's eyes in the back of my head. Then I knocked on the door and waited for Karl to give me a mouthful. When he opened it, he just grinned all over his face. "Hello, Dad," he said; "come in and have a cup of tea. What do you want?" ' Les told his son that he was sorry for what he had done and asked Karl if he would come back into the family. Every word cost him an effort.

Karl and his wife smiled. They'd known all the time, they said, why Les didn't want them to get married and they'd be only too happy to become part of the family again. That Christmas, they all sat round the same table. 'It was a marvellous time,' said Vera. To Les, the whole business was incredible. This simple idea of listening worked, despite his ideology. From then on, he began to have a regular time of quiet every morning.

In the New Year, one of the leading functionaries of the Party called at Les's home and asked him to sign up again. Les told him he had decided to pack the Party in. He had already been shaken by the Russian intervention in Hungary in 1956 and the exposures about Stalin; his recent experiences had made up his mind. 'What?' said the Party official. 'Have you gone soft? Are you turning your back on the struggle?'

'No,' retorted Les with conviction. 'I want to stay at the heart of the struggle.'

How, he himself still was not sure. The Labour Party, he felt, didn't offer him an alternative: it was a political party, not a revolutionary ideological force. He had met some of the local Labour leaders and labelled them opportunists, people out to make a name for themselves, not to create a fundamental change in society. He felt lost, in a vacuum, stripped of his entire reason for living.

He also had to face a good deal of ridicule at work. Men would twit him by asking if it was true that he had 'seen the light'. When his mates discovered that he had a time of quiet every morning, they would ask him, 'And what were your thoughts this morning, Brother Dennison?' Nevertheless, like Vera, they recognised that there was something different about him, and at the next stewards' election he won an increased majority.

Soon, they began to have a good deal more respect for the thoughts of Brother Dennison. The conviction came to him one morning that, in future, he should do a moral day's work instead of a legal day's work. 'You can get away with murder doing a legal day's work,' he said, 'but I thought, "There are twenty-seven thousand people in this city who need houses, so why don't we set out to meet that need?" ' He put a resolution to that effect on the agenda of the weekly site meeting. There were 160 at the meeting, bricklayers, carpenters, plumbers and labourers, and they passed the resolution unanimously. Les had taken the first step on a road which in many ways was a good deal more revolutionary than the one he had trodden before.

After the meeting, some of his mates were more doubtful about how it would all work out. 'You're bloody right, Les,' said one of them, 'but how do we sort out the gaffer?'

That was one thing which worried Les too. The 'gaffer' was 'Smudger' Smith, an extremely blunt Yorkshireman and senior superintendent on the site. Les's next conviction was to apologise to Smith for all the aggravation he had caused him. It took all the courage he had got, and it did not prove to be a cordial encounter.

'Who the hell's there?' yelled the superintendent when Les knocked on the door of his hut and, when he saw who it was, he asked Les brusquely what he wanted. It was not an encouraging start, but Les said that he had come to say he was sorry for all the clashes of the past and that, in future, he wanted to fight on the basis not of *who* was right but *what* was right . . .

'Get out of this office,' shouted the superintendent. 'What are you trying to pull now?' Outside again, Les was fuming; as he said, he 'felt like hell'. Then the thought came to him that he had done what he had been told in his quiet time and that he should just go down to the site.

A few days later, he was fixing some lead flashing to a roof. Suddenly, to his astonishment, he heard the superintendent's voice. 'Good morning, Dennison,' he shouted. It was the first time Les had ever heard him say 'good morning' to anyone. 'Did you hear that?' said one of his mates incredulously. 'Smudger said good morning to Dennison.'

Thereafter, Les decided that the boss was not going to be his main target; that he needed to fight *for* the boss not against him, that the gulf between the boss and the workers somehow had to be bridged if they were to make the meeting of the community's needs their first priority. 'You'll never get rid of the conflict,' he said; 'it'll always be there, so it's the permanent bridge you've got to keep building all the time. The other side may not always be conscious of it, but they fight the class war just the same. I'd dropped the class war and I wanted them to drop it, too.'

He was soon put to the test. Two terraces of houses were ready for occupation, apart from the fact that they had no water. There was a shortage of general labourers and none of the ditches had been dug. In the past, Les would gladly have used physical force to stop anyone but labourers digging those ditches. But, as he stood there, he thought, 'You're morally obliged to complete those houses for the people of Coventry' — and he jumped into the ditch and started digging himself.

When the other workers noticed what he was doing, they downed tools. Soon, most of the site was at a standstill. 'Hey!' said the bricklayers' steward. 'What do you think you're doin', Dennison? That moral day's work is OK, but this is different.' Les replied that there were no labourers and that people were waiting for houses. The bricklayers and plasterers then had a meeting to talk it over and decided that, on that basis, they were willing to go along with Les. The rest of the plumbers then joined him in the ditch.

On another occasion, a sub-contractor dropped ten thousand tiles a hundred yards away from where the men were roofing some flats. Rain was pouring down, but the tilers were quite happy to work on provided the tiles were brought closer. The foreman ordered three labourers to move them, but they refused and Les went to see the site agent. The labourers either did the work, the agent said sharply, or they got the sack. Les flared up. 'If they're fired,' he snapped, 'we all go.' And he started to walk away.

Then he remembered what he had come to say before they had started arguing. He asked God to give him strength and went back into the office. He'd had another thought, he told the site agent. Supposing all the men, 'brickies', plumbers, tilers and labourers, pitched in, they could move those tiles inside ten minutes. The site manager was amazed; so were Les's mates when he explained the idea. People were waiting for those flats, he told them; if the tiles weren't brought in, the work would be held up for days. 'Come on, then,' said one of the labourers gruffly. 'Let's get on with the bloody job.'

This was Les's revolutionary conception of worker participation, 'Where you as a trade unionist take full responsibility for the management and the jobs and the men you work with.'

Slowly, attitudes on the site began to change. The men became aware of what they were doing and felt a real sense of pride in it. 'They weren't out to screw the employers or dodge the column,' said Les, 'but to do their best for the community.'

Traditionally, the 'brickies' shouted 'Muck up!' when they wanted mortar in the early morning. Now, when the labourer who did the job was late, they started the mixer for themselves. At night they loaded up the scaffold so they could make a prompt start next day. Men who had been laying between four hundred and five hundred bricks a day were soon laying one thousand two hundred, and both productivity and wages shot up. Before long, they were completing a dwelling every five and three-quarter days.

Les also tried to apply the same principles when it came to wage negotiations. He had begun by wiping his own slate clean. He wrote to the boss of one of the motor companies he had worked for, told him about the things he had stolen from the factory — if someone had wanted a carburettor, for example, Les would slip one under the railings during the day and then collect it at night — and offered to pay the bill. The man didn't even answer the letter. Les put it down to the fact that he'd had all his green-houses built by people from the factory in factory time.

Then he remembered another occasion, more recently, when he'd taken a works-study engineer for a ride. The engineer had come to estimate the time it would take to fix some steel box guttering at a school, and Les had deliberately put a worn blade into the hacksaw to make the job take longer. He reckoned that had boosted his earnings by £13, so he went to see the engineer and offered to pay the money back. It was stopped out of his next bonus.

When it came to negotiations, Les's basic principle in the past had always been to get as much as he could, regardless. If the company lost money as a result, so much the better: that showed the men that the capitalist system didn't work. Now, he decided to operate on the basis of a fair day's pay for a fair day's work.

'Before,' he said, 'I used to go in and ask for £2 when I knew we'd accept £1. On the new basis, I went carefully into average earnings and productivity before I made a claim, and then I'd go in to convince the management that the men were worth extra. Usually, the proof of it was plain, because we kept finishing jobs on time, and often before time.'

If a job took longer because new materials were being used, Les expected the management to make extra payments. For example, they used Flemish Bond brickwork for a police station when the price had been worked out on the basis of half-Bond; the men were given a substantial bonus when Les protested. He also expected his own side to show a comparable degree of fairness. On one occasion, a price had been fixed for nailing weatherboarding to some houses. Then a nailing machine arrived which made it possible to do the work so much more quickly that, one week, a man earned a bonus of 700 per cent. Les told them bluntly that it wasn't fair and the job should be retimed. He wasn't popular, but the change was made. He faced the same angry reaction when he stood up to three men who had been booking false times. One said they'd bury him under twelve feet of earth, but all three amended their time-sheets.

As he took more responsibility, Les also began to recognise some of the things in himself which had made him so critical of management. 'I realised,' he said, 'that I had always been very ambitious to get on in the Communist Party and the Labour movement. Whoever I was supposed to take orders from, I was always convinced of their incompetence, and thought I could do the job far better.

'Then I thought in one of my quiet times, "Why not be honest about the level of your own incompetence?" and I started running through the jobs of the people of whom I was most critical. "Could you do the site agent's job? No", and so on. The more I realised the ramifications of cost comparisons, the more I realised I was out of my depth. After that, my ambition declined, but somehow I felt a new sense of authority and peace. I've nothing against managers now. If they manage in what I think's the wrong way, then I try to help them without crawling. If more workers did that, there'd be more managers on their toes.'

Meanwhile, Les had also started mending his fences at home. He wept with bitter shame as he told Vera about all the other women, and apologised to his son Alan for the misery he had caused him. He saw that, when he came back from Singapore, he'd wanted the boy out of the way so that he could 'catch up on the frustrated sex-life of three and a half years in three and a half months'. He told Alan he'd been jealous of his relationship with his mother. Alan smiled. He'd known that all the time, he said.

Even so, there were still rows. 'Hard as I tried,' said Les, 'and I did try desperately hard, I often slipped and reverted to my old self, lost my temper and then they'd say, "This is him, this is the real bloke." '

It was then that he valued so much the help that his new friends gave him in understanding the meaning of Christ's life and the Cross. 'What Christ and the Cross mean to me,' wrote one of them in a letter, 'is that I have to forget myself and do God's will, crossing out my own.' He told Les of a postcard he had once been sent which had a crib in one corner, and a Cross in the other and, in between, the comment, 'What a wonderful life, thirty-three years and not a second spent thinking of himself.' That, said Les, helped him understand that the Cross was a fulfilment, not a denial.

In the same way, another of his friends helped him after he had been savagely attacked by his old comrades as a management stooge, and felt he could stand it no longer. 'Les,' said the man, 'if you're not being attacked, you're not where God means you to be.' In due course, Les felt grateful. 'Miracles,' he said, 'only come via men and women who will administer strong doses, which are actually as painful to administer as they are to take, people who're prepared to accept the reaction of the person they're trying to help and who go on pin-pointing the things which need to be dealt with.'

But it was not until he went to India to work with his new friends that he felt what he calls 'Christ's second touch'. 'That trip brought back all my memories of past years,' he said. 'The sheer delight I'd taken in shooting that Malay kid as he ran across the *padang* — I could remember him looking up at me. Then pushing that Nip into the River Kwai — and the time when I forced Vera to have an abortion. It all flooded back and I felt for the first time just how deeply I had done wrong.

'I thought I couldn't possibly be forgiven and for four days I went through hell. Much of the time I was just lying on the bed in the most awful depression. I wouldn't talk to anyone. Then I told one of my friends, who'd been a shipyard worker in Clydeside. He just said to me, "You need forgiveness", and the next

day he came in and threw a Bible on to the bed and told me to
read the 51st Psalm.'

Les opened the Bible and read the psalm again and again.

> Have mercy upon me, O God, according to Thy loving
> kindness: according unto the multitude of Thy tender mercies
> blot out my transgressions.
> Wash me thoroughly from mine iniquity, and cleanse me
> from my sin . . .
> Behold, I was shapen in iniquity: and in sin did my mother
> conceive me . . .
> Purge me with hyssop and I shall be clean: wash me, and I
> shall be whiter than snow . . .

'When I read it,' he said, 'I saw that God could forgive even a
man like me. I went to sleep that night and felt free of the whole
thing. Next morning, God said to me, "*You* can never heal those
things, but *I* will heal them in my own time." ' Then he wrote to
Vera and told her that he was praying that God would somehow
heal all the deep wounds he had inflicted upon her.

From that point on, their relationship began to mend and,
slowly, a love which Les had thought he had killed for ever, began
to come to life again.

'He's a different Les now,' said Vera happily; 'there's no doubt
about that. As each month goes by, a new thing adds to him. Now,
I can honestly say I love and respect and admire him.

'God meant Les and me to be together somehow. He saved us
just in time, and brought us together. I thank God so much, I
can't thank Him enough for it. Heaven knows what would have
happened if we hadn't found this.

'In a way, I was as much to blame as Les. I've been such a self-
centred woman, so full of my own self and what people thought
of me. I had no faith and I felt sorry for myself. Deep down, I'd
not given much real love to my children either.

'I pray to God every day to help me and He does help me an
awful lot. I ask Him to take away all my fear and my jealousy and
my bitterness, because that's me — and when I've said my prayers,
I know He will look after the children and the grandchildren and
I feel so free inside. I only wish we'd given the children a Christian
upbringing. To me, Christianity is giving to people.'

'There's a warmth and a closeness I've never felt for any person before,' said Les. 'I come into the house now and she'll be singing, of all things. "Hello, Mr. Dennison," she'll say. "Hello, Mrs. Dennison," I'll say, and she'll come up and give me a kiss.'

Nor has Les lost any of his passion to change the rottenness of the system, its injustice and its corruption. The difference is that he now believes a new world can only be built on the foundation of new men. 'I still feel the hurts of history and society so intensely,' he said. 'When I hear of what's happening in places like Northern Ireland, it gives me real nausea. Maybe when you've been hurt so deeply yourself, you feel the pain of it all the more.'

On 27th March, 1975, almost thirty-seven years after they were first married, Les and Vera had their marriage blessed in a church, St. Peter's, Dunchurch, which stands in a place where there has been a Christian church for more than a thousand years.

In church that day there were so many of the family, Karl and Alan and their wives, their daughter Lesley and her husband, and six grandchildren, and there were messages from their two twin sons, one in New Zealand, the other in Ireland. Vera's face was full of an unforgettable joy and radiance: Les's had a sparkle and a warmth and a love which no one who had seen that photograph taken twenty years before would have thought possible.

8

The Rich Rewards
of Failure

BY THE TIME he was in his early fifties, Walt (that's what we'll call him) had risen pretty nearly to the top of the academic tree; there wasn't much doubt about that. His books and articles on economics were influential in the financial and political worlds, and he was greatly respected by the specialists in his own field. When he moved over into administration by becoming Academic Dean of the State University, he made quite a success of it at first.

There was a rapid expansion of numbers, new departments were set up and his transatlantic connections brought in a flow of distinguished European intellectuals either to teach or as part of their American lecture tours. On the face of things, Walt had ample reason to feel pleased with himself.

His elevation to the Dean's office had been the culmination of a lifetime's ambition, something he'd toiled towards with unrelenting zeal. For the best part of three decades, he had worked a sixteen–eighteen-hour day – weekends included – almost as a matter of routine, and most years he took no vacation at all. At Christmas, he would allow himself only a few hours off. He scarcely knew what it was to be tired, had a feeling of unlimited energy no matter how long he worked, and relied on pills to get him to sleep, the wheels were turning so fast.

His desire for knowledge was omnivorous, not merely for its own sake, not merely to keep ahead of his peers, but because it gave him a sense of control over what seemed a chaotic world.

His own field was economics, but his interests spilled over into history, sociology, philosophy and political science. He kept an eye on more than a hundred learned journals, and his studies on campus and in his home were filled from floor to ceiling with books which ranged across a dozen disciplines.

Walt expected the same kind of dedication from his staff as a matter of course. He was not openly tyrannical, just totally demanding. His junior colleagues voluntarily worked long hours of overtime and he rarely thanked or complimented them. He assumed they worked day and night for the same reasons as he did: enthusiasm for 'the program', 'the deadlines are crowding us.' So far as he was concerned, that sort of work schedule was normal.

Some of the motives which lay behind these drives were obvious enough, others more obscure, rooted in the traumas of Walt's childhood experience. Coming from a relatively poor home, he had a passion to be accepted by people of superior social status and intellect, and an insatiable desire for ever more conspicuous achievement.

Walt's desire for approbation was increased by a deep sense of insecurity and worthlessness, which also had its origins in his early years. It may, he now thinks, have been connected with the fact that his mother, a hysteric type, had frequently threatened to commit suicide. He could remember her saying, during one of her nervous breakdowns, that she had walked down to the river to throw herself in, but decided to give them all another chance. He also remembers being told, years later, that he had almost died in the first few weeks of life because he was unable to digest any standard form of milk.

So far as Walt could see, there were only two possible reactions to what seemed, from the first days of his existence, such a hostile cosmos. Either you became hysterical or you developed super-control or super-indifference. Walt's answer was to use his brain to try to exert some control over an anxiety-producing world in which he somehow had to claw out a place for himself.

This undefined but limitless measure of control was to be achieved by prodigies of effort, and these prodigies of effort were yet another way of winning approval from higher-status social and academic groups. Any approval he attracted, however, merely spurred him to greater exertion. Since he considered himself basically worthless, each accomplishment aroused his sense of guilt. 'Why didn't I do twice as much?' That, in turn, led to redoubled effort, still more tension and even greater anxiety.

Walt's recurring nightmare was of himself bicycling on a high-wire over Niagara Falls. He had to keep pedalling faster and faster to stop himself falling off. His wife Eleanor had often fought to get him off a career-treadmill which was constantly gaining speed, but he wouldn't listen.

Inevitably, there were emotional and physical crack-ups. Walt had come close to a breakdown during his mid-thirties, after his day-and-night work schedule had led to a near breakup of his family. A decade later, he suffered a coronary thrombosis which brought him to the door of death. The specialist told him he had never known anyone so willing to play Russian roulette with his life. A photograph taken at the time shows a man with a haggard, hollow face which is almost a death mask.

After he had recovered, he rushed back to work much sooner than the specialist recommended and worked even harder than before to make up for lost time.

Walt also prided himself on the fact that he was always (or almost always) under control. He could only remember losing his temper three times in the previous twenty years. On each occasion, it had been a flash of anger brought on by a colleague letting him down on something relatively trivial. That had shaken Walt because it gave him an uncomfortable feeling that his well-ordered world was spinning out of control. If they could fail him on small things, what else might they have done which he had not yet discovered?

That was one reason why getting the top job had been such a relief. Now, thought Walt, he was no longer vulnerable, he could control everything. Never again would problems be brushed under the carpet, decisions drag on for months. He also confidently expected the highest academic office to free him from the snake-pit of factionalism which he'd seen in his own and other faculties. Naïvely, he believed he had left behind for ever that squalid atmosphere.

He would weed out—with due decorum, of course—the incompetent and the half hearted along with those who politicked—and the people he brought in to replace them would, like himself, be both hard-working and above politics.

Not that Walt had ever been very good at human relationships. They were too messy and too difficult to handle, so he avoided them as much as possible—words on paper were so much more malleable. Work was his world, a protected world to which he could escape from his anxieties, something he could control; why risk dealing with people's unpredictable personality traits?

In any case, Walt didn't regard people as individuals but only as representatives of categories or types. He had chosen Eleanor to fit a category. He had wanted a bright, beautiful wife and she had done very nicely. No, when he thought about it, he didn't have an intimate knowledge of anybody. He didn't even see Eleanor and the children very clearly.

The effect of all this on Walt's family life was disastrous. His family life, in fact, was quite zero. Eleanor and the children had very little social life, no trips to the theatre—people who went to the theatre, Walt felt, couldn't be very interested in their work—no real recreation, very few holidays.

He and Eleanor might go out for dinner to a friend's house perhaps twice a year and she might come along when he was entertaining a visiting celebrity, but those occasions were focused on the celebrity, not her. In a sense, he had never really spent an evening with her for decades. Evenings like that, after all, were unproductive; they didn't advance Walt's career. To Eleanor, it was like living in purdah but, struggle as she might, she had not been able to shift Walt.

The hard fact was that he just didn't care about his wife and children as individuals. The children hadn't turned out quite the way he would have wished, but that was part of the price of getting where he wanted to go.

When he reached the top of the academic tree, Walt adopted the role of the tough, no-nonsense executive. He actually felt a sense of accomplishment in getting rid of people he thought incompetent. He was unsparing and that gave him satisfaction because it reassured him that he was strong and in control. Before long he was intoxicated by his own success. Life was difficult, there were problems, but nothing he couldn't cope with.

Then one day, quite suddenly, it happened. Three of Walt's most influential colleagues asked to see him and told him flatly that they thought he ought to step down as Dean, and make way for someone else. He had sanctioned unwise expansion programmes which would shortly, in their view, create a budget crisis; they were unhappy about some of the appointments he had made; staff morale was very low . . . and so on. They made it clear that they were not just speaking for themselves but had both the backing of a majority of the senior faculty and the blessing of the University Administration.

While Walt listened in horror, they went on to say that they were not asking him to resign precipitately – that wouldn't look good, and in any case, a search would need to be made for a successor. What they suggested was that, in due course and with suitable public explanation, he should announce his desire to return to his rank as a professor.

Next day, it became plain that the three men had not been bluffing. A majority of Walt's senior colleagues did indeed want him to step down; a few were sympathetic, but none was prepared to fight on his behalf.

A wave of panic overwhelmed him – 'frozen panic' was how he thought of it later. This was total disaster, absolute ruin. Oddly, perhaps, he didn't feel rage or bitterness, just that his stainless-steel shell had collapsed and that he was totally defenceless. He had a devastating sense that his whole life up to that point had been a cypher. Ahead, he could see nothing but ignominy and humiliation.

At first, he had a strong impulse to consign his lifetime's accumulation of data to the incinerator in the basement. The pursuit of knowledge had let him down. The man who lusted for control had lost it. He felt as if he were going to his execution.

His mind sought desperately to grapple with possible escape routes. It was as though he were slipping on the edge of a cliff, clinging with his finger-nails to stop himself going into the abyss. It was Eleanor's reaction which probably saved him from plunging into it. 'What a relief,' she said when Walt told her the news; 'now we can spend time together and enjoy life.' In retrospect, that had been a life-saver. If she had turned on him, Walt thought afterwards, he might have done a disappearing act, in one way or another.

Meanwhile, life dragged on. Walt assumed that everyone knew and was secretly gloating over his humiliation. Soon, he couldn't look anyone in the eye. It was hardest with the campus gardeners and janitors because he had the feeling that *there* was the real snicker. 'He's back at our level,' he imagined them saying behind his back. 'Now *I* have the job and he doesn't.'

As the days went by, Walt began to feel more and more like a leper. The people who used to drop by his office almost daily avoided him. Colleagues who normally joined him in the Faculty Club at lunch drifted to some other part of the dining-room. In his office, too, he had a growing sense of isolation. The phone seldom rang; there seemed to be very little in the in-tray, and his once-crowded engagement book began to show blank pages.

Worst of all were the end-of-semester parties. After one, where he had barely managed to get through the usual glad-handing routine, Walt walked home, collapsed on to his bed and started to spin out into irrationality, to the borders of sanity. He felt as though he was drowning in a whirlpool. It was a very real temptation to succumb, to let go. The misery, to be exposed to a crowd like that! It took the most superhuman act of will on Walt's part to slow down the whirlpool and claw his way out of the vortex.

As he wondered whether he could possibly go on, he remembered something a boyhood friend had once said when, as teenagers, they were talking about goals in life. 'What kind of death would you like?' someone had asked. 'Death at the stake,' Walt's friend had replied, to everybody's astonishment. 'That would really add to one's experience!' This was one of the things which made Walt decide that he, too, would try to live through the fire.

'In those early days,' he said, 'I could have chosen to disappear or go into my shell, or just walk around in a bruised state. Instead, I just made a pledge to myself that I'd take whatever came. I wondered if it was like riding a bicycle — if I could retain my balance at the start, perhaps it might become a habit.'

Walt didn't have any set of orthodox religious beliefs to fall back on and he felt that his primary need was to cling to rationality and restore some semblance of order to his mental processes. With that in view, he began to analyse his position on paper, to put down all the thoughts that came into his mind — hopes, speculations, fears and decisions. If an idea occurred to him during the day, he would grab a piece of paper and jot it down. In the evenings, since he couldn't bear to read, watch TV or go out, he would often spend an hour or more scribbling away in his room.

The process came naturally enough to him, because he'd always been a notes-on-paper man, but at first it took a real effort to hold his thought-process steady for even five minutes, because his mind was still spinning like a catherine wheel. Other parts of his brain seemed to be whirling off, and the fear of disaster and ruin kept creeping in.

Putting everything on paper, Walt found, not merely helped give his ideas some kind of logical coherence—they weren't then, as he put it, 'just puffs of smoke in the air'—but also acted as an indispensable release valve. 'It was a deep wound,' he said, 'and it had to be cauterised, with daily dressings, cleansing, healing and picking off the scabs.

'At first, I wasn't capable of calm, detached analysis, I was just trying to create order out of what had become the utter chaos of my life, to bring together the scattered pieces to get a coherent view. At that stage, all I could think of was survival. There was no room for anything else.'

Most of Walt's first jottings consisted of 'pledges' to himself. He had a deep fear that, at any moment, he might lose control, and the 'pledges' were a way of trying to hold himself steady. Night after night, he would promise himself that he would do this or not do that. He pledged that he would set aside an hour every day for 'cogitating time', that he wouldn't take any impetuous decisions, and so on.

He also made up his mind that he was not going to waste time blaming other people. Malevolence of that kind, he felt, merely cheapened one; and, even in those first desperate days, he was convinced that mentally castigating his colleagues was not going to solve his problems.

First week after the crash:—'Pledge to myself—say nothing negative about the institution or the way they have treated you or about the people who work for it.'

Second week: 'Pledge to myself—no trace of self-concern, anger or bitterness; no recrimination, no protest, no whimpering, no request for favour.'

Third week: 'Worst fears have not been realised—my morbid imagination has outrun reality ... Do not treat colleagues as if facing enemies—the majority want to be constructive and human ... Develop a little zest for what is ahead. So many plusses can happen.'

Fourth week: 'Crash was inevitable . . . was living in a fantasy world . . . became crotchety and out of touch with colleagues.'

Walt was also tempted to think remorsefully about other jobs he had been offered in the past but had turned down. He felt instinctively that it was unmanly and unfruitful as well as unhealthy to pine for what might have been, so he took comfort from the fact that others *had* wanted him, and then he honestly faced the disadvantages which the other jobs would have had. In that way, he 'deflated the Shangri-Las that might have been'.

Sixth week: — 'Futility, sinking into "if only" speculations — those are comparable to a gambler agonising over "if only I had stopped when I had the jackpot", when he would never have had the jackpot to lose if he had not indulged in gambling excesses in the first place.'

Eighth week: — 'Quit struggling. Look back on career as fascinating kaleidoscopic series of stages. Don't worry about big achievement now. Relax and see what the next ten years will bring — why assume that nothing but black nightmare lies ahead? This is an unrealistic and morbid view in the light of the richness and variety of the past decades.'

Tenth week: — 'Note change from frozen panic to calm composure.'

Twelfth week: — 'When you find yourself out of your depth and can't swim, the only thing to do is to tread water and keep your mouth shut.' (Quotation from a 'thriller' he had read.) 'Be ready to shift gear into new work, be ready to discuss any assignment — no reason to doubt ability to adapt — made very successful adaptations before.'

Soon afterwards, Walt was offered a professorship in a smaller but high-quality college in another state — a college with which his own university had always had close ties. He accepted. Apart from anything else, it brought priceless relief from the daily humiliation of continuing on his own campus shorn of all authority. If he'd had to go on doing that, with all those people avoiding him, Walt thought afterwards, he probably wouldn't have made much progress.

Nevertheless, he suffered fresh agonies in meeting a new group of colleagues, all of whom, he felt sure, considered that he was a 'wash-out'. As he went into each of their offices, he imagined them saying to themselves mentally, 'Here's the biggest failure in education.' He was constantly bracing himself to face an unspoken attitude of contempt.

The fear that he might fail yet again drove Walt into frenzied attempts to get on top of his new job in record time, and into a panicky whirl of engagements. At the same time, this fresh humiliation impelled him to try to shed some light on what he later called 'the black mystery of my failure'. Until he understood that, he felt, it would continue to haunt him.

To do that involved facing the truth about his own character and motives. For Walt, this was a journey into the unknown. As an academic he had been exposed to a substantial number of brilliant people, Nobel Prize winners and the like, and he couldn't remember a single one who had shown real self-perception, that penetrating vision of self which he now sought.

What Walt had in mind, he said, was not a self-indulgent ego-trip, spurred by clichés like 'Know thyself', but a desperate search for the truth about himself. He wanted to find the real person behind the shattered frame of the once-successful man.

He therefore began looking at his own mistakes to see what they could tell him about his character, and he did it with considerable rigour. He had to know the worst, he felt, before he could face it, grasp it and surmount it. As the months went by, he struggled to get a clearer and clearer picture of himself, using his whole mind to probe both his deepest motives and the causes of his downfall.

It was particularly important, he discovered, to accept his own areas of incompetence. That, again, meant discovering limitations he hadn't previously known he possessed. He now realised that he couldn't have had any realistic idea of what his weaknesses were. After all, *he* hadn't been wasting his time in bars or messing around with women. *He'd* been on the ball eighteen hours a day.

Fifth month: — 'Realise I had been cold, remote, detached in delegation of authority and responsibility.'

Sixth month: — 'I now want to be sure I understand the past to make sure it is not repeated in the future. I want to put it in the past so that I can get on with the present and the future, so that the future will be more orderly and constructive ... Has whole career been a search for status and ego-satisfaction?

. . . Selfishness index – failure to help failing colleagues rather than replacing them.'

Seventh month: – 'Today can write of *post*-crisis – sense now of having weathered 90 per cent of a crisis of proportions that, at the beginning, I was certain I was incapable of handling.'

Eighth month: – 'Significance of my emptiness when my job was lost and my reaction of "nothing to live for" – is this not the mark of an excessively self-centred man who couldn't accept that, like billions of others, he was doing his job to support his family? Need to put sense of humiliation and failure behind and then develop a sense of enjoyment with family.'

Ninth month: – 'Shockingly poor picker of people. Never did solve staff problems – latter were patched over by "inspiring" and energetic leadership'.

Tenth month: – 'Beginning to be amused with plunging, unplanned career. Now look back gratefully on the fantastic breaks I had . . .'

Eleventh month: – 'Why assume that it is so important you have easy, gravy-train final decade of career? Why not be tested by adversity and humiliation, like others?'

Twelfth-month summary: 'First, am alive, not extinct as could have been; second, family not crushed or ashamed; third, looking forward to next decade; fourth, physically healthier than for decades, off the coronary road; fifth, Eleanor happier and healthier than for years.'

One of the consequences of Walt's crash was that, for the first time, he shared his life fully with his wife. He began to spend evenings with her and later, when he stopped working at weekends, they took short holidays together. 'The treadmill had led to disaster,' he said, 'so I thought I might as well try the holiday-life. For the first time I was ready to acknowledge that it is more important to have a plus-plus relationship with family, colleagues and friends than to make it in a career.'

'It was wonderful trying to channel him into more relaxing ways,' added Eleanor with a smile. 'Walt had always felt guilty about taking time out for pleasure. His key word was duty, but I'd always thought that dour stuff was strictly for the birds!'

For the first time, Walt got to know Eleanor as a human being and, for the first time, they became a partnership. And, as he saw himself and the way he had behaved more clearly, he began to feel a profound sense of regret for the way he had neglected his wife and children.

The crash not merely opened Walt to himself and his family; it also made him increasingly aware of, and sensitive to other human beings. He suddenly realised how tender people's feelings were — 'Through my own pain, I began to know what pain I'd inflicted on others' — and, having fallen so far short of perfection himself, was no longer so demanding of it in those around him. 'I was such a bruised pulp myself,' he said, 'that I could no longer bear to hurt anyone.' If only, he told himself, he'd treated his staff generously — if only he'd reassured them when they were anxious, instead of regarding them with such cold indifference.

His first secretary on the new campus tried hard, but had marked inadequacies. Walt, however, had decided that he would never fire another person and was now, as he put it, 'sensitive to distress signals, listening with a third ear'. He noticed that the woman had problems of her own and decided to put up with her deficiencies and help her. At the end of a year, she had become first-rate.

Walt also discovered, much to his delight, that not everybody in his world thought of him as a second-rater, despite what had happened. A visiting scholar of considerable international reputation who did not know the inside story of Walt's dismissal told him that his work had made a great contribution to his own researches. It was this single reassurance, said Walt, which gave him 'the final heave back on to my feet' and made him feel that he could again move about as if he were a normal individual and not a crushed, empty husk.

As the months went by, Walt's enlightenment about the past and his sense of inner freedom continued to grow.

Thirteenth month: — 'Recognition of own limitations produces huge sense of relief — free from sense of obligation to create another approval-winning career.'

Fourteenth month: — 'Hindsight on past, foresight on future — what was gained by going through the crucible? Proved ability to recover from crushing defeat. New value system. Now generous in human relations. New poise, confidence in ability to take shattering blows, some inevitable in future years — e.g. one's own death.'

Sixteenth month: — 'May have been better to have gone through the "flames", and to know self to a degree that would never have been possible if had enjoyed additional success.'

Eighteenth-month summary: 'Liberated from treadmill. Liberated from careerism. Liberated from "obligation" to achieve what the public considers "successes". Liberated from concern with image among colleagues. No longer dependent on others' approval.'

Twentieth month: — 'Had no genuinely close relationship with any person in decades. Individuals were counters.'

Twenty-first month: — 'Now see that I behaved in contradiction to my highest idealism, and set out in ruthless pursuit of success ... Realise that for three decades I was a walking career-disaster on its way to happening ... super-energetic, super-rigid, grindstone-preoccupied ... incredible I did not crack sooner.'

End of second year: 'Can now celebrate recovery from life-long, near-fatal illness — self-destructive illness that, if had not been halted by failure, would have brought even bigger disaster. Should be able to savour family, friends, nature, and chuckle at lifetime delusion about "success", prestige ...'

During third year: — 'Throwing off the contemptible attitude that the only thing which counts in life is "winning it big", even at the price of coldness towards colleagues and family ... replacing this with what counts is how one plays the cards that life gives one, whether with dignity in both set-backs and triumphs. The crash was self-therapy for an already sick man ... For first time, a life of satisfying enjoyment ... Did not realise insatiable hunger for approbation. Now looking forward to future without fear, without need to conquer and win approbation from academic world. Relieved to be able to be amused at reputation-inflating drive of past decades.'

Despite all the progress he had made, Walt still had a lingering doubt about whether he had penetrated to the core of his problems. He had, he knew, put himself through a piece of self-analysis involving the most intense mental effort of a lifetime, which had clearly brought him back from the brink of disaster. Even so, he asked himself, might not an amateur effort like that prove to have been totally wasted and misleading, an exercise in self-delusion? To make sure the analysis had been adequate, he sought professional help.

He was looking for an academic psychiatrist (more likely to be sympathetic, he felt), someone who was neither a charlatan nor a doctrinaire Freudian. He discovered, on the new campus, a perceptive and sympathetic friend in the College's Department of Psychology who was also a professional psychiatrist outside the classroom. For Walt, it was yet another stage in his passionate search to find out what had gone wrong. Walt scheduled a series of review 'seminars' with his new colleague. Before each session, he drew up an agenda and invariably took along a notepad with half-a-dozen topics to discuss. He also asked the psychiatrist to recommend technical books which might help him understand himself better. Later, the psychiatrist told him he had never worked with anyone who had done so much work on his own. Walt found these sessions very fruitful, 'a lively give-and-take between us and the literature'.

Third year continued: — 'Equilibrium emerging from self-examination and new self-knowledge. Seminar — "Chairman" (the psychiatrist) sees the suppressed areas of my personality rebuilding by natural processes ... Have cut out cancer-like "cells"; healthy "cells" of personality are rebuilding ... My failure as Dean was the biggest "success" of a lifetime; saved me from another (perhaps fatal) coronary or breakdown ... Driving at 75 m.p.h. along winding cliff-edge was unfair to self and family. "Chairman" says naïve to fret over hard-driving personality. "You have to have some neuroses; otherwise you'd be a vegetable!" ... If a neurotic is unable to learn from his mistakes, I am fast becoming de-neuroticised by learning from my mistakes. This is why I went through my prolonged analysis of mistakes: not morbidity, but the only way to neutralise, learn from, and overcome them. Hypothesis: psychological wound needs several years to drain; longer than physical wound ... Paradox: sense of personal worth restored in failure.'

The next summer, Walt made what he still thinks of as his greatest discovery. It happened after he had been injured while driving in a resort area, where he and Eleanor were taking a holiday. There were no private rooms available in the local hospital, so he went into a ward with six other patients. One was a sheriff's deputy, another a store-keeper, and there was also a mechanic from a garage and a salesman. None of the six knew Walt or what he did. To them, as he said, he was just Joe Blow.

For four days, nobody asked what his job was and he didn't volunteer the information because he wanted to be just 'plain citizen'. He didn't want to put a barrier between himself and the other patients. He saw they were 'plain Joes' in terms of status and he didn't want to be separated from them.

To his astonishment, Walt found that his fellow-patients involved him in their chatter without knowing anything about his profession. It had never occurred to him before that anyone could accept him simply as a human being. After he had lost his rank as Dean, people he had regarded as intimate friends, senior colleagues who had often visited his home, had even dropped him from their Christmas-card list. Now, in the hospital ward, he discovered that he didn't want to have any signs of status.

'All my life,' he said, 'I had tried to get a rub-off from distinguished people. I wanted to be in their company as much as possible. In that hospital, I found I was able to get a rub-off from the humanity of ordinary people. I discovered the worth of plain unadorned humanity; the qualities of the ordinary man.

'Today I generally value ordinary people more than high-status people. Take the janitors on this campus. You just can't help but be impressed with what some of them are doing — for example taking this as a second job in order to help educate their children. Many have a basic cheerfulness I don't often find in hard-driving Big Shots. In fact, if I had to make a choice — as genuine human beings — between four of our janitorial staff and four of the college presidents I know, I'd have to pick the janitorial staff. They're just nicer people.

'It's not because I romanticise working-class people — I came out of that milieu and I didn't find it nobler or better. It's just that I now value the straight-forward no-nonsense person, whoever he is, and whatever his occupation.

'One of the greatest curses of this world is the assumption that prominent people are more admirable people. For example, I'd always had a most naïve, romanticised notion of superior intellect. I assumed that the super-learned person was also a person of super-character. But, of course, just because a man becomes the greatest authority on a subject doesn't make him a great authority on himself, his wife or his children — or his colleagues, for that matter. Men like that often achieve great stature by means of an unbalanced life which destroys their family and the people around them.

'The fact that they are world leaders in their own professions doesn't mean they are world leaders as human beings. So many of the "distinguished authorities" I have known were twisted personalities, miserable and self-deceiving.

'It is almost impossible for a person to maintain a balance if he becomes a "celebrity". It is one of the nastiest words in the language, a cheap word, and a cheap role. Just think of the life a person like that leads. He is showered with attention, he attracts shallow-minded hero-worshippers. He can spend his whole life going to seminars and conferences. He is no longer a person, but an institution on two legs. There is no man living who can carry out that role and remain a well-balanced human.

'People still ask what I think of certain scholars, and I have to answer that, having known and worked with so many, I never ask that question alone. The first and most important question is—what do you think of x as a person, as a husband, as a parent, as a member of the human family? Accomplishment alone is the wrong measure. Humanity is the right one.'

In his jottings at the end of the third year, Walt noted: 'Paradox —felt better about self, not by regarding self as superior but by regarding self as ordinary. Fame is printed on Kleenex—fragile; to be sneezed in and discarded.'

On his new campus, Walt has devised some simple rules to ensure that he doesn't revert to his old 'treadmill' working habits. 'I do no working-reading after dinner,' he went on, 'that's my curfew. During the day, when I find myself getting steamed up, I switch to something else. I do get carried away from time to time, but I know how to recognise the signals. And I don't use pills to get to sleep!

'I'm finding the rich rewards of plain human existence, of really trying to consider other people. I'm becoming a student of human nature for the first time, and there's an openness to people that was never there before.

'My family are no longer just objects in classified boxes. They've become three-dimensional people—much more interesting than I ever realised. My aim with Eleanor is to make up for the years I wasted and forced her to waste. I wish I had done it years ago.

I have a crushing sense of regret about the way I neglected her. Every day I feel it.

'I realise now that if one is excessively demanding of one's self, one tends to be excessively demanding of others . . . and by what right? My measure now is: harmony with people and the universe. Not a sterile harmony, but a rich, warm, affectionate harmony with people around you and the universe as a whole. To be much more warm and generous and outgoing, not to be a harsh judge. Judgmentalism is part of the accomplishment syndrome—harsh with yourself, you're harsh with everyone else. My image of my successful years was like Mark Twain's description of the Mississippi: two inches deep and two miles wide. I now aim to be two miles deep and two inches wide!

'I certainly wouldn't describe my previous life as genuine living. There was always that frantic, "driven" quality to it. This is like being born again. What I needed was a crash severe enough to break the shell, but not destroy the contents of the egg. Had the fall been less severe, the shell would not have broken. I needed to expose the "yolk" of my personality to the healing effects of self-examination.

'Now I see that the biggest "success" of my life in worldly terms led to my downfall, and that the greatest "failure" in worldly terms brought the greatest rewards.

'Whatever I've discovered came from an honest and passionate search for the truth about myself, and then a determination to put right things that were wrong. I don't think you can really come out of the things that happened to me if you pave over the past with ego-flagstones.

'People dose themselves with salves. The usual thing with career-failure is to blame it on the other guy. Certainly there were faults on the other side, but, if I'd blamed other people, I never would have discovered myself.'

9

The Still Centre

BARBARA PITCHFORD REMEMBERS Tuesday, 10th December, 1963, only too well. She spent the morning hurrying round the town of Ndola in Northern Rhodesia trying to finish her Christmas shopping. With the rest of the family — Alan, her husband, then a doctor with a successful practice, and their four young children — she had just come back from a month's holiday sailing and swimming in the Indian Ocean and she didn't want to get behind with the Christmas shopping.

Barbara was not the kind of person whose presents arrived late. A radiographer before she married Alan, she was fastidious about everything she did. She dressed immaculately, and ran their home like clockwork. Even though they had two African servants, it was Barbara who scrubbed the walls and carpets and did all the washing. She was, as her younger daughter Karen put it, very well organised; she had to be — there always seemed so much to do.

Life in Ndola was certainly full. Every weekday morning, Barbara was up at quarter to six — the children had to be at school soon after half past seven — and then there was the social life. Everybody, said her elder daughter Julia, thought mother was pretty, with her slim figure, auburn hair and blue-grey eyes; and there was a constant round of parties — children's parties, parties at the boat club, dinner parties. In Karen's memory, her mother always seemed to be going to dinner parties and she always seemed to have a new dress.

Every Sunday, Barbara sent all the children to church, though she didn't feel she had the time to go herself. All her family were ardent Methodists and she and Alan had gone to Sunday School together in Wolverhampton in the English Midlands, but life in Ndola was a little too hectic for that sort of thing. Neither Alan nor the children had forgotten how Mummy had driven their Ford Consul into an anthill because she was in such a rush ('The ants never came back!' said Alan); and once, in a moment of exasperation, she had thrown one of her shoes through a window.

So 10th December was just another busy day in the life of a young woman in her early thirties with four children under the age of seven and a great deal to do. Suddenly, however, Barbara was struck by a blinding headache; for a moment, she thought of going home, but remembered how far behind she was with the Christmas preparations and carried on. Later, she noticed an item in the local newspaper about polio and knew instinctively that that was the cause of her headache.

At that moment, Barbara didn't feel particularly worried. Several years before, Alan had taken six months off medical school because of polio, but his legs had only been slightly affected, and everybody Barbara knew who had had the disease had fully recovered, Despite her training, she had no idea that people actually died of it.

She also felt reassured by the thought that the children had already been vaccinated. They had been the first priority, but she and Alan had talked about following suit. By the time she arrived home, laden with parcels, the pain had become acute, and her neck was becoming more rigid.

On the Wednesday evening, Alan called in a specialist who asked an anaesthetist to carry out a lumbar puncture. The pathologist thought he had found something suspicious, but wasn't sure. Barbara, meanwhile, did not tell Alan that she knew she had polio – she didn't want to cause any unnecessary fuss – but by midnight that night she was already finding it difficult to breathe.

Next morning, she was worse. She couldn't get to the bathroom without help, she couldn't hold a tea-cup and she couldn't eat. Karen remembers her mother asking for some cold peaches, but, when Karen tried to feed her, Barbara wasn't able to swallow and, soon, both were in tears. Barbara managed to walk to the car in which Alan took her to hospital, but, by then she could hardly breathe at all.

The doctors anaesthetised her and breathed for her through a tube until a respirator was brought. Then they carried out an emergency tracheostomy to open a way through to the main air-passage below the vocal chords, and then this was connected so that the respirator could pump air direct into and out of Barbara's lungs. At first, she had hoped she might be out of hospital in time for Christmas; now, she was totally paralysed and fighting for her life. She prayed fervently that God would not let her die.

She could not breathe for a second without the help of the respirator, which Alan was afraid would fail at any moment, and she had to be fed, first intra-venously then through a tube. A rota of doctors and consultants from all over Northern Rhodesia kept watch at her bedside twenty-four hours a day. All of them were volunteers, all of them men and women who were running practices of their own. It was their self-sacrifice which saved Barbara's life in a situation where there was neither a respiratory specialist nor a special polio unit. Apart from anything else, she had to be turned over every quarter of an hour to stop pressure sores developing.

Then, in the middle of an operation to examine and clean her bronchial tubes, one of the nurses noticed that Barbara's heart was no longer beating. A French nurse struggled to bring her back to life with heart massage for what seemed like hours but was probably about a minute, and, when Alan had almost given up hope, his wife at last began to breathe again.

As the battle to save Barbara's life went on, Alan felt a sense of utter emptiness. Two weeks before, they had been sunning themselves together on a beach; now he had no idea whether Barbara would live or die. As soon as she went into hospital, he had called Barbara's mother in England and asked if she would come and look after the children. Frances Westwood was already in her sixties but, within hours, she had packed and was on her way to Rhodesia. She took over the running of the house, and it was she who woke Alan at four in the morning so that he could take his place at Barbara's bedside.

The children, of course, were even more deeply disturbed by what was happening to their mother, even though they had spent Christmas with Barbara's cousin. They were not allowed to visit the hospital and, what was almost as bad, scarcely ever seemed to see their father. When another little girl asked Karen what was wrong with her mother, Karen simply burst into tears. She didn't know, she said, she just knew it was something terrible.

As the weeks went by, Barbara showed no sign of improvement, and it became obvious that she needed treatment in a specialist unit and that she would have to be flown to either Capetown or London. Alan decided that London would be best.

This in itself was a perilous operation, because she couldn't breathe for a moment without help. At the airport, Barbara had to be transferred to a completely new respirator because the aircraft operated on a different voltage from the one she had been using, but this was provided by a local mining company, just one example of the spontaneous generosity of the whole community. Then, as they were crossing the Mediterranean, the pilot had a radio message from London to say that the airport was closed because of fog and, after a hurried consultation, Alan agreed that the best course was to land in Malta.

Even this was not without its hazards. The pilot knew that the aircraft would have to keep its engines running until Barbara's respirator had been switched to a source of power on the ground, and he also knew that Malta had no such source available. The Royal Air Force, however, produced a generator at three in the morning and, as soon as the fog at Gatwick had lifted, they flew north again.

When Barbara arrived in England, she was overwhelmed by despair. She had left sunshine and light; now she became aware of an awful greyness. Nobody seemed to be smiling and the sun, when you could see it, was a red ball in a grey, grey sky. Her hospital room looked out on chimney-stacks and black walls. Everything seemed hopeless. She tried to tell Alan she didn't want to stay, but could only make the appropriate lip movements and hope he understood. Alan stayed with her for a fortnight and, during that time, had a tremendous piece of luck. He met the head of a German pharmaceutical company who told him that they wanted to set up a medical department and offered Alan the job. It seemed like a godsend because Alan had always been keen to do research. Before he left, he had made up his mind to accept.

The next months were amongst the most difficult of Barbara's life. With Alan back in Rhodesia and the children being cared for by close friends who actually gave up their jobs for two months to do so, her only contact with her family was through visits from her mother and aunts, who faithfully travelled from the Midlands every Wednesday. For the rest, there were only the photographs of Alan and the children which stood on her bedside table.

Often her spirits sank very low. She could see nothing ahead but 'a great big void' and sometimes thought it would have been better if she had died in Rhodesia. The nights, she found, were the worst. Then, there was time to lie and wonder what would become of the family and how Alan was managing to cope alone.

There was one consolation; the treatment she was given in hospital was superb. There was the physiotherapy three times a day, Sundays included, to try to bring back the use of her limbs, and she was given a rocking bed, which moved up and down at her normal breathing rate, to help her breathe without the help of the respirator.

In the spring, the hospital staff began taking away the respirator for short periods. At first it was fifty seconds, then two minutes, then twenty minutes, and before long Barbara could survive without it for two hours. She also began to eat normally and recover the use of her legs.

By that time, the children had come back to Britain in the care of a friend and were living with relatives in the north of England, the girls in Leeds, the boys in Selby. So the family had been fragmented still further.

Meanwhile Alan was busy clearing up their affairs in Africa. It was a heart-breaking business. Seven years' hard work in building up the practice went down the drain. So did their yacht *Josephine* and all the other trappings of comfort.

Alan sold the yacht and put his home on the market. Again, luck seemed against them. The coming of independence that same year (Northern Rhodesia became Zambia), sent house prices tumbling and eventually Alan had to sell at a considerable loss.

When he flew back to England, he had no home and his new job meant frequent journeys to Germany. He divided his time between this, visiting Barbara, making hurried sorties to Yorkshire to see the children, and tramping round estate agents' offices hunting for a house he could afford. Altogether, he looked at about fifty. Some were unsuitable, others were beyond his means, and some turned out to be 'unavailable'. Once, he thought he had found a promising flat in Sussex but, when the upstairs tenants heard children were coming, they objected and the offer was withdrawn.

By now, Alan was desperately short of cash — the house in Zambia was still unsold, and he would have found it hard to make ends meet but for the generous help of friends in Africa. At last, he found a bungalow in rural Sussex. Barbara's mother agreed to set up home there for the children and brought with her Jackie Palmer, an eighteen-year-old girl who also came from their home village.

By this time, the children were bewildered and disturbed. They had seen their father only twice since he came back from Africa, their mother only once; they were desperately lonely; they found their new schools strange and difficult to adjust to; and underlying everything, there was a growing fear that the family might be breaking up. Julia, who—as the eldest—felt very responsible for the others, had begun to wonder what would become of them all, and Alan's flying visits left her so miserable that she secretly thought it might have been better if he hadn't come at all.

Nor did the experience of settling into their new home raise their spirits much. Nigel, the youngest of the four, was sick on the journey south and when they and Alan arrived at this strange house at the bottom of a rutted lane, there was no mother to greet them, only grandmother and this unknown girl dressed in a blue overall. Just like a film, thought Julia.

Barbara's mother and Jackie had done what they could to make the bungalow welcoming but, in the absence of carpets and the family furniture, which still hadn't arrived from Africa, it was a thankless job. So when the children arrived there were bare floor-boards, bare light-bulbs sticking out of the walls, hard cushions instead of pillows on the makeshift beds and, outside, a garden which was nothing more than a great, untended mud heap.

What was worse, they felt marooned in this wilderness. Alan had to have their only car and every time Barbara's mother or Jackie wanted to go to the shops, they had to pilot Nigel's push-chair through the mud and puddles for what felt to Julia like miles.

Each weekend, Alan took two of the children to see Barbara. For the children, it was a traumatic experience. Often, one of them was ill. Karen remembers being very sick several times in her father's lap—and, at first, she found the sight of their mother, lying there with her pale face and tubes going through an opening in her throat, both frightening and embarrassing.

Everything was always so clinical, said Karen. There was the smell of the hospital and Mummy, lying there in the middle of it. It was so sad. Nor could Barbara even speak to them. They had to try to lip-read what she wanted to say and since, as Julia said, she and the other children were hopeless at lip-reading, they had to depend on Alan who interpreted for Barbara as she struggled to tell them how much she loved them.

Barbara, indeed, was finding it desperately difficult to keep up her own spirits. On Good Friday, she felt thoroughly fed up and said so to a Catholic member of staff. 'Good Friday—and *you're* fed up?' he replied. That brought Barbara up short. He's right, she thought, it *doesn't* make sense.

In February 1965, more than a year after she had arrived back in Britain, her morale hit rock-bottom when she was moved to another rehabilitation hospital. There, she knew nobody and nobody knew her; the level of technology was still high, but Barbara felt it was impersonal and soulless, with consultants who often seemed to treat her as an interesting object, and she was put in a ward for acute orthopaedic cases, whose entire population seemed to change every fortnight.

People were arriving and departing all the time, but it was never her. Will my turn *ever* come, Barbara wondered?

She could sit up in a wheel-chair for short periods, and her voice was almost back to normal after successful plastic surgery, but nothing raised her spirits for very long. By now she had been in hospital for almost two years.

Finally, Alan decided there was only one thing to do. Somehow, he had to find a way of bringing Barbara home. A local doctor told him the idea was madness. Barbara, he said, would run the risk of catching every infection which afflicted her children, and it might easily prove too much for her. Barbara, however, was only too happy to take whatever risks might be involved, even though at first she had a respirator of somewhat antiquated design.

Barbara was deeply thankful to be home again, but the transition proved almost as hazardous as the doctor had predicted. For a long time, she picked up a lot of the chest infections which the children brought home. She was also afraid that something would go wrong with her breathing apparatus when no help was at hand, though someone was always within call. As she lay gazing at the ceiling, her fear and frustrations sometimes knew no bounds.

The physical dangers, however, were only one of Barbara's anxieties. Back at the heart of her domestic empire, she instinctively wanted to take up again her role as the busy, brisk, highly-organised mistress of the household. Now, however, she was utterly dependent on other people, and felt appalled at the extent of her helplessness. Far from being able to rush around in the old way, she could not even scratch her own nose when it itched.

At first, her helplessness made her frustrated and bitter. She resented the fact that she wasn't able to do more, that others could go out when she couldn't. She even resented the people on whom she depended so much, those who did things for her which she could no longer do for herself. It took years to conquer that resentment.

The children, too, discovered that, although mother was home again, she was not the same mother whom they had known two years before. This became evident in the simplest and most basic things. Barbara, for example, was no longer able to fling her arms around them, and the children often felt starved for lack of physical affection. Karen, in particular, used to lie in bed and cry for hours. She longed to feel sure that somebody loved her. 'When you're little,' she said, 'toys aren't enough.'

Often, the children took out their resentments on the newcomer in their midst, Jackie. Julia remembers that she sometimes spoke cruel, cutting words which she now bitterly regrets.

Alan, too, who had done so much to hold the family together in its first crisis, needed to find a fresh impetus now that the crisis had been weathered. He and Barbara had been married twelve years, and he found it hard to go back to what in many ways was a lonely existence, while still bearing all the responsibilities of a married man. He could not forget that once, not so very long ago, they had been a couple doing ordinary, everyday things together and that, now, he was doing them alone. There was nobody to turn to for comfort and he still had to bring home the necessities. In his worst moments, Alan found himself asking why he should go on. After all, he told himself, he wasn't going to live forever. At times, he confessed, he was overwhelmed by self-pity. The thing which held him steady was a profound conviction that 'the only sane unit in an insane world is the family'. In a universe where people were prepared to lie and cheat to satisfy their passion for material things, the love and loyalty which a family could provide seemed to him the one abiding refuge, and he was prepared to sacrifice anything to hold his own together.

He also drew courage from advice which his father had given him. 'If you start something,' his father had said, 'have the guts to go on and finish it.' For Alan, this homespun wisdom summed up his distaste for an age in which, he felt, every relationship had become disposable. Too often, he thought, people simply gave up just because they were bored and tired or because a relationship had become too difficult.

He told Barbara that, whatever their own misfortunes, the children's lives must not be allowed to suffer. Two of his maiden aunts, he remembered, had spent virtually their whole adult existence nursing an invalid mother, and he was determined that that should not happen to his own children.

Yet, although Jackie shouldered the main burden of the household chores – shopping, cooking, washing, cleaning, often working from six-thirty in the morning until ten-thirty at night – there was still a good deal she couldn't do. Then the children, particularly Karen and Julia, who were nine and eleven by the time Barbara came out of hospital, had to step into the breach.

On Saturday, which was Jackie's regular day off, they had to do everything for Barbara. They washed her, cleaned her teeth, emptied her bed pan, took her to the toilet, helped to get her up when the district nurse didn't come, cooked all the meals – and then washed the dishes and did all the dusting and cleaning. Sunday, in Julia's memory was always a day when she felt totally worn out.

During the rest of the week, the children made their own beds and occasionally cooked supper or fed Barbara. In the mornings, Christopher would give her breakfast while Jackie took the girls to catch the school bus; and when he became older,

Nigel would feed her at supper on the nights when Jackie was out. It was, to put it mildly, a testing experience for the two girls. The first time Julia helped her mother, she was horrified by the way Barbara's head and shoulders slumped because she had no control over them. Karen, for her part, hated taking her mother to the toilet. 'I was such a fuss-pot,' she said with a grin.

At different times, both the girls rebelled against the constant chores and having to look after their mother at a time when, instinctively, they thought *she* should be looking after *them*. Julia remembers asking herself the question, 'Why us, why her?' and feeling bitter because her mother's incapacity seemed to be disturbing everybody's life so much.

As she grew older, she also resented the fact that she wasn't free to go out on Saturday, when all her friends seemed to be 'raving it up', because that was Jackie's day off. Even though she and Karen agreed to take alternate Saturdays when Julia was doing her 'O'-level examinations, she can't remember going out much at all until she was seventeen.

'We always used to argue,' said Karen. ' "It's not my turn!" "It's not *my* turn!" — I was terribly selfish. The mornings weren't so bad, but things began to weigh on us in the afternoons and evenings, when we were tired. I often got very bitter and twisted because I wanted to go out.'

Barbara, for her part, did everything she could to ease the burden on the rest of the family. The British Polio Fellowship provided her with a specially adapted typewriter and, although she had only a slight upward movement in seven fingers, she taught herself to type. That meant she could at least take a greater part in simple household tasks. Every Monday morning, she typed out the menus for the following week, and then a shopping list to match.

As she became more proficient, she also took on the job of typing letters for a nearby hospital and school for handicapped children. The man she was working for put his letters on tape, Jackie fed the paper into the machine and Barbara did the rest. It was marvellous, she said, because it gave her a degree of independence. She was no longer, she felt, just a useless lump of flesh gazing at the ceiling all day long.

At the same time, the British Polio Fellowship also provided Barbara with a 'Possum' machine. The word 'Possum' is short for Patient Operated Selector Mechanism and the machine enabled Barbara to do all sorts of things she could not do before. Using only the toes of her right foot, she could call for help by ringing a bell in the kitchen, raise and lower her bed, switch on (or off) her electric blanket, radio and TV set, read microfilmed books and make telephone calls.

Her health improved along with her morale. Typing helped bring back the use of her fingers; she can now walk the few yards to and from her car; and she has gradually regained control of her neck muscles.

Although breathing is still a conscious effort and there have been days when it has been so difficult that Barbara is afraid she will pass out at any moment, she can usually manage to survive without her respirator from mid-morning until seven in the evening, when she goes back to her room.

But it was Barbara's mental attitude to her physical helplessness which made the task of caring for her bearable. When she first arrived home, she resolved that, whatever her limitations, she would actively try to be as little trouble as possible. 'Whine whine, want, want,' she said. 'We invalids can become that very easily. It's obvious that I'm in need, but I decided that I'd try to make sure that that need never turned into a demand.'

Instead, she waited to be asked what she needed, to such an extent that her own mother was quite concerned at first that she should ask for so little.

'You often get chronic disabled,' said Margaret Green, the former district nurse who used to visit Barbara regularly, 'who're always saying, "Move this, move that; this isn't comfortable; I want that", but you never find that with Barbara. She's not a bit demanding.' 'I've nursed quite a few arthritics,' added Jane Wilmshurst, a neighbour who helped out once a week, 'and where some would snap "I *must* have that hook done up", Barbara would simply say, "Just give this a hitch up, will you?" A lot of it is that she's free of self-pity; she just doesn't have any. If invalids do, it puts a wall between you and them, and you can't cope with that. It's more of a burden than the ailment itself. People accept Barbara as one of them just because she is free from self-pity.'

'Mother has always been the sort of person who wanted to bother others as little as possible,' said Julia. 'She was never one of those demanding people who are always resenting the situation they're in, and she was *never* a martyr.'

This is partly because Barbara has never lost her sense of gratitude for being able to be at home again with her family, or an awareness that only a narrow thread separates her from being forced to go back into a hospital ward. Being in hospital with people dying around her, she said, helped teach her to appreciate life and not to demand too much. 'Just being at home with the children has been wonderful; it's such a privilege and I've enjoyed them so much.'

Barbara's lack of demand also sprang from a conscious decision to give herself wholeheartedly to the family, to concentrate — as she put it — on 'getting the children over their hurdles, trying to smooth their way and praying for help for them'. She realised very quickly that, precisely because of her physical disability, she had much more time to devote to them. She was always available to talk over problems and, when she knew one of them had a hard day at school, she would spend a good deal of time asking God to give them courage for whatever was in store.

In doing that, she discovered how important it was for her, confined as she was, to be able to look outside herself. 'If I concentrate on someone else's needs,' she observed, 'my own don't seem half so bad.'

Curiously, Barbara's immobility made the children feel more, not less secure. She was, quite simply, always there. 'During the day,' said Julia, 'we knew exactly what she was doing and she knew what we were doing. And we always knew she'd be there when we came home. I had a much greater sense of security than most of my friends.'

Barbara also found she had ample time to look back at the way she had lived before she was disabled, a chance to review her whole philosophy of life. She began to feel that it had had a great many shortcomings.

In Africa, for example, there had been so much to be done. The telephone was always ringing (usually when Nigel was in the bath) and she recalled how grumpy she had often been, particularly when Alan was called out at inconvenient times. She had often not thought of the other people involved, only how annoying it was for her to be left alone. How bitterly she regretted the thoughtlessness of those years!

Looking back, she could see how she had wanted to keep
their family life in a nice little, water-tight compartment away
from Alan's practice, and how she'd resented people who weren't
seriously ill, but just needed somebody. In that, she thought,
she had really failed Alan. If only she had given up more time
to people and to Alan's work ... and then there had been the
big blow-up in the Congo with the refugees pouring into Ndola
in their thousands, She knew at the time that she should have
opened her home to them, but she hadn't.

And then she began thinking about her faith, and what had
happened to it over the years. It had always been there, because
she'd been brought up that way, and she'd believed in God
and she'd prayed—but always for what she wanted and not
for what He wanted (she thought with a smile how she'd never
gone into an exam without praying first!); and she'd certainly had
no time to listen to find out what God wanted *her* to do.

If she had listened, she reflected, she wouldn't have rushed
round like a mad thing washing carpets and walls and everything
else in sight, because she would have seen that all that was not
so important. As Alan told her, she'd been so busy living, she
hadn't stopped to enjoy life.

Then, one day, an Anglican parson who had come to their
local church as a stand-in, called on her. When they had become
friends, he suggested to Barbara that her disability and its consequences might be even harder for Alan to bear than they were
for her. After thinking it over, Barbara came to the conclusion
that he was right. If she put herself in Alan's place, she thought,
she couldn't have coped with all he'd had to bear—the new job,
the desperate shortage of money, the crippled and helpless wife.
That realisation changed Barbara's attitude towards Alan. It
made her appreciate even more the magnificent job he had done
in keeping the family together, when so many would just have
cleared off or given in, and it helped her to face up to his enforced
absences in a quite different spirit. Before, she had always assumed
that she, and nobody else, was entitled to his time and energy;
she wasn't going to share him with anybody, he was hers. Now,
although she didn't like the thought of Alan going away ... to
Germany, to Austria, to South Africa, which he had to do because
of his job, she found that she felt far more deeply for what he
would be facing.

She decided that she was going to give up clinging, wanting to own Alan. As soon as she did so, she found that not only was Alan a freer man, but also that she was a freer woman — that, although her body was bound by her wheel-chair and her respirator, her soul was at liberty.

Barbara also began to find a faith which was deeper and more real than anything she had ever had before. 'When something goes wrong and you're in my condition,' she said, 'you have to find the answer to it within yourself, you can't just jump into a car and drive off. You just have to say, "God, I can't do another thing, please take over".

'For example, I sometimes get terrible fears of being left alone (although in fact I never am), or that Jackie might break her leg and I'd be shut in so I couldn't get any help. When that happens, there's only Him to lean back on, and so I lean. When I feel low, I pray to God to send me somebody, and very often someone comes. One day, for example, three little children from up the road came and had biscuits and squash with me. They just rang the bell and said, "May we come and see you?" They just wanted some company and so did I!

'And there are days when I rebel and say, "I'm not going to let God through to me." Those are days when I have to turn to Him to straighten me out.

'But, you know, the truth is that I'm much happier person than I was before I was disabled. I used to live in permanent turmoil. I felt far more martyred then than I do now — driving myself to scrub walls and carpets and clean windows all the time. At least half the things I did were ludicrous and unnecessary! If I hadn't been disabled, I don't think I'd ever have realised that. Now, I've got time to concentrate on essentials.'

The children, too, feel that, despite all the drudgery and difficulty the last years have been a priceless experience. 'Looking back,' said Julia, now a radiantly cheerful young woman of twenty-one, 'it was nothing but benefit. I wouldn't have missed any of it, even the hard times. I learned so much, it was the making rather than the breaking of me. After all, there aren't too many girls who've learnt to make bread at twelve or run a house by the time they are thirteen!

'I had friends at school who were in families which seemed to be breaking apart, and I couldn't understand why they had such terrific problems. They seemed to argue over such stupid things — like what time they ought to be in by, and so on. That just didn't occur in our house; we were so united, we never seemed to experience the generation gap. I think it was because we all knew how much Mummy needed us.

'And it was always an extraordinarily cheerful home — I've never been afraid to bring anybody here. People say, "Gosh, the atmosphere's a lot happier than it is in my own home." '

At school, Julia had begun to feel there wasn't much purpose to life beyond the rat-race of examination success, and could envisage nothing for her own life apart from looking after the family. She was, indeed, well aware that she had already begun to use looking after her mother as a way of hiding her adolescent shyness. Then, through a school friend, she became a Christian. She asked Christ to become a reality in her life, and told Him she didn't know where she was going. The decision had a marked effect both at home and school.

'The first year I was head girl at high school,' she said, 'I shared the job with another girl, and I always wanted to do more than she did. The second year, I decided to do it quite differently, for the good of the school and not my own. Then, somehow, everybody approached me very differently; even the little tots used to come up and talk to me. My attitude to Jackie changed completely too, and I began to see Karen much more as a friend.'

When she left school, Julia became a nurse because she wanted to do something for people. The early days of training in London, however, were not easy. Barbara and Alan both told her it would be better if she didn't stay at home, but she still found the break very difficult. There was one weekend when she told her mother and father that she wasn't going back. 'If they hadn't sent me,' she said with a chuckle, 'I wouldn't have gone. They really had to push me out!'

Eventually, she came to love the work and discovered ways of applying her faith in all kinds of practical ways. 'I've found out that it means standing up for what you believe to be right,' she said, 'particularly in situations where you know what is right for the patient but it isn't being done. Patients should always get the best we can give, no matter how long it takes, no matter what paper-work gets left.

'The other thing is that, every day, I try to make my life more steady and stable. If you're up and down like a yo-yo, you're not going to be any use to anyone else. I've noticed that if people get up-tight about their boy-friends or social life generally, their work deteriorates rapidly.

'I think I am more able than I was to put other people first. And I try to think how I'd do it for mother if she was there. I am there to help people, to try and show by the life I lead that there is more to it than existing from day to day. I feel I was prepared for it with mother.

'What happened to Mummy wasn't so bad so far as I was concerned. For a start, I wouldn't have come to God if it hadn't happened — nor would Mummy or Karen for that matter.'

Like Julia, Karen prays and reads the Bible every morning, and also has a time of quiet. When she was at school, which meant leaving home soon after seven, she used to begin at six — 'I've found it helps to have a prayer time-table, although that sounds terribly organised, doesn't it?

'Without a faith, I just couldn't have coped,' she said. 'I was driven to something deeper. When I was eight or nine, I used to lie in bed and pray that Mummy would get better. Nothing happened and I thought God wasn't listening. Then I prayed to be able to accept things and find some of the jobs I had to do less repulsive. That worked, and it made me a lot more tolerant. I got the feeling, "There are more things in me that need to change", not "I can't put up with this."

'When things went wrong at school, I'd always blamed it on Mummy and not having enough time because of all the house-work but, when I thought about it, I knew it wasn't true and that really I had plenty of time. So, after reading the Bible in the morning, I'd come down in a good mood, having thought I must be helpful to Mummy and the others rather than bitter and twisted.

'Another thing is that I'm lazy if I think I can't cope. If I run into difficulties, I tend to switch off, to panic before I even attempt something — but, when I began reading the Bible, I felt I could do my school-work for His glory. You can't let Him down, can you? So, when I got very depressed because at one stage I felt I was doing the wrong A-levels, I thought at first, "I can't cope", but then I felt inside I should press on and try.

In the end, I had a sense that I was doing it for more than myself.

'I find my faith also helps with loneliness. I used to be extremely lonely, and now I actually enjoy being alone sometimes. God's very good company!

'If we'd stayed in Africa, we'd have been so busy living our lives, swimming and sailing, that so much would have passed us by on the spiritual side. If there'd been lots of money around, we'd all have been terribly spoilt and we'd have missed the most important things. So many people never have anything in their lives to help them realise what the really important things are.

'Daddy's never said he wished he'd trotted off. He feels so much we're here to serve other people; if not, there's no reason to be here at all. He also speaks his mind freely at work – and that helps us to know he's not just a stern businessman.

'We're all so very fond of each other. Christopher, for example, he's a natural leader like Daddy. He's not vain or big-headed. Even if he's successful, he never puffs himself up.'

Christopher, who was head boy of his school and is now training with a diamond company, feels that they are so close because they know what it is like *not* to be a family. Nigel, a sensitive and charming thirteen-year-old, is also quite sure that his mother's illness has brought them all closer. 'It's made us go together more and listen to each other's problems.'

Unknown to the others, Nigel began to read the Bible every day when he was eleven. 'Things aren't always easy at school,' he said, 'and I thought Jesus would help. Reading the Bible helps you think about things and, well, sort of keeps you company. Prayer helps too – on my own or with my sisters, it just helps. I know every other boy has a mother who is ordinary, and sometimes I wish mine could get up and move around, but I don't mind, so long as I've got one.' Watching Nigel feeding his mother is a profoundly moving experience.

To Alan, the lessons seem plain enough. 'Most children today,' he said, 'are so protected from reality. All our kids were faced with stark reality, and they came through it by themselves. It's left me with a feeling that adversity is an enriching experience – that people who've been through tough times are more human and understanding and willing to help.'

'I think helping gave the children a feeling of responsibility,' said Jane Wilmshurst. 'If Barbara had been too demanding –

"You must stay in; I must be put to bed"—it would have been a burden. None of the children ever get resentful now—you never get the feeling they're thinking, "I *have* to stay at home with Mum."

'They certainly think about each other a great deal more than most families, and they're far more united. So many families pull away from the nucleus, but this one seems to have drawn closer together. They are all going their own ways, but they are still a family.

'It's a pleasure to come here. I always feel better for it. I come up here and I think, "What the heck are *you* feeling so gloomy about?" Barbara is such a normal, free person that you're not even conscious she's sitting in a wheel-chair.'

Jane Wilmshurst is by no means the only person who finds new hope from visiting Barbara and her family. All kinds of people go there to talk over their problems and shed their worries. Barbara, as she says herself, has the time to listen, when so many people haven't, and, as is evident to all her visitors, she is neither absorbed by her own problems, nor looking for sympathy.

'Pity is the last thing I want,' she said, 'because pity drives me to self-pity. You feel so much better if you're not feeling sorry for yourself. Pity's what you get from do-gooders, and they're doing it for their own satisfaction and not to help you.'

When you walk down the narrow Sussex lane to the bungalow near the bottom, and you are greeted first by Jackie, then by Max, the Pitchfords' wire-haired dachsund, and then by Barbara and the children, you feel instinctively that they're not expecting you to do something for them but that they want to do something for you.

And you think of everything that has gone into the making of a home like the Pitchfords' and of the modern miracles it displays. You think first of the human qualities—Barbara's grace and ever-deepening insight, Alan's faithfulness and fortitude, Jackie's selfless service for more than a decade. And then you think of the faith of generations in those Methodist chapels in the English Midlands where Barbara's grandmother sat in the same pew every Sunday for eighty-four years, where Barbara's mother followed her, where Jackie's mother and father were Sunday School teachers and Jackie found her own faith. Only

a few miles away, in another Methodist chapel, Barbara and
Alan first met, and found a faith which has held firm and borne
fruit at times of great crisis.

In one way the Pitchfords are an ordinary family, unpreten-
tious, unpious, unsentimental. But through sacrifice and pain,
disappointment and sorrow, they have laid hold on truths and
riches hidden from millions apparently more fortunate. 'You
have to fight your own way out,' said Alan. 'Where you find the
strength from is another matter.'

10

The Eye of the Needle

I TRIED FOR two solid days to phone Baba Amte from Bombay. The telephone number I had for him was Mul 10. When I finally discovered where Mul was, I understood all, but for the whole of those two days it appeared that Mul 10 was engaged, unobtainable because the lines were down, or unobtainable for other, more mysterious reasons. I began to wonder if my journey to India was going to prove a complete fiasco.

After forty-eight hours of mounting frustration, I decided the only thing to do was set off for Nagpur (the nearest airport to Mul 10) and hope that the local newspaper editor, A. G. Sheoreoy, whom I had managed to contact through a friend, would somehow have let Amte know I was on my way.

I need not have worried. Mr. Sheoreoy was at Nagpur airport to meet me with a colleague; they had spoken to Amte on the telephone; they had even hired a taxi to take me to his place which, they said, was about sixty miles to the south. I began to feel that providence was, after all, on my side.

Five miles down the road, on a slight incline, the taxi began to exhibit obvious signs of weariness. It was, indeed, a nonagenarian among public conveyances, but the driver insisted that such a thing had never happened before in its long history and began poking ineffectually under the bonnet.

Eventually, I flagged down a passing car. Two men climbed out, hooting with laughter at our plight, fixed the trouble and went on their way in as good a humour as they had arrived. The rest of the trip was relatively uneventful, although every upward gradient was a potential hazard.

The countryside was unremarkable. Much of it was unfertile-looking scrub; only the occasional village, with its gaggle of bullocks and men gathered round an open-fronted café and a petrol pump, showed much sign of life.

Soon, the driver announced that we were getting close to Anandwan, which means 'Forest of Joy'. I felt relieved but apprehensive. I had never been to a leprosy colony before and certainly not one in the middle of India. I was nervous, but determined not to show it. We drove along a dusty track past a collection of low, white buildings and stopped abruptly in a little compound.

A man stepped forward, stocky, with thick, grey hair and the face of a warrior, fierce eyes and a powerful nose. He wore a white cotton shirt outside his dhoti. This was Amte. As we shook hands, I didn't think to ask about Mul 10.

At lunch, I met Amte's wife, Sadhana, a slight woman, with classic features and an air of great determination, and his elder son Vikas. We would have a rest, said Amte, and then we would talk.

When I saw him again, he was lying on a bed on the verandah. At first, I wondered if I had disturbed his rest, but it turned out that, since 1965, he had been suffering from cervical and lumbar spondylosis, which brings a gradual degenerative process of osteoarthrosis and, for seven years, had worn a steel collar and a fearsome collection of belts to try to ease the pain. The year before, he told me, he had thrown all of them away. Now, he cannot sit for any length of time without suffering agonies, and he prefers to stand or lie down.

During his childhood, he said, his life had been that of an upper-class landowner's son. His father was a *jaghirdar*, a British government servant responsible for the administration and revenues of an entire district; he had been given a sizeable estate for his services.

As the *jaghirdar*'s son, Amte was treated with considerable deference. When he went out, people ran in front of his bullock-cart to show that someone important was coming; for four years, he had a private teacher who talked to him about Indian mythology and being a well-behaved boy; and he was only allowed to play with the sons of government officers or high-class farmers. Whenever he attempted to mix with anyone of a lower class, his parents reminded him sharply of his elevated caste and status. He was not supposed to talk to people like that ... after all, they pointed out, he was a high-born Brahmin. When he tried to take food with the family of one of their six house servants, he was thrashed and told he would not be given any evening meal if he behaved in that way. The prohibition had little effect. Since untouchables were not allowed in the family kitchen, Amte fed with them on the verandah.

'There is a callousness in families like mine, which are well looked after,' he said. 'They put up strong barriers so as not to see the world outside – and I rebelled against it. My whole life has been spent wrestling with the leviathan of my inner bondage. Tradition ... caste ... family. All-in wrestling!', he added roaring with laughter and writhing on his bed with amusement.

Then, when he was thirteen, he decided to visit the slums on the day of the Hindu festival of Diwali. On the way home, he came across a blind beggar. The man was shouting, 'He who gives will be blessed by me, and he who does not give will also be blessed by me.' One *paisa* would have been a normal offering, but Amte had a pocketful of small change and emptied it all into the beggar's bowl, making a considerable clatter.

'You naughty boy,' shouted the beggar, 'you're playing with a poor blind man, you're throwing stones in there.' When he put his hand into the bowl, however, he soon realised they were not stones and began to count them incredulously again and again. The look of astonishment on his face and the way his hands scrabbled frantically among the coins made a deep impression on the young Amte. To think that a man could be so overwhelmed by the gift of a few small coins, to experience for a moment that life in the dust, to imagine himself in that position ... the boy ran home in tears.

He did not want to stay in 'the golden prison' of his home any longer than he had to. That same year, he began to run away during the school holidays, and in the period of the British occupation, travelled all over India – Delhi, Calcutta, Hyderabad. For a day at the beginning of the holidays he would take meals with the family and then disappear, having secretly assured his mother that he was not running away for ever. Sometimes he would be away for ten days, sometimes for a month; soon he was spending a quarter of each year wandering round the country. His father was angry, his mother anxious, but they could do nothing to stop him.

'I ran away,' he said, 'because I wanted the experience of life, because I wanted to mix with the common man. To me, the common man's society is a maskless society. He doesn't carry that thick mask which we—the professional people, the upper classes—wear so that we'll look nice and beautiful. Even if he tries, he still betrays something.'

By the time he was fourteen, Amte had his own rifle and was hunting wild boar and deer. His 'hunting *guru*' was Talatule, who had shot scores of tigers by standing on the ground and waiting for his quarry to approach the bait. Not for him the safety of the *machan*, the platform built in the trees where 'hunters' sat while the tethered buffalo screamed in fear below.

'That "instant *shikar*" I always hated,' said Amte. 'It is like trying to shoot your evil at arms-length—"I have given so much to charity, I have been so good", showing yourself at church. The one who pits his dug-out against the mighty roar of the sea, he is my *guru*, not the one in the motor boat.'

In due course, Amte was sent to a Christian Mission School in Nagpur. The obligatory Bible classes seemed to him a dreary ritual and Christ, he thought, was just a myth. The missionaries, too, bored him but he was reluctantly impressed by the behaviour of some.

One day, the economics teacher, a Scot called McFadyean, took him for a drive in his Baby Austin. They came across a Morris Eight parked on the roadside with two women, one carrying a baby, standing desperately beside it. 'Why stop?' said Amte, as McFadyean braked. 'Let us go on.' McFadyean, however, got out and said to the women, 'Can I help you?' The simple sentence stuck in the boy's mind.

Eventually, he left the Mission School, and went on to college in Nagpur. His ambition was to become a doctor (even his initials, he said, were MD) but, when he was a baby, an astrologer had prophesied that he would be a lawyer, and so his father forced him to give up science and transfer to the arts faculty.

At college, he lived in the style to which he had become accustomed. His lodging was in the quarter where British members of the Indian Civil Service lived—'tar roads, dogs must not enter, that sort of place', said Amte with a grin—and his father insisted that a carriage with a driver should collect him every morning when classes were over. Riding five miles each way on a bicycle, he argued, might damage a young man's health. Later, Amte drove a twin-carburettor Singer sports car with white mudguards, a long green body and cushions covered with panther skin, and was dressed by Rosario, tailor to His Excellency the British governor.

He was also a cinema addict and often took in two or three performances a day. As a reviewer for the *Picturegoer* magazine he behaved on these occasions with a proper sense of his own importance. He always bought two tickets, so that he could put up his feet without fear of rebuke and, when an attendant had the temerity to disturb him by asking him if he wanted something to eat, he bought up the entire tray and told the man to trouble him no further.

These extra-mural activities, left little time for study. When the roll was called, Amte would reply 'Yes, sir', and then climb out of the window.

Nevertheless, he graduated and took up practice in the nearby town of Chattisgarh. His heart, however, was never in it. Why, he thought, was he wasting his talents defending criminals? A client would admit he had committed rape and he, Amte, would then be expected to obtain an aquittal. Worse still, he was expected to attend the celebration party if he succeeded. He became increasingly restless and his father suggested it would be better if he avoided criminal cases and concentrated on civil law. He also persuaded his son to move to Warora, a town only a few miles from their family estate. There he could develop his practice during the week and look after the affairs of the estate at the weekend.

In theory, it was an excellent way of inducing a volatile young man to settle down. Amte had three houses at his disposal in Warora and there was a club where, his father thought, he could occupy his leisure time with bridge, tennis and other pursuits befitting his station.

The stratagem, however, misfired. When Amte visited his father's estate at Goraja, he was appalled by the naked poverty he saw around him and nauseated by the parasitic life he was supposed to lead. He had never planted a single seed on the

estate, yet he was expected to stay in the comfort of the farmhouse while those who had toiled there daily all their lives had
only the meanest hovels. He refused and, instead, moved into
a little thatched cottage.

He began to study the way in which the poor lived. He took
his meals with the untouchables, the *harijans*, and went to prayer
with them. He discovered that they were even forbidden to
draw water from the village well, for fear they might pollute
it. At first, Amte assumed that the richer people of the neigh-
bourhood had become exceptionally callous, and walked to another
village where there was a big landlord. There, however, he found
conditions were still worse.

That summer, when the courts had risen, he tramped round
seventy of the neighbouring villages with only a blanket, a stick
and a small bag. Afterwards, he felt he could no longer delight
in fine clothes and good living. 'That microscopic look at village-
life,' he said, 'taught me to hear the heart-beat of reality.' Against
bitter opposition, he opened the Goraja well to the *harijans*.

In Warora, meanwhile, he had begun to organise various groups
of workers – weavers, sweepers, and the despised carriers of
night-soil, the latrine cleaners – into unions and co-operatives
in an effort to stop exploitation. He also offered his services
to any *harijan* who wanted to be represented in court. After
two years, he was elected vice-president of the municipality.

Amte also became involved in the struggle to get the British
out of India. He organised the lawyers to defend those imprisoned
by the British, smuggled arms for the Indian Revolutionary
Party and, in 1942, was thrown into jail at Chanda for singing
the Indian national anthem.

By this time, he had grown a long beard like a *sadhu* or holy
man, and forsworn marriage. How could he bring children into
such a tumultuous, unstable world?

In 1946, however, he met a girl who made him rethink all
his ideas. Sadhana Guleshastri came from a family which, for
seven generations, had been producing Sanskrit scholars. Attending the wedding of her elder sister, Amte watched from an upper
window as Sadhana slipped away from the party and went into
the scullery to wash clothes with an elderly servant woman whom
everyone had been scolding. 'Don't tell anyone,' he heard the
girl say as she went back to the celebrations.

At that moment, said Amte, he felt married to Sadhana already because he was sure they could do something together in life.

A few weeks before the wedding, thieves broke into the Guleshastris' home and Amte fought with them. He was taken to hospital with sixteen stab wounds and appeared at the marriage ceremony swathed in bandages. The sweepers whom he had befriended sent presents by the cart-load.

With his new wife's agreement, Amte then disowned the property he would have inherited and tore up his licence to practise law; he had decided that he never wanted to go back to that life. Instead, he and Sadhana set up a commune on an abandoned small-holding near the Mohammedan cemetery and invited labourers of various castes to join them.

'After murmuring "your honour", "your lordship", to magistrates for all those years,' said Amte, 'I started shouting "your Lordship" to the real Lord.'

Before long, more than twenty people had joined the commune. They included untouchables (one of whom brought three wives), professional beggars and two Christians, one a shoemaker, the other an umbrella repairer. Amte put all his own savings into the venture. Everyone agreed to share the work and pool their incomes.

'I said we will share and we will have good company,' he recalled, 'and I will get real experience, not just talking about society but living it.' For three months, he washed all the dishes every day. Sadhana, who before her marriage had never worn anything but silk saris, never again felt the touch of silk on her skin.

Several months later, the night-soil carriers went on strike. Their quota of work was excessive, they said, and they wanted a change in the laws which governed the use of latrines. Would Amte help them fight their case? He agreed, but said he wanted to do the job himself for a year so that he could find out the difficulties at first hand.

There were very few flush toilets in Warora and the night-soil carriers had to empty the pits under the latrines, shovel the night-soil into wicker baskets and then dispose of it. It was a task which Amte found utterly repulsive. At the same time, it represented a tremendous challenge, and he wanted to share the life of these men who were regarded as the untouchable of untouchables.

One night, working in torrential rain, he noticed what he thought was a heap or bundle in a monsoon drain. As he came nearer, he saw that it was a man and that he was still alive. When he looked more closely, he found to his horror that the man was in the last, agonising stages of leprosy. Where his nose had once been, there were now only two holes, his fingers and toes were raw stumps, and maggots were eating at his eyes. Amte was gripped by a paralysing fear; like so many others at that time, he believed that those who passed close to a leper might catch the disease.

'Imagine,' he said, 'me, the night-soil basket on my head, passing by this living corpse. I wasn't afraid of the night-soil, but I was afraid of this heap of flesh, this man. What I did, I dragged a piece of bamboo matting from the wall, put it over him and then hurried away. I was afraid even to move him from the gutter. I just patronised him. That Baba Amte whom everyone called a fearless man was really the coward of cowards.

'For six months, I was very restless. Then, one day, it dawned on me — "Suppose your loving wife or your dearest Vikas (his elder son) contracted leprosy, would you leave them in the gutter?" and I said, "No!"

'So I sought out a Mohammedan lady, who was living in a broken-down cottage surrounded with weeds near to the cemetery, and who was also in the last stages of leprosy. She had lice all over her face, maggots in her nose and eyes, she was almost blind, and looked like a skeleton.

'We said, "Mother, we have a commune here, please come," but this inner struggle to leave her place was far more difficult than any battle in the trenches with bombs. We told her she would be given nice broth — "No", she said. "Why?" I asked. "Baba," she said, "I was a tribal and in my village one good-looking man used to bring bangles. I fell in love. He was a Mohammedan. My family would have killed me, so I eloped with him."

"I have stayed by this cemetery so that, when I die, I may be buried with him. If I go with you, the Mohammedans wouldn't bury me. There will be no union in my grave with my husband, so let me die here. This body was seen by him alone." . . . Clad in rags, riddled with disease and maggots! What a faith!'

Instead, Amte took her food and water every day, washed her and cleaned her sores. She died in his lap. When the commune ran out of money because so many of the labourers had gone down with malaria, Amte decided that he would give his life to the care of leprosy victims. When he told Sadhana, she said only that he must follow the dictates of his heart.

He began by reading all the books he could lay his hands on. The way lepers had been treated over the centuries – in the fourteenth century they were commonly burnt alive – appalled him; the sacrifice which others had made to help them stirred him deeply. There was Father Damien, a Catholic priest, who had given his life caring for leprosy victims, and Miss Read, an English lady who found that her twelve-year-old Indian servant boy had the disease. At first she told him he would have to leave. When she asked what he would do, he replied that he would commit suicide like his parents. Miss Read prayed all night, wrote down the thought, 'I dismiss the idea of dismissing him', and then began nursing the boy herself.

Amte went twice a week to a leprosarium at Dattapur run by a disciple of Gandhi, and then opened his own clinic outside the hospital in Warora. At that time, nobody in the town was treating leprosy in any systematic way: a sweeper had been detailed to distribute tablets, but that was all. Now patients began to turn up in hundreds and soon Amte was busy from eight in the morning until late afternoon, diagnosing, giving injections, cleaning out ulcers with a knife, removing decomposing bones and dressing wounds. The government labelled him a quack, but there was no one else.

In 1949, against considerable opposition, he was given a place at the Calcutta School of Tropical Medicine for a leprosy orientation course. There, he heard a lecturer say that one of the greatest barriers to curing the disease was that they could not grow leprae germs in the usual animals. Perhaps, he added with a smile, human beings would be the best laboratory specimens.

It took Amte two days to think it over. Then he stood up and said he was prepared to be the human guinea pig. 'The halo of Father Damien was before me,' he said, 'and I knew that Sadhana would nurse me.'

First he was injected with lead bacillus emulsion taken from smears gathered from positive cases of leprosy and, when that was not effective, with the live bacillus itself. Even that failed to take hold, and the experiment had to be abandoned.

By the time Amte had arrived back in Warora, having come first in a course made up of medical students and qualified doctors, the treatment of leprosy had been revolutionised by the discovery and availability of the sulphone drug known as DDS. The cure, however, was a very lengthy process, and the danger of highly infectious patients passing on the disease still remained.

Amte saw that what was needed were colonies where long-term patients could safely be treated; such colonies, he felt, should also help leprosy victims rediscover the self-respect which constant rejection had usually taken from them, and perhaps also provide a permanent home for those too disfigured to return to normal life. His vision was based on giving these unwanted human beings not charity, but a chance. Charity, he believed, destroyed, but work built a man; where Schweitzer had put patients to bed, Amte decided to put them to work. Work would help them lose their sense of helplessness and recover their sense of dignity. They would learn to love life again through labour. There was, he felt, no occupational therapy like hope.

In 1950, he asked the State Government for land which could be used as both a leprosarium and a farm. Their response was to offer him fifty acres of disused rock quarry and forest infested with tigers and leopards, part of what had once been the hunting estate of His Excellency the British governor of Madyha Pradesh.

Amte accepted. He persuaded six leprosy patients, all with serious deformities of the hands or feet and all of them either beggars or unemployed, to join him. Together they set up camp in the forest with Sadhana and his two sons (the younger Prakash, was just two and a half). They had no bullocks, no plough, only a few simple hand tools—hoes, shovels and axes—one lame cow and fourteen rupees (75p).

It was a perilous environment in which to rear two small boys. Leopards carried off three of the family's dogs and Sadhana frequently killed fifteen or twenty eight-inch scorpions a day, but she never doubted her husband. 'He loved the children, he loved me and I knew he wouldn't expose us to danger,' she said.

They built two simple shelters which had roofs made of bamboo matting and leaves, but no walls; the six patients lived in one, the Amtes in the other. Then they began digging a well, hacking away at the iron-hard earth with their shovels and crowbars in temperatures which never fell below 100°F and were often as high as 120°F. They dug for seven long weeks and to a depth of well over thirty feet before they found water but, at last, they struck it. As they stood, utterly exhausted, with claw hands grasping their crude tools, unable to believe their own success, Amte sensed that a miracle had begun at Anandwan; a miracle fashioned on outcast land by outcast men, men rejected by their families, unwanted even in their own homes, ruins of men able still to snatch victory from the jaws of defeat.

In those early days, it seemed a fragile miracle. 'We were so short of money,' said Sadhana; 'we had no milk, no curds, no broth, and vegetables only once a week.' Amte was so desperate that he went to a rich man's house to ask for help. The servants said the man was not at home, though Amte knew he was. He left almost in tears and decided that he would never again ask for money.

There was only one way to survive and that was to produce their own food. Amte threw himself into the work of clearing the rocks and the forest with ferocious energy. He often worked eighteen hours a day while Sadhana cooked over a wood fire and cleaned all the pans. When she fell ill, Amte did the cooking himself for three and a half months.

Somehow, they survived. After a year, they were given a pair of bullocks so old they could only be yoked to a wooden plough; after two, they were self-sufficient apart from sugar, oil and salt; at the end of three years, there were sixty patients and six wells.

By that time, the need for better accommodation and treatment facilities was becoming critical, but Amte could find neither carpenters nor masons to help him. Then he discovered that a team of young volunteers from thirty-six countries was engaged on a building project at Gandhi's old *ashram* at Sewagram, sixty miles away. After they had finished, fifty of them agreed to come to Anandwan. Three months later, Amte had a new clinic and two new wards for the hospital.

When the buildings were complete, Amte decided that he would never turn away a homeless human being; that he would never think of his budget or say he had no food to spare but, instead, in faith take in everyone who asked for shelter.

The coming of the Europeans also transformed the relationship between Amte's struggling colony and the inhabitants of Warora who, till then, had largely shunned it. None of the local children would play with Vikas and Prakash and Amte found it almost impossible to sell his produce in the local markets, though its quality was excellent and its price tempting. Even the doctor who came to Anandwan to treat diseases other than leprosy always cleaned his bicycle thoroughly with Dettol afterwards.

When the Europeans appeared, however, the local people began to wonder if they had after all been mistaken. Some ventured to visit Anandwan and discovered that it was a good deal better run than most of the farms they knew. From then on, Amte found it much easier to sell his vegetables.

During the next years, Anandwan flourished. Patients flocked to it from all over India, the State Government gave Amte another 200 acres and new crops and buildings sprang up almost every year. In 1961, Anandwan became the first leprosy colony in India to allow marriage between patients – provided both had become negative and the husband was willing to undergo vasectomy – and, with money from Swiss Aid Abroad, seventy-eight dwellings were built in blocks of three to house them. Two of the units were for couples, the one in the middle for elderly single patients.

By the early 1960s, there were almost 600 patients at Anandwan and Amte was treating as many as 4,000 at a dozen weekly clinics in the surrounding villages. In 1968, he opened a school for blind children near his own house at Anandwan; and in 1972, with the help of an Englishman, Arthur Tarnowski, set up a training centre for the physically handicapped.

He was also determined that Anandwan should be as much like a normal village as possible, and make the same sort of contribution to the outside world as any other good community. In 1962, when the Chinese invaded India, the patients staged a drama which raised 2,000 rupees for the National Defence Fund. In 1964, they set out to build a college as a gift for the local people. They erected the buildings, made all the furniture, did all the fittings. The cost was 250,000 rupees, most of it raised by the sale of produce from land once regarded as useless. The college is now affiliated to Nagpur University and can handle 1,400 students.

When you visit Anandwan today, you have no feeling that

it is an isolated enclave, cut off from the rest of humanity. It bustles with activity; the fields are covered with rich crops of vegetables, wheat and cotton (the yield is twice the local average); there are 500 hens whose eggs go daily to the local restaurants and a dairy herd which provides milk for Warora and manure for Anandwan; a flour mill; an engineering shop which makes all the beds and operating tables for the hospital as well as furniture for the homes; workshops where milk-powder tins bought for four annas are turned into lamps sold at four rupees; a tailor's shop which clothes all Anandwan's 1,500 inhabitants, and a cobbler's shop which makes all their shoes; a post office, a school and a community theatre built without benefit of architect and with only minimal help from outside craftsmen.

Anandwan's doctor is Vikas, Amte's elder son, a fierce, cheerful young man in his twenties. 'I was more interested in engineering,' he said with a smile, 'but there was a dearth of doctors here – and, in any case, because we're short of mechanics, I have to treat both bodies and engines! Father never suggested I went to medical school, but I knew what a fix they were in, so I read medicine and then went to on the National Institute for Leprosy in Madras.'

Vikas doesn't say so, but he won his entire medical education through scholarships, and his father, who now receives a modest salary of 400 rupees a month ($£21$) from the trust which administers Anandwan, turned down a gift of 5,000 rupees ($£275$) to pay for his son's education.

Vikas treats 200 patients a day, 150 of them leprosy cases and he gives part of his government salary to Anandwan. He took me first to his surgery, a neat white building which, like the hospital behind it, is steadily being surrounded by a delightful garden, with roses, hollyhocks, marigolds and lilies among the orange and mango trees. His chief assistant in the surgery, Karim, is himself a burnt-out case of leprosy who has had the toes of both feet amputated. His principal helper in the hospital is Gitabai, a small, elderly woman with all the grace and dignity of a nun, who first came to Anandwan as a patient twenty-three years ago. Gitabai is illiterate – she was never able to go to school – and she is now responsible for all the daily dressings and injections.

The chief gardener and assistant medical officer is Shaligram, who is thirty. Before he contracted leprosy, Shaligram was a school-teacher. The man hoeing beside him in the burning sun has his feet swathed in bandages. He too has a broad grin on his face.

The patients who wait near the hospital shrink back shyly at our approach, but almost all of them look cheerful and many of them smile. It reminds me of what Mother Teresa said to me later in Calcutta about the leprosy victims she and her sisters serve. She had never, she said, heard one of them utter a single word of bitterness or of complaint. That, she remarked, was true greatness.

Inside the hospital, the operating rooms and wards are simple and spotlessly clean. An old woman lies groaning beneath a blanket. She has cataracts, says Vikas, but as in so many other cases, he cannot perform the operation because they don't have money to buy instruments. It takes 600,000 rupees a year to run Anandwan, and government grants provide only 200,000.

In the tailor's shop is Ramchandra. He suffered from leprosy for thirteen years and, because of it, his wife divorced him. He had lost an eye and what fingers he has left are either truncated stumps or bent like claws, but Ramchandra has trained twenty-five other tailors and helps make clothes for 1,500 people. Anandwan gives all its inhabitants a new set of clothes twice every year.

At the flour mill, a woman with stumps for fingers sifts through the millet to take out grit and other dirt. She, too, is a burnt-out case but, as Vikas says, society will not have her back. Both the flour mill and the dairy are run by Deoman, whose hands and feet are so totally disfigured that he can no longer balance properly. 'It hasn't affected his voice, though,' says Vikas as Deoman issues orders in ringing tones, 'so he still makes a first-class administrator.'

The former patient who runs the metal shop, Giridhar, once had the most virulent form of leprosy and has been at Anandwan for twenty years. He was a cow grazer but, by taking courses, has turned himself into a first-class engineer. It is he who makes all the hospital furniture, he who has just built Anandwan's newest seed-sowing machine.

The priest and headmaster of the school is Dahake Guruji, a burly, cheerful man who has been at Anandwan eighteen years and was one of the first patients to be married there. He also doubles as postmaster. About 600 of the patients, he says, keep post-office accounts and all of them send money regularly to their families. 'The joy in Anandwan,' as Amte says, 'is more infectious than the disease.'

Anandwan was to be only the first of his ventures. In 1956, the State Government gave him land at Ashokwan, only a few miles from Nagpur. Again, it was rocky ground which neighbouring farmers did not think worth cultivating but Amte opened a second centre there. Ashokwan now has seventy patients and its land has become so fruitful that it is entirely self-supporting.

Then, in 1967, Amte was offered 2,000 acres at Somnath, seventy miles south-east of Anandwan. Much of it was dense forest and there were no roads from the nearby village. Worse still, Amte was by then suffering almost continual pain from the spinal disease which had been diagnosed two years earlier. He had been fitted with a steel collar and belts to try to ease his torment. Nevertheless, he could not resist the challenge. He wanted to create something quite new at Somnath—a workers' university on the same site as a leprosarium. To begin with, a hundred students would each be given two acres and then allowed to keep the proceeds from their crops, minus only the cost of fertiliser and meals. 'A teacher,' said Amte, 'is he who gives you the chance to hatch your own eggs.'

The Amtes moved into Somnath in March with Vikas, Prakash and their third, adopted, son; ten cured leprosy patients from Anandwan went with them. They slept in the open and began to dig a well. Amte was in such pain that he could do very little manual work, but he was able to walk and map out the area. In April, they found water and, the following month, with the help of a *harijan* builder from a nearby village, they finished the work just before the monsoon came. By then, however, Amte's adopted son had fallen seriously ill. He was taken to hospital in Nagpur and Sadhana went with him.

One day, a man from the village brought news that the boy had died. Amte set out for Nagpur immediately. The virologist who had been treating the child said he had been killed by a mysterious disease which he called simply 'the Somnath virus'; he urged Amte to leave the area and to take his workers with him.

Back at Somnath, Amte gathered his patients together, told

them what the virologist had said and added that he himself
had no intention of leaving. Four or five of them, however,
said bluntly that, having been cured of leprosy after so many
years, they didn't have the courage to face another deadly disease,
and walked out. When they got to the nearest village, one of
the older men in the group said that they had lived through
difficult and desperate times with Amte, so why should they
leave? With that, they turned round, walked back to Somnath
and told Amte that they were ready to live and die with him.

The following year, students from all over India came to
help develop Somnath and soon twenty-five acres were under
the plough. By that time, however, local opposition to the project
had become intense. Why, some of the villagers demanded, had
the land been given to strangers and not to their own landless
labourers? The fact that nobody had been interested in the
land until Amte came was completely forgotten.

One night, he was warned by a village policeman that a mob
of a thousand armed with axes and stones, had set out for Somnath with the intention of evicting him and his workers for ever.
He ran down through the forest to confront them before they
came too near, followed by some of the patients from Anandwan.
As he ran he prayed.

At one point, a narrow stream crosses the track to the village
and it was there that Amte came upon the advancing mob. He
shouted to them that they would cross it over his dead body,
and sat down in their path. 'Come on,' he yelled. 'Kill me.'
One of the men from Anandwan, a Bihari with claw hands and
ulcerous feet, leant over him protectively, like an umbrella. The
policeman, who had given the alarm, urged the patients to escape
while they could, but the Bihari said, 'Jagdish will not run away.'
When he heard these words, Amte said to himself, 'I am protected
by the Lord in the form of this patient.'

The mob wavered and one of their leaders began to harangue
them, declaring that as disciples of Gandhi they believed in
non-violence. When someone shouted that the police van was
coming, the entire mob disappeared into the forest.

Amte had won a battle but lost a campaign. Persistent local
pressure eventually forced him to hand back over 700 acres
of the land which had been given to him, together with valuable
brook water which would have irrigated large parts of it. It

was a shattering blow but, although he had to abandon his scheme for an agricultural university, it didn't stop him and his patients from turning Somnath into a model farm. Now, it provides a home and work for 200 leprosy victims, many of them married and living in attractive houses built with the help of more money from the Swiss; and it produces bumper crops from the 225 acres which are being farmed. The average rice yield for the area is five quintals to the acre; in 1974, Somnath produced no less than twenty. It has become so prosperous, in fact, that it is able to send very substantial subsidies of food and money to Anandwan.

There are modern go-downs to store the vegetables and rice; a dairy herd with 100 cows and buffaloes and 30 pairs of bullocks, although the Somnath virus and marauding tigers have killed off 70 cattle over the years; and outside the main farmhouse bungalow, which is Amte's house when he's at Somnath, are flowers, trees, a fountain and, incidentally, Mul 10.

'We have no secretary, no executives, no graduate agronomists,' said Amte. 'So why are government farms, which have them, losing money? In the beginning it was a work strewn with boulders, with wounds, with blood, but it became a trail of light.'

Success has also helped transform the hostility of the villagers into a reluctant admiration. Many come for advice about seeds and farming methods. 'It's stencil knowledge,' said Amte, 'anyone can copy it now.'

The man who manages Somnath is Shankar Jumde, a small, shrewd man of fifty who first came to Amte as a patient in 1953. He had then already been suffering from leprosy for twelve years. Cured at Anandwan, he became one of the pioneers who opened up Somnath. His wife, Sindhu, is also a cured leprosy patient. They married at Anandwan and, since they could not have children themselves, adopted two sons of leprous parents. It would be difficult to find a kinder or more loving mother and father. Sindhu is also Somnath's chief medical worker, responsible for all the daily dressings and injections.

'These,' said Amte, 'are the mute inglorious Miltons. Shankar is as fresh as a new-minted coin. He could leave at any time for 1,000 rupees a month but he only takes 250 and he doesn't want any more. "I have no sons," he says; "what would I spend it on?" Then there is Sindhu, mother to two children not her own, the children of leprosy victims, scarred herself but looking after the health of the whole camp, and not a *pie* she is paid.

'It is like mining. You can see the rich ores in their lives. The common man, he is *un*common. It was after seeing the greatness of people like these that I became convinced God is always there in the heart, sleeping like a baby.'

Frequent journeys along the pot-holed roads and rutted tracks between Anandwan and Somnath did nothing to ease the almost constant pain which Amte was now suffering. He went into hospital in Bombay in 1969 and again in 1971; later that same year, friends subscribed to fly him to London for an operation which replaced a piece of degenerating bone near the top of his spine with a graft taken from what Amte calls 'an anonymous quadruped'. He spent the whole of 1972 in bed, much of it in agony. If he wanted to get up, he had to put on his steel collars and belts immediately. As he said wryly, 'I looked like an astro-naut with all that on.' Forcibly confined, he began reviewing his life and work. So many illuminating insights came into his mind that lying in bed no longer seemed such a waste of time. 'At first,' he said, 'I thought my bed was a coffin, but then it became a womb.'

He thought often of the tribal people he had first discovered when he was a college student, the people who lived in the remote region of rivers and forests south-east of Warora. Some of them he knew, were so cut off from the outside world that they had never heard of India, never seen a wheel or a grain of wheat and survived on a diet of lizards, termites and edible leaves.

In 1973, with his newly married son Prakash—like Vikas, a doctor qualified to treat leprosy—he began exploring the region. They soon discovered that the disease was endemic. In one village alone, there were 90 cases in a population of 170. Gonorrhea and syphilis were spreading unchecked. So was tuberculosis, because of the shortage of milk and vitamins. The sick, they found, were often left to die; in that primitive and largely noma-dic world, the herd did not wait for them.

In December, when the rainy season which cut off much of the tribal region for six months of the year was over, Amte, Prakash and his wife, Manda, set out from Anandwan with sixteen leprosy patients, including three of those who had been pioneers at Somnath. They made camp at Nagepalli, 110 miles south of Anandwan, and next day went along the jungle tracks for another eight hours to Hemalkasa, near the confluence of three big rivers. There, as at Anandwan and Somnath, they began to dig a well and erect simple dwellings, in the meantime sleeping in the open on bamboo mats. Because of the danger from wild animals, they kept a fire throughout the night but, even so, one of the men was savaged by a bear and had to have sixteen stitches.

When they heard the newcomers were doctors, the tribal people began coming to Hemalkasa with all kinds of ailments, and often from great distances. Amte and Prakash treated them as best they could; Amte had to stand as he examined them because sitting down was so painful.

By the time the rains came in May, the well was ready and some paddy had been planted. Amte had to go back to Anandwan, but Prakash decided he would stay behind alone at Hemalkasa throughout the rainy season, although he himself was suffering from a hiatus hernia which draws the stomach up into the food passage. It meant being separated from his new wife for several months and giving up the chance of going to England to become a surgeon, but he felt the need for a doctor was so great that he could not leave.

That same spring, the doctors told Amte he was developing a condition known as 'bamboo spine' and that, soon, he would not be able to bend at all. His best hope, they said, was to throw away his belts. For two or three months, he did not have the courage but then, having vowed that he must endure the pain without cursing it, he did so. The result, he said, was a miracle. Although he is often in terrible pain, he still somehow manages to travel on a mattress laid in a truck driven by a cured leprosy patient, and he still takes on new projects with the same passionate energy.

'My pain never makes an appointment with me,' he said, 'but my work does. I have often thought that, compared with all the pain and misery in the world, mine is negligible. I don't want to be divorced from His work. Those who remind me about the state of my health are my worst enemies – I don't want to remember.'

In the winter of 1974, he was back at Hemalkasa. By the following spring, twenty acres of land had been cleared and planted with rice, *brinjals*, vegetables and chillis. That year, Hemalkasa was able to send twenty-five quintals of rice to Anandwan.

Amte, Prakash and Manda, who is a highly trained anaesthetist, also started a system of 'canoe clinics'. Whereas, during the wet season, the rivers are so swollen that, as Amte says, even death-bed cases would not cross them, in the dry months they are the region's only roads. The three of them travelled from village to village, drawing up a disease census for each one, running clinics and getting to know the tribal people. Serious cases were taken back to Hemalkasa for more prolonged treatment. There, providing he can raise the money, Amte plans to build a sixteen-bed, in-patient hospital with brickmakers brought in from Anandwan. Meanwhile, they manage as best they can.

Amte also wants to revive his plan for setting up an agricultural college at Somnath so that tribal boys can be taught how to farm. 'To fight ignorance and hunger,' he said, 'they must grow food.' He hopes to take twenty-five of them to Somnath, give them the use of land, bullocks and go-downs, train them and then share with them the proceeds from their crops. If any of them want to stay, they will first have agree to help train ten more tribal boys each year.

'Wherever God has pointed the way with His finger,' said Amte, 'He has also cleared the way with his mighty palm. Now Vikas and Prakash are off to catch the sun and I have confidence that they do not have wax wings.

'I'm a Hindu Brahmin, but I'm also a follower of Christ. I want to be a contemporary of Christ, not the sort of Christian who says, "I have an executive meeting at four-thirty" while there is a man dying in the gutter. The moment you are His contemporary, you remember Him every second of your life — the man who, when He was born, had no place to rest, the fisherman who did everything with the common man, who shared the mattress of fodder with the donkey. I love that description of Him, "He lived for others."

'The Cross is the emblem of crucifying one's own life to make others happy. It asks us to yield up the love of life for the life of love; to back our conscience with our blood. Where is fear is no love. Fear of leprosy, fear of loneliness in the tribal belt, this scarecrow of fear cannot be allowed to guide your conscience.

'Everyone should attempt to walk in the shadow of that Cross. That means you are in the company of that life which scuttled itself to save others. I haven't the arrogance to say I can carry the mighty load of His Cross, but I do try to walk in its shadow.

'He wants to carve your life like a crucifix. Every calamity is a crucifixion, crucifying your ambition, your lust. Each is a tiny lesson, and then the imprint of the crucifixion is on your life.

'What is your plan of sacrifice today? You and I, petty souls, sacrifice for our children. Christ sacrificed for tomorrow's whole world. Do not substitute promises for action. You don't become a Moses by parroting the Ten Commandments. We are all doing this parroting—"Marx said this, Lenin said that"—my god!

'Whenever I see slum-dwellers, with their hunger and poverty, that obscene poverty, I feel He is crucified like that. When I come across a leper, foul-smelling, ulcerous, I can see the imprint of His kiss on the forehead. That is *all* I can see, just the imprint of His lips, His kiss. What did they not do to lepers in His time, yet this carpenter's son cared for them and touched them. That hand is an emblem to me—that hand which cared for the lone-liest and the lost.

'The Christian is also he who not only lights the darkest corner in the world but also the darkest corner in his own heart. It is no use talking about the afflicted and being a moral wreck yourself.

'When I prattle to my wife or the young people, He says to me, "I have not seen your words in the company of deeds." To me, Christ is that goad sitting on my neck, telling me, "You said this in the meeting, but what have you *done?*" How He goads me! He tells me, "Don't bluff." When I was a politician, I was talking we must do this or that, and not doing it at all! I can so easily bluff on a platform but not with Him.

'I also have a chronic temptation to vanity—my ego feels very nice when someone gives it a massage, but I know it's numbing, not curing.

'I pray daily for success *and* defeat. I crave both equally because the ebb and flow makes you scale new heights. I don't always want to be condemned to success. Success is like an ash-can. The cigarette-butts glow for a while, but in the end it is all ash.

'You have to strip yourself of your vanity, your pride and the blistering ulcers of dishonesty. It requires great courage to face one's own self but, in all these things, honesty and courage are twins.

'The worst in you is very intimate with you. I want to hide certain things from other people for my own gain—and, if I go on doing it, I become very intimate with the liar in me. The best in me I shun—"Go away, kindly make an appointment", which I never keep! The worst in me, I flirt and conspire with.

'So many people suffer from mental leprosy. The physical signs of leprosy are a hypo-pigmented patch and loss of sensation. Then, later, there is thickening of the nerves. Now, in so-called healthy society, you can see a lot of injustice and poverty, yet you are not moved. You have lost your sensation, your feeling. The mind is so dull, the heart so unfeeling—thick-skinned like a hippopotamus—that's mental leprosy.

'Yes to God is also *no* to the whole empire of greed and lust. It is "No" to all those who want to exploit, to stultify, to enslave.

'Class war? No! Even when affluence brings thick-skinnedness in a man, that man is still a creature in His kingdom. I can't imagine He feels hopeless for such a man.

'The problem is not solved by elimination. The leaders of Russia and China came from the soil, yet the worst atrocities have been perpetrated not by capitalists but by labourers come to power. They have not answered the basic question: how to build a man? Love alone can resurrect a man, whether labourer or capitalist.

'Without it, that Judas, that Doubting Thomas are still there inside. Why then this *class* war? There is an *eternal* war between good and evil going on in my heart, isn't there?

'Great heroes of history are nothing to me. The uncommon thing in the common man, that is my hero. I don't want to be a great leader. I want to be a man who goes round with a little oil-can and, when he sees a breakdown, offers his help. To me, the man who does that is greater than any holy man in saffron-coloured robes. The mechanic with the oil-can, that is my ideal in life.

'If I died now, I would like them to put on my grave a line like the one on crossed cheques – "A man who said responsibility is not transferable".'

11

'And Death shall have no Dominion'

MYRA MACNICOL DIED of cancer on 2nd February, 1972, less than three weeks after we had last talked together. She was fifty-five years old. By the way she lived and died, she exemplified for me the most sublime words ever spoken by a woman, the words of Mary, mother of Jesus, when she was told that she was to bear God's son, 'Behold the handmaid of the Lord. Be it unto me according to thy word.'

Myra died in a small, stone-built cottage in the North of England, with roses at the door in summer and a bird-table where sparrows and blue-tits came to feed outside her bedroom window. It was a triumphant end to a journey infinitely more significant than any of man's travels in space, a giant step forward in the realm of the spirit.

Myra was the daughter of a south London butcher. Looking back, she could remember nothing happy about her early years at home. The family lived over the shop and there were rats in the basement, cockroaches in the kitchen, and blood and sawdust in the shop. She was a naturally fastidious child and, from the beginning, rebelled inwardly against the smell and gore. She never invited friends home and, when she went out, hoped that she didn't reek of raw meat.

Myra's unhappiness was made worse by a sense that she was an unwanted child, 'something of an after-thought'. Her consolation was that she was her father's favourite, and her happiest memories were of sitting on his knee and being fondly kissed.

When she was four, however, even that had to come to an end. Her father found that he was suffering from cancer of the mouth and his doctors prescribed an extremely painful course of treatment using radium needles. During the next fourteen years, he underwent no less than fifteen operations and was constantly in and out of hospital. Myra came to dread visiting him. In later years, even a whiff of disinfectant reminded her of the hospital ward where she had seen him, often in great pain. To shield herself from the misery of it all, Myra hardened her heart towards the one who loved her most. Soon, she couldn't bear to go near her father.

Despite the slow spread of the disease, he went on running the shop in his usual hard-driving way. At Christmas he might even sell the family's own turkey to please a customer. Nor did he ever, in Myra's recollection, take the family away on holiday: the biggest treat she ever had was a bus-ride to the terminus and back on a Saturday afternoon.

It was a hard life – by the time she was seven, she had already begun to cook for her brothers – and she was ashamed of her home and parents. She hated her mother coming to school because she dressed in such an old-fashioned way and, when visitors came, Myra would often run to her room. Her parents then had to bang on the door to make her come out. Until she was thirteen, she shared a bedroom with them and often listened to them quarrelling when they thought she was asleep.

In these circumstances, it was hardly surprising that Myra's dearest wish was to get away from home. She was regularly top of her class at school and it came as a considerable shock when she failed to get into university. Eventually, she managed to find a place in a social science course at the London School of Economics. Her aim was to become an almoner. That, she told herself, would be useful work. It also provided an excuse for leaving home.

Then, in 1936, one of her elder brothers met the Oxford Group, a religious movement which gained many converts in Britain during the 1930s. He left a book about the group lying around the house. It had the intriguing title *For Sinners Only*; Myra read it and wanted to know more. All the family were staunch Methodists and Myra knew many of the Sunday School hymns off by heart. What she had never experienced was the kind of Christianity which challenged the core of her will. The gaiety and dynamism of the Oxford Group caught her imagination. So, too, did its appeal for a total surrender to Christ, its claim that the Holy Spirit could speak to and direct a person, and its aim of creating 'God-guided personalities, which make God-guided nationalities, to make a new world.'*

She experimented with the idea of 'listening to God' for a year without telling anybody. The results were remarkable. In those morning 'quiet times', she began to think of her attitude to her home and her parents and realised that she had never been grateful for what they had done for her. What was more, she had never even thought of what they must have suffered through her father's long illness. 'I always said my prayers,' she recalled, 'including God Bless Mum and Dad, but I was so selfish and callous to them. All the hurts had closed my heart.'

Slowly, Myra's heart began to open again. She apologised to her mother for her selfishness — her mother replied rather patronisingly that she had always known Myra would eventually see reason — and began to feel a new love for her. When she left the house in the morning, she kissed her mother goodbye and even helped in the shop on Saturdays, despite her dislike of its clinging odours.

She also faced the fact that the LSE course was beyond her intelligence and left, giving the excuse that she was needed at home to nurse her father. Even though it wasn't the truth, she felt God used the decision because, during the last month of her father's life, she found a new love and compassion for him.

Nevertheless, she still longed to get away from home. When a young man whom she had met at church proposed to her, she eagerly accepted, the engagement was blessed by the church and soon her mother was proudly displaying the presents which poured in from their friends.

Then came the second turning-point in Myra's life. One of her friends in the Oxford Group, an older, married woman, asked her bluntly whether her engagement had really been

* The Marquess of Salisbury, speaking in the House of Lords, 20th March, 1936.

'guided by God'. Myra knew the honest answer was 'no', that she didn't really love the young man and that she was marrying him merely so that she could leave home as soon as possible. Eventually, she told the other woman what her real motives were.

Breaking off the engagement went very much against the grain, but Myra came to the conclusion . that that was what God wanted her to do. Her friends in the group tried to help her and her fiancé, but her own family were furious, her fiancé was deeply hurt, and Myra herself found the break hard to endure. She walked the streets of London, saying to God, 'I accept Your Will, I accept, I accept' over and over again.

In 1940, Myra began working full-time with her friends in the group, which by then had been renamed Moral Re-Armament. Like them, she worked without salary and depended on gifts from those who believed in their work. She spent the war in Britain, much of it in London as a member of the Fire Service.

After the war, she was invited to a newly opened MRA conference centre at Caux in Switzerland. Soon, however, she had a cable from her brother saying that her mother had had a heart attack. The thought of leaving Switzerland to live at home again didn't appeal much to Myra, but she was quite sure she must go immediately. When she arrived, she told her mother she had come to be with her indefinitely.

The next eight months were among the most rewarding of Myra's life. She gave herself wholeheartedly to nursing her mother and prayed that, before she died, she might find a real experience of Christ. One morning, her mother sat up in bed and told Myra that she knew of so many things in her own character which needed to be different. She then changed very deeply and her last words were 'Jesus shall reign'.

Before she died, Myra told her that at Caux she had met, and fallen in love with, a young Scotsman called Henry Macnicol. 'If Henry ever asks you to marry him,' her mother replied, 'tell him you can cook, you can sew and you're never idle.'

Henry, who had become a full-time worker with the Oxford Group in 1937 after winning first-class honours in English at Edinburgh University, hadn't fallen in love quite so conclusively. He was a rather earnest young man who was determined to seek

God's will for his life and who, at this point, was torn between resolving to lead an ascetic, single existence and being ready to get married. One day when (as he says) he was 'feeling dead inside', he prayed that he would be ready if God wanted him to fall in love with a girl. When he next saw Myra, he had the clearest thought that she was the girl he was going to marry.

He also had the thought that he should not speak to Myra about his feelings until God told him plainly to do so. The result was that when, in 1948, he was invited to work with Moral Re-Armament in South Africa, nothing had been said between them, although both were aware of a bond and indeed sent each other news from time to time.

Then Myra began to feel that her life was too much governed by whether a letter had arrived from Henry and decided that, although she was still in love with him, they should stop writing to each other. Henry accepted the decision with a heavy heart. He didn't know that Myra was still deeply in love with him and, indeed, more convinced than ever that one day they would be married.

She wrote down in a series of notebooks the thoughts which came to her during her morning 'quiet times'. 'What a wonderful thing it is,' she wrote in October 1950, 'to have love in the Lord's keeping, like flowers or trees He makes grow. In His time you see the fruit or flower, but growth and fullness of life are there all the time. You will grow in these months in grace, love and wisdom to maturity. Henry . . . needs a woman at peace, wholly satisfied by the Lord, in the line of Mary, to inspire him with greatness of heart and fun, far away above correction and protection, to laugh at herself and laugh at him.'

Henry, of course, knew nothing of this. Each year, he secretly hoped he might be able to go back to Europe to see Myra, but in the third year, when the chance did come, he found that she had already left for America.

One day a friend who knew of his feelings asked, 'Are you still in love with Myra?'

'Yes,' Henry replied, rather to his own surprise.

'Well,' said his friend, 'are you being guided by God or by propinquity?'

Henry thought it over, decided he was being influenced by the fact that Myra was several thousand miles away and that this was, indeed, the right time to propose. His cable read simply, 'I love you with all my heart. Will you marry me?'

Three weeks earlier, Myra—who had begun to feel she would never marry—had knelt down with two or three of her closest friends and surrendered her hope of ever becoming Henry's wife. She told God that she was ready to stay single for the rest of her life, if that was what He wanted.

Unfortunately, Henry's cable took a long time to reach her. It was forwarded to the address in San Francisco where she had been staying, but arrived after she had left. As the days went by, Henry became increasingly edgy. Had he been wrong? Was Myra going to turn him down after all? Then came her reply, as simple and direct as his proposal: 'Yes, with all my heart. God's perfect gift.'

They were married in 1952. Frank Buchman, the American who had founded the Oxford Group and MRA, gave them his recipe for a happy married life. 'My word for you,' he said, 'is "No fights, no secrets and no bluffing".'

The early years of marriage brought Henry and Myra the joy of working together in many countries, particularly in Africa, but there were disappointments too. Their greatest sadness was that they had no children. Myra had miscarriages and both she and Henry eventually came to feel that they were not meant to have any children. What they should do, they decided, was care for all the children in the world as if they were their own.

Nor did Henry's work go smoothly. In Africa, particularly, he felt he had failed because of a drive for human success. 'What ran me,' he said looking back, 'was a quite unreal ambition. I had always wanted to please my mother and I thought the way to do that was to shine in public.

'Myra reached my heart, which came slowly and creakily alive, but she suffered a lot in those years, because I tried to push my ambition on to her, so that she would be a credit to me. "Those were the years," she told me later, "when you wanted me to be your Big Wife!"

'When the failure of my work became evident to everybody, one of my friends wrote and said, "Your wife will help you." It was a new thought to me but, somewhat reluctantly, I began to let her do so.

'She took Jesus seriously, but she refused to take *me* too

seriously! When I would tell her of some mistake I had made, or confess some sin I had fallen into, she often remarked with a brisk smile, "Grunt, grunt—what d'you expect from a pig but a grunt?" And she always encouraged me to sing and be merry. She felt, usually much to my annoyance, that it would often do a lot more for people than the serious words and earnest sentiments I was planning to give them.'

Henry nicknamed her Mrs. Twinkle and tried to express what he had learnt from her in a poem:

> The English girl who takes a Scot
> Is tackling an awful lot:
> His pride, his cold and hard ambition;
> His sense of Man's Almighty Mission;
> His independent way of life—
> Which sometimes may include his wife;
> Those unnamed fears and longings deep
> Which round his conscience creep,
> While he with speech prophetic, strong
> Tells where the whole world's going wrong.
>
> But she is just the one for him—
> Gentle and gay when he grows grim,
> Sensitive, quick to serve, or heed
> A friend whose heart's in any need;
> To her own deepest nature true
> Hiding not tears or fears from view,
> Finding in Jesus riches rare
> Which with her man she loves to share.
> So, Scotsman, raise your heart and voice—
> Break through your Scotch mist, and rejoice!

In the summer of 1966, Henry and Myra were staying with friends in Scotland. One night, as she was undressing, Myra's hand brushed against a small cyst on her left breast. Since it was quite painless, her first reaction was that it couldn't be anything important and she said nothing about it to Henry until they were having breakfast together next morning. When they had a 'quiet time', however, both had the thought that they should take the cyst seriously and see the doctor immediately.

He, too, could see nothing to be alarmed about. 'I don't think it can be anything,' he said, 'but maybe it had better come out.' The operation was a relatively simple affair and, after a few days, Myra came out of hospital again, expecting that she would soon be going to the out-patient department to have her stitches removed.

The day after she arrived home, the telephone rang just as they were finishing breakfast. It was the doctor. 'We've had the pathologist's report,' he told Henry. 'At first they thought it was benign but, when they made a closer investigation, they found there were a few doubtful cells. I'm afraid it means having the breast off. She'd better come in again tomorrow.'

When he put down the telephone Henry, whose own father like Myra's had died of cancer, felt numb. Somehow he managed to walk back into the sitting-room and tell her what the doctor had said. They looked at each other with great fear and dismay and Myra wept quietly, the tears welling up into her eyes.

Henry wondered if God was punishing him for being a rotten husband. Then he said, 'Let's be quiet.' It had been the daily practice of almost thirty years and, at this moment of great crisis, it seemed the natural, indeed the only thing to do.

Myra wrote down, 'God is a god of love and mercy. Trust Him.' She also saw that behind every fear lies a demand and that, in her case, it was the demand to hang on to life and, in particular, her life with Henry. Naming the fear, she said later, was the key.

Then they prayed together, 'Father,' said Myra, 'I do give you my demand, the right to live and the right to hang on to Henry.'

'Father,' said Henry, 'I do accept your forgiveness and mercy.' When they got up from their knees, their fear had vanished.

'I just needed to give my demand to God,' said Myra, 'facing the demand in myself and giving it to God. It took less than five minutes.'

'It was incredible,' added Henry, 'but so natural really. From that point on, fear had no hold over us.'

Ten days later, Myra had her breast removed. At the same time, the surgeon also took away her ovaries – because in women of her age, ovarian activity seems to enhance the malignancy of breast cancers – and she was given a blood transfusion. When

Henry first visited her in hospital, she looked—he remembers —'all yellow, like a corpse', but the worst was over and she was still alive. Myra could barely speak but she noticed, through the window, a thread of white smoke drifting upwards from the hospital's incinerator. 'Look,' she whispered to Henry with a faint smile, 'I'm going up in smoke.'

As soon as she could hold a pen, she reached for her notebook and wrote, in a shaky hand, 'Once anyone has had God's experience of pain and victory, it is proved available for anyone . . . anything you and Henry have experienced is available for all.'

A few days later, she wrote, 'Thank God can now read. God's love amazing. I didn't need to make any effort. He showed each detail to meet my need at every point. He keeps us in touch with Him. It cannot be and isn't our effort. There is no fear or loneliness in death. And how marvellously He cares for those we love.'

One of the things which amazed Myra was that her fear of hospitals and physical pain, so deeply rooted in her childhood experience, seemed to have completely disappeared. She made a habit of putting others' needs before her own and simply went on doing so in hospital. Her notebooks are full of concern about the ailments of the other patients—'Mrs. M. needs a permanent cure for her ulcer'—and about the doctors and nurses.

There was a ward-maid with a cleft palate who, because nobody could understand what she said, tended to be regarded as something of a nuisance. Myra took time to listen to her, and they became close friends.

Then there was a doctor who, Myra felt, made technical comments on her wound and ignored her as a person. She decided to say 'good morning' to him every day. At first there was no response but, after a few days, the doctor actually looked at her and returned the greeting.

There were the usual irritations of hospital life—'O, give me love in my heart for all these snoring ladies!' Myra prayed one morning—and, after a staff nurse had behaved in a hurtful and thoughtless way, she wrote, 'Let go your bitterness about Staff Nurse X. Why be surprised about human nature let loose in a ward? The frustration of women who do not know how to let their hearts be healed, though they may know everything about physical healing!'

And each morning, when she woke, she honestly faced up to any new fears which came into her heart. 'You want to hang on to your's and Henry's life,' she wrote. 'All our lives are on a thin thread and, if it is Heaven for either of us, truly accept it as God's gift. "Thou, O Christ, art all I want, More than all in Thee I find." '

And on another day, 'Your fear of other cancer is a real thing —you must expose it and let God in His mercy give grace to overcome. It is really the resistance to suffering and discomfort. His grace would be adequate. But live in the victory of cure.'

During her convalescence, Henry had to go to Switzerland for a week. Myra stayed with friends, in a bedroom where she looked out over the Firth of Forth. One morning, the loss of her breast, the loss of her ovaries and her loneliness swept over her. Was this the end of her as a woman and a wife? What had she left to live for?

As she looked at the sea, she remembered a children's chorus and with tears streaming down, she sang it again and again:

> Wide, wide as the ocean,
> High as the heavens above,
> Deep, deep as the deepest sea
> Is my Saviour's love.
> I, though so unworthy,
> Still am a child of His care,
> For His word teaches me
> That His love reaches me
> Everywhere!

For the next two years, all was well. Myra recovered steadily and soon she and Henry had begun to think that the time had come for them to settle in Edinburgh. They had never had a permanent home; Myra had always longed for a place of her own and Henry himself suffered from a chronic chest condition. They found a flat with a glorious view across the Forth in a beautiful crescent near the city centre. It seemed made for them.

The only problem was that they had little money of their own—their only regular income was £20 a month free from covenants—but when they told friends about their hopes, gifts began to pour in. Soon, they had £3,000 towards the cost of buying a flat. Then Henry had a letter from a man he describes as 'a faithful friend' questioning whether they were doing the right thing. At the same time, they had an invitation to live and work in Newcastle, with the use of a flat in the city. Myra knew the flat well and her spirit sank at the thought. It was in an old Victorian house; the rooms were large, dowdy and old-fashioned; the carpets didn't fit and the bathroom was at the top of three steep flights of stairs. 'I shall never forget her look when I told her,' said Henry. 'She said almost nothing — just "That awful flat, I can't face it." ' Everything in her rebelled against the idea.

Unwillingly, she agreed at least to take a look. Their friends in Newcastle could not have been more welcoming or understanding, but the flat was even more depressing than she had feared. In the hall were three buckets catching drips from the ceiling, the wallpaper in the kitchen was peeling, the carpets in the sitting-room were folded under to make them fit and she hated its faded curtains and chintzes. She and Henry were in dismay as they drove back to Edinburgh. Henry had become convinced that they ought to go to Newcastle but, try as she might, Myra could not face the prospect. For weeks, she wrestled with her feelings. Then, one morning, a letter arrived from a friend who knew the struggle she was going through. Like Myra, she had thought the invitation from Newcastle was too much to ask until she read a poem by George MacDonald. She enclosed a copy.

I said, 'I will walk in the fields',
He said 'no, walk in the town'.
I said, 'there are no flowers there',
He said, 'not flowers but a crown'.

I said 'But the air is thick
And fogs are veiling the sun';
He answered 'yet souls are sick
And souls in the dark undone'.

I took one look at the fields,
Then set my face to the town.
He said, 'my child, do you yield?
Will you leave the flowers for the crown?'

Then into His hand went mine
And into my heart came He
And I walk in a light divine
The path that I feared to see.

When Myra read the poem, something clicked in her heart. 'On that basis,' she said to Henry, 'I will go.' It was still a struggle to yield her desire for her own quiet place and leave Edinburgh. At the farewell party, she said, 'Please don't ask me to speak.' With the agreement of the donors, she and Henry decided to give the money they had received to a team of their friends who were going to work in India and, at the age of fifty-two, they put their few simple belongings in store and set out on the road again.

At first, Myra found the going hard in Newcastle. She felt depressed every time she woke up, but she gritted her teeth and carried on, and, as she and Henry began to get involved in the lives and needs of people, they discovered what Henry called 'an extraordinary gift of contentment'.

Then, in the early summer of the following year 1969, Myra found a tiny cyst on her collar bone while she was dressing. She mentioned it to Henry, who felt his own to see if he had something similar. Again, they had the thought to take it seriously and act immediately. This time, they had to fight to persuade their doctor that something must be done quickly, but further examination revealed clear evidence of the spread of cancer to the lymph glands in Myra's neck and into her left armpit.

Her doctors prescribed an intensive course of X-ray treatment. At the end of a week of daily visits to the hospital, she was utterly exhausted.

Henry and Myra's first reaction to the reappearance of the cancer was disappointment rather than despair, and a sense of annoyance that the pattern of their lives had been disturbed. Soon, however, waves of fear began to sweep over Myra, dread of an increasing spread of the disease, of intense physical suffering and death, dread above all of separation from Henry. She felt a passionate desire to grow old with her husband and to care for him always in his earthly life. She told Henry about her fears, yielded again her demand for life, and felt a deep sense of assurance that not only was God in charge of her destiny, but also that there were countless friends who would happily give Henry a home.

Nevertheless, what Myra called 'evil cells' continued to attack her imagination — 'They were death to my spirit just as the malignant cells could be death to my body.' A simple mathematical calculation told her that, if the disease had moved eight inches from breast to collar bone in three years, in another three it could have reached her throat.

This, she felt, was the Devil and, believing that the best way to defeat him was to expose his work, she revealed her new fears to Henry. Terrified himself, he told her not to be silly. Then Myra's dread poured out in a flood of what she called 'self-pity and revenge'. 'What will you do when I'm gone?' she asked Henry tearfully.

That night, Henry apologised for his callousness. 'I'm so sorry I laughed at your fears,' he told Myra, 'You must always be honest about them, and then we can find faith together.'

The spread of the disease certainly did not make Myra blind to the need to deal with weaknesses in her character. When she and Henry went to meetings, she liked sitting at the back while he always wanted to go to the front. At a meeting in London, one of the speakers talked about people who held back when they should have spoken up. As they came out, Myra said to Henry, 'He was talking about me.'

They sat on a bench in Hyde Park. 'Why don't we apply what we learnt about cancer?' said Henry. 'That at the bottom of every fear there is a demand, something you want that you won't give up.' Suddenly, Myra saw that the thing which kept her silent was her pride, the fear of making a fool of herself. She and Henry prayed together, she surrendered her pride, they walked back into the meeting and Myra sat at the front beside the man who was leading, and took responsibility with him for the afternoon session.

'God giving me warnings of cancer attacking my body,' she wrote in her 'quiet time' book. 'It was exposed and by surgery and deep-ray therapy killing hidden bad cells. Claim the equivalent exposure and healing in cancer of my spirit — dishonesty and pride which keeps me from giving everyone my best and fighting for all I know to be right all the time.

'Let go completely wanting our own home. My will was crossed on this a year ago, but now let God take the deep desire. Obey God with no limitation in health and strength in doing God's will with my whole heart.'

And again, a few days later, 'The constant love of Jesus to transform your loveless nature when circumstances and people cross your will. You have tried with your own effort all your life, but only Christ can change your self-centred disposition that is proud, touchy, impatient, self-righteous, critical of others' faults, callous and cruel.'

Afterwards, she and Henry went back to Newcastle and tackled the flat and all its problems with a completely new zest. They decorated the kitchen together and were planning to do the other rooms when an invitation came to live in Tirley Garth, a small country estate near Liverpool which had been given to MRA as a centre for its work.

By this time, Myra did not really want to leave Newcastle, but felt it was right to go. At Tirley, she could be given the care she needed. There, too, she found herself living in a community of thirty or forty people (many more at weekends and during conferences) and it meant opening her heart in a new way to the needs of those around her.

'If I have fear,' she wrote in January 1970, 'the other person feels my demand. God, use my whole heart as a mother all the time with all the people You give; care equally as if my own children—and the men, to care for as my husband ... making the whole world my home again and Jesus central in my heart as my security and joy, because anything smaller is not His Will anyway. What others will miss if I don't.'

She also tried to pass on to the women of Tirley all that she was learning about the essential nature of Christianity and the meaning of the Cross. 'The Cross for us women,' she wrote, 'is our calling, and the channel for all God wants to create for others. So often, we accept the calling, but then want to decide our own way of carrying it out. Creating our home, or putting our children first rather than the children of the whole world. How small and deadening for all around if we want anything for ourselves! God sees what we secretly want!

'Without the Cross, we women love the power and satisfaction of a man putting us first. It actually crucifies Christ in the men and holds them back from mature manhood. Early in our marriage, I knew that any demand on my part for physical love would crucify Christ in my husband. Only recently I have learnt that any demand of the spirit crucifies too.'

In the early summer of that same year, while she was dressing, Myra discovered another cyst, this time on her right side. She went into the Christie, the Manchester hospital which specialises in the treatment of cancer, for further examination, and it soon became clear that the disease had spread to the lymph glands in her right armpit. That meant removal of both the right breast and the affected glands, followed by a lengthy course of X-ray treatment.

In that part of England, even a mention of the Christie makes people drop their voices in fear but, by this time, Myra had found an extraordinary freedom. 'You and all your age-group friends will probably face death in the next thirty years,' she wrote in her notebook. 'Why worry if it is sooner rather than later? It's a place where people close their hearts so much, bound by fear and demand for life and security in the known things and people. But just think of the love of God through your life – and, when you die, it will be His crowning gift. "An inheritance incorruptible and undefiled and that fadeth not away, reserved in heaven for you." '

Her regular visits to the Christie were far from being gloomy occasions. 'I really enjoy my visits to hospital,' she wrote while having her X-ray treatment. Before each visit she and Henry would pray together in the car park; and under the machine, Myra would repeat to herself lines from a favourite hymn:

> Let the healing streams abound,
> Make and keep me pure within.

'How God has poured out his love and grace over these weeks,' she was able to write towards the end of her treatment. 'Hospital has been a faith-filled and really merry time with patients and staff.'

When Myra first went to the Christie, she took on a 'ministry of prayer', and kept a special notebook to make sure she did not forget the people and situations she took on her heart. 'I find it a very relaxing exercise,' she wrote to a friend, 'and so much part of being in touch with God's healing power for me.' Joy, she often wrote in her quiet-time book, means Jesus first, Others second, Yourself last.

She was deeply moved by the obvious needs of the other patients. 'Think of all the sad, burdened faces,' she wrote, 'especially the well-dressed ones who look so bitter and closed and do not have peace.' The outstanding care of the nurses and doctors, too, stirred her very much—'Pray for Doctor C., every day,' she wrote. 'She carries a great deal, the patients who don't get better and seeing their families.'

Soon, she had made friends with all kinds of people. There was Adassa, the West Indian maid whom Myra heard humming a spiritual to herself: soon Adassa had agreed to sing a different spiritual to the whole ward every day. There was Beryl, a cheerful north country girl, also suffering from cancer, who said of Myra that 'She just sits in bed and radiates "thoughts" to us all.'

And there was Sally (as we'll call her), an eighteen-year-old ward maid who dabbed at the floor rather than cleaning it properly. Myra wondered how she could help her, and the simple thought came to tell Sally that she had a good voice and a bad voice inside and she could choose which one she listened to. 'That's exactly what the mistresses at school used to tell me,' said Sally, and told Myra of her unhappy home, the trouble she'd got into with the police and the problems she had with her boy-friends. Even when she was moved to another ward, she would come back to talk to Myra—diving under the bed when she heard the sister approaching.

'Myra and I were together less than a week,' said Madge Dunkerley, another patient, 'but I thought she was wonderful. There was a complete serenity about her. Never for one moment did I think she was concerned about herself. She had the sort of smile which gave you hope just to see it. She helped me when I felt at my lowest.

'To look at her you would have thought there was nothing wrong with her. There was no suggestion of fear—she was just going on as usual, thinking of other people. When you're ill, you naturally indulge in self-pity—Why should this happen to me? and so on. You never felt Myra asked herself that question —it was always other people.'

The staff too, soon realised that Myra was no ordinary patient. 'I've seen thousands of people over the years at the Christie,' said a consultant who worked there for over a quarter of a century, 'but I never met anyone else with the same peace of mind as Myra. The nurses couldn't understand how a patient so seriously ill could be so appreciative, so uncomplaining, gay and cheerful.'

The only complaint from Myra's doctors was that she told them too little about her symptoms. 'It's very hard to find out what the situation is with your wife because she makes so light of it,' the specialist who was treating her told Henry. Myra took this remark as a rebuke and, thereafter, made a point of being more forthcoming.

She made the same impression on her local doctor at Tirley. 'She slipped into the surgery one day,' he recalled, 'and we discussed her illness very frankly – you never had to play hide and seek with her. She wasn't frightened and needing constant reassurance, like so many. As a doctor you sometimes realise that people are putting on a face, but with her it was quite different. I never felt she was demanding anything, just the opposite. Her farewell, with a smile, was always an apology for taking up my time. The result was that she seemed to be doing more for me than I was for her.

'I'm not a religious person, but Myra Macnicol had something you could really envy. You felt her saying, "Don't worry about me, doctor, I'm all right." The main trouble for a doctor is bridging the gap between what a patient wants and what he or she actually needs. Well, she didn't want anything and she didn't somehow need anything either.'

All the time, Myra was reaching out in her spirit for new truths. 'I have been too superficial,' she wrote one morning, 'more conscious of Henry's untidiness and rush than of his deeper need to be a wholly God-centred man. I am ashamed that God has had to use my illness more than my health, because it has forced the Cross on us more deeply than I would voluntarily accept – and I did put my security in Henry and his love rather than truly placing God first . . . How closer than breathing God is. It is only wilful not to turn to Him.'

And again, when Henry had just come back from a few days away from home, 'Our companionship is a marvellous thing to enjoy but only with true satisfaction and security being in God alone. Last night such a joy having Henry back, but had to give to God my deep, deep longing to be his fighting partner and care for him (wash shirts etc.) for all his earthly life. I can only ask for healing, unconditionally wanting God's Will as Jesus did ... Dearest Henry and all he gives—do not clutch on in case life is short, but let God truly hold.'

The next year, 1971, was to be a critical one for Myra. She was still, as she said, 'playing to win'; and if she 'lost', she intended to 'lose' honourably. It was to be a year when she felt a growing passion that others should find the experience she had had, and a year when her horizons, far from shrinking, grew even broader. Her views on current social issues were as pungent as those about herself.

2nd February—'Women's Lib'—the extremity of women on the get. A false dividing line as in race or class. All because we get away from God's eternal laws. Hating because I do not get what I want, and dividing off from humanity. On this basis, women will still be enslaved by their own hate and selfishness. True liberation lies in facing where we have been wrong, putting it right and living differently. I would like to pioneer the liberation of men from women's domination in moods, demand and nagging.

'Mary—"Be it unto me according to Thy Word"—this is the most satisfying way for all women. It is only selfish ways which cause misery and destroy manhood.'

9th June—'Always needing God. Of my nature, as I wake in the morning, do I look forward to life with great joy?—seldom. I always have to come just as I am. Then I do not need to think of myself and thoughts begin to come for other people.'

28th June—'Illness either gives us a colossal self-concern or fear—or, in the redemptive power of Christ, it gives us a super-sensitive quality of thought and care for others and, in having to depend wholly on God, we are in a unique position to pray for others.'

Myra's doctors now discovered that the cancer had spread to her neck, spine and abdomen. The surgeon who examined her decided the growth was so large as to be inoperable, and a course of deep-ray therapy was prescribed.

13th August (her birthday)—'More ray treatment. Strength for any suffering today. What a coward I am!'

14th August—'How truly blessed ... what a rich day yesterday, and how minimal the suffering compared with all God's richest blessings and, above all, His own love and power He gives me all the time. You feel so much the riches of God given in suffering. It is only the ease and comfort of spirit which we demand that keeps us from God's riches, until suffering of body forces us to find His deepest truths.'

16th August — 'Forgive my temptation when at lowest physically to want to give up the battle with suffering. I did turn to "Fight the good fight with all thy might". What a triumph God has given in these days here at the Christie, advance and growing links with so many.'

17th August — 'Thanks presence of Jesus in night. The abundant gifts of his grace, as if it means that I am not going to live long. Wholly wanting God's Will, but not a half-resignation to death yet. "Fight the good fight with all thy might". Fight the good fight wholly against evil of body or spirit.'

28th August (in a letter to a friend) — 'I need a miracle of healing now, if God's Will, and would be grateful for your prayers, as a fresh attack of cancer in my spine has been diagnosed. I have just been having deep-ray treatment for it and can only trust now. God gives so richly of Himself and a deep sense of all His Love, and He has renewed in me the spirit of playing to win.'

29th August (thoughts for a woman who constantly worried about her husband's health) — 'Why do we women control? How my illness over these years has helped break yours. It is a God-filled life we most need to give our husbands to inspire them. Worrying wives, and I have been one, are the worst form of controlling wives.'

One day, the physiotherapist took Henry aside and told him they were not making progress, and a consultant friend confirmed that, medically, there was no hope. Henry decided that it was best to say nothing to Myra at this stage and took her for a holiday to a friend's house at Abersoch in North Wales. There, they had three weeks of unbroken sunshine in a part of the country where the summer weather is often changeable. 'This is so lovely,' said Myra, 'it makes me think it is God's special gift for our last holiday together.'

She had breakfast in bed, and often spent the afternoons sitting in the garden. Each night, she and Henry chose a different continent and prayed for all their friends there.

26th September – 'Ask R. (a consultant friend) re head pains. Not-self-centred, but be responsible.'

27th September – 'So conscious of my need for liquid love, yet to be so straight that others cannot take you off God's guided beam in thought, conversation or letter. At peace, an instrument used by God, completely in His hands, not in a hurry to write all the letters I want to write to so many in case I do not have much time left. That is your human control.

'Almost constant head pain on left side and top, worse when tired. Back pain when move about or wake up.

'Last night, I was not sure whether I was awake or dreaming, I had one flash of terror about further suffering I might have and death. And this morning I realised how God has given me His grace. The care and passion for people, God-given, makes pain easy to bear. My last hospital visit was very painful from ray treatment but, on the basis of JOY, God told me what to give to every next person who came to my room, and the life and adventures were such fun and are continuing.'

The pains in Myra's neck and head indicated an extension of the disease into the bones of her neck and skull. Soon, she had begun yet another course of ray treatment.

10th October – 'Only give Henry God and His victory, not your struggles. You have no right to absorb him in inessentials – it sometimes wears you out rather than refreshes. Going to God together in any attack of the Devil is different – then you need each other – but always be in touch with God first. Always have rich creative times together thinking of other people.'

Same day (in a letter to a friend) – 'I thought the other day I want to be a mother shepherd. Though it sounds strange, it's expressive for me as it seems God wants us to use our whole hearts as women, whether married or not, with children or not, to care for the children of the whole world, including those of all ages we are given wherever God has put us.'

15th October – 'Playing to win, wholly trusting. Human determination to get well can be self-will. You have wholly put your body in God's hands, cell by cell, trusting in His almighty power. It is still FAITH – Forsaking All I Take Him – as it has been for 30 years, whatever it was you needed to put wholly in His hands – engagement, pleasing my family, marriage, home, children, reputation, now life itself.'

28th October — 'Pride now same as always, and the Big "I" needs crossing out. That's the only reason you feel a burden and a nuisance. Fight the good fight. No harder for you, because Christ gives the strength for the need, whatever it is. If you don't accept God's victory, it is just as cruel and callous to Henry and your friends.'

24th November — (in a letter to friends) — 'God gave me a marvellous Spirit-filled week in the Christie. One morning, I could not get the verse out of my mind —

At Thy feet, O Christ, we lay
Thine own gift on this new day;
Lest it prove a time of loss
Mark it, Saviour, with Thy Cross.

'By afternoon, the back of my neck was marked with a thick purple cross as they decided to give some ray treatment there! I chuckled, as I have found how God reveals His love with a sense of humour.

'I was thinking of how in physical weakness I feel my complete need of God. I realise it is the only way He can use us, in health or sickness. I *have* to say, "Have mercy on me, O God", because I feel so helpless. Then I know my body is in His Hand, and my spirit is free for prayer and thought for others. In health, how slow I was to learn this lesson! I wanted to be competent, to prove myself, anything but have a pure passion for souls. In weakness is our strength, and God is all in all to us. I begin to understand a little how Mary's strength and joy came from her meekness in so totally accepting God's Will right through His suffering on the Cross.'

Same day (in Myra's notebook) — 'You need all God's strength today for X-ray treatment and blood transfusion. Truly relaxed in Him.

'Can you help Henry not to slouch in chair? It doesn't pay people due respect. Dr. T. is a senior consultant . . . our honest care for each other prepares for this life and the next.'

25th November — (after transfusion) — 'Great thanks for all the bountiful care I had yesterday, it couldn't have been more lavish, with God's love and sunshine pouring in and through everyone all day. "My yoke is easy and my burden light"—how true this is, whatever we go through.'

28th November—'You are marvellously at peace. If no more hope, you would face and accept it, with gratitude for 55 years and especially gift of last 20 with my dearest eternal partner. I would need to be ready to trust for whatever advance Heaven is on my own world.'

Myra's consultant friend now began to feel that she had weeks rather than months to live, but didn't feel he should tell her. Two days later, she said to him, 'I think God has told me I am not going to get better.'

'She wept a little,' said the consultant, 'but that was all. Most of us would go into a state of tremendous depression.'

2nd December—'Have mercy on me. Into Thy hands. A little bit of a sense of the unknown, where the enemy might strike next. So near my head. Perfect trust in God's Will.'

11th December—'Mary—"my soul doth magnify the Lord and my spirit had rejoiced in God my Saviour"—what a perfect pattern for any woman's heart!'

'I went to Tirley to see her,' said Madge Dunkerley, Myra's friend from the Christie. 'I just had the urge, though I didn't know whether she had died or not. There she was, serene and placid as usual, absolutely no suggestion of fear or feeling sorry for herself. Fear had lost its hold because there was nothing to grip on to. "Just hoping that a miracle is going to happen," she said—even that with a smile on her face. I don't think anyone has made such an impression on me in such a short time.'

By now, Myra's legs were like sticks, her body was wasting away and her weight had begun to fall rapidly. 'They should take a photograph of me for "feed the hungry",' she said to a friend with a laugh. One of the effects of the X-ray treatment was that she only needed to use deodorant under one arm, and this too she found immensely funny.

Although her head always felt sore, she usually slept well and only needed very small quantities of drugs. She and Henry were living in a cottage several hundred yards from the main house at Tirley and friends took turns to nurse her, including Meili Gillison, the daughter of a doctor who had worked in China and who had herself recovered from cancer.

On Christmas Day, a choir of young people came to sing

carols for Myra. Much to everyone's surprise, as an encore she chose not one of the quieter carols but a West Indian calypso. When the singers had gone, she talked quietly about the new world and how, by the next Christmas, she would be watching all of them. On Boxing Day, she noted in her 'quiet-time' book: 'You must give to everyone your experience of the satisfying relationship with Christ.'

31st December – 'Henry, tuck me up by 8.30 p.m. and go up to the big house for Hogmanay. He ought to sing for the children. Thank God for this year, a quiet one for you with God's loving, providing care, so generous and bountiful for every need. Marvellous care at the Christie and your joyful times with your many friends there.

'Henry's loving, merry care right alongside you day or night, sharing God's magical gifts like Abersoch and our sunny autumn drives to the Christie. Sharing in the great events of Tirley, especially the industrial conferences, as well as the day-in, day-out training of our young crowd. Your new year wish for each is to be firmly rooted and grounded in God for the rest of their lives. It is the decision of wholly giving their wills that counts, so God can always satisfy, lead and use them.'

That night, however, as Henry was tucking her up before going to the Hogmanay party, Myra suddenly said, 'Henry, I can't say it – I can't say "Happy New Year".' She looked utterly forlorn. Then she said, 'This is evil, this is rebellion' and she and Henry prayed together, Myra asking forgiveness for her rebellion and yielded her will afresh to God. A moment later, said Henry, she was full of joy again and insisting that he go up to the party and dance some reels.

1st January – 'Last night showed your complete need. How you wouldn't let go, so it was His strength made perfect in weakness. All your old nature and ambitious striving left behind in 1971, your strong self-will wholly given.

'The gifts of healing that has freed you from pain – "who forgiveth all thine iniquities, who healeth all thy diseases, who crowneth thee with loving-kindness and tender mercies" – how He does all that for you.

'You have always wanted to hold on to the known ways, and now for you it is the greatest step into the unknown you have ever taken. Feed on God's promises – e.g. "These are they which came out of great tribulation and have washed their robes and made them white in the blood of the Lamb." '

'She looked so serene and full of fun,' said a friend who saw her at about this time. 'She said with a laugh, "I wonder sometimes how Henry will manage without me. I think I am so indispensable! But God has told me that the richest and most fruitful years of his life lie ahead of him, without me, without ME!"

'She spoke too, of our trust to bring people into a living relationship with God. "If I could have my time over again," she said, "that is what I would live for all the time. I have been so busy with things and what there is to do. That is what I want to live for in the rest of the time I have here." '

6th January – 'How I need to give God my will at the start of every day! As life gets a little more of an effort, it takes an even firmer decision to obey and turn to God immediately at every point of need, with no lapse into even a moment of self-pity, resentment or jealousy for your friends who still have life before them. What marvellous gifts God has given you in the midst of the battle these last five years.

'I must let go of Henry completely, as I had to decide years ago. The more abundant life for you, which God will use to enrich Henry's life too. Accept it as God's gift in faith. It means for me completely letting go of this marvellous life God has given me, especially the privilege of being at Tirley these last years with Henry. They have been the richest times.'

7th January (in a letter to friends in Scotland) – 'What marvellous friends you are, with all your constant generous care and thought, and we feel very close to you. I couldn't help feeling we will have our joyful reunion in our more abundant life together.

'God is very near for every need of spirit and body. Since my ray treatment, I am quite free from pain, which is such a gift, and I sleep well, taking only half a sleeping pill when I wake about 1.30 a.m. Henry sings me hymns about 8.30 p.m., always finishing with "Leaning on the Everlasting Arms", which sends me off! He is such a wonderful companion in every way, and I do now know his finest days are ahead too. What a joy when he gets to Scotland for you to look after him!

'As I write, sitting in my chair, I see the robins and sparrows on the bird-table, and the tits at the coconut. I get a face looking in at my window at intervals if the table is bare.

'Your letter, with all your loving, faith-giving thoughts just came – a great help. "God will choose his own time" helps me to relax and trust. Your generous gifts provided me with so much, from warm nighties to brandy for my egg-nogs – and we keep buying pounds of nuts for the birds!'

9th January – 'This nearness to Heaven does give perspective on our earthly treasures and how God must truly come first in all our lives if ever He is to use us to change this wicked world. "I take, O Cross, Thy Shadow, for my abiding place."'

One day, a woman who had been bitter all her life about an unhappy childhood came to see Myra. As she came out of the room, Henry said to her, 'Are you ready to shed your bitterness now?'

'Yes, I am,' she replied and, before long, had gone to Belfast to try to bring an answer to bitterness there.

The next weekend was the one when I went to see Myra. I went full of apprehension. I thought of what it might be like visiting a house of sickness which was soon, I knew, to become a house of death. Along with anxiety went an inbred scepticism. Would I be met by a kind of grim fortitude which is really only a brave front concealing the despair beneath?

Nothing could have been further from the truth. I could never have anticipated what I found in that cottage in Cheshire. Everyone was so welcoming, so genuinely cheerful, so free of any sense of burden. Departure was in the air – as if everyone there knew that a much-loved friend was about to set out on a momentous journey – but not death. It was a house not of sickness and darkness but of joy and light. Afterwards I could scarcely believe what I had seen.

The first member of the household I talked to was Meili Gillison, Myra's helper since the holiday in North Wales. She told me something of Myra's day. 'Henry takes her a cup of tea about seven in the morning,' she said. 'Breakfast is at eight and then there's a good hour of "listening to God". At ten-thirty she has a bath – we have to help her more and more with that – and an early lunch. Afterwards she sleeps and often wakes, rather exhausted, at four. Usually she sits up for an hour over tea and sometimes she watches a little TV. Then it's supper on a tray and we sing hymns together. Henry sings to her every night.

'She can look very normal or very grey, but her cheerfulness is totally genuine. If she's not feeling good, she'll tell you. Then she listens to God and finds freedom. She notices every detail, flowers on her tray, everything. "Oh bless you!" she says. And she notices every little thing about you, whether you're happy or not.

'She can't read, except the Bible for a short time in the morning, because reading makes her feel sick, but she has visitors most days. She tells people she hasn't got much longer and she has such peace of heart, though she often says she finds it terribly hard to face separation from Henry.

'She doesn't like talking about her illness or her problems; you have to draw it out of her. She makes light of it. Half a sleeping tablet is the most she'll allow herself. I find it so refreshing to see her and all the girls feel the same, they can't have enough of her.'

'To me,' said Sylvia, a cheerful young Scots daughter of the manse who had been visiting Myra regularly, 'she seems more free, more at ease, as the months go by. I find it hard to believe it's so serious. She thinks so much about my future. Even when her face is white, she always has that radiant look, I can't explain it.'

'I've often seen people at this stage lifeless in face, listless in attitude, no light in their eyes at all,' added Lorna, a trained nurse who had helped look after Myra for three months, 'but her eyes sparkle even when she's tired. She doesn't make a big thing of her health and going to see her isn't a draining experience because you get so much from her. Somehow, your sense of values gets straightened out.'

'In all the times I've seen her,' said Renske, a Rhodesian girl who had been coming to set Myra's hair each week, 'she's only talked of illness once. She said, "I know I'm finished, I know I'm going, so I take each day as a gift and thank God for it." It's been such a faith-building time for me—I've never felt fear in her, she's so tremendously gay and she's poured herself out for me the whole time. I always feel when I go in that it's a God-filled room. There's such a peace about the place and, if there's something wrong in me, she spots it immediately.'

At this point, I heard Henry come into the cottage. 'How
are you, Mrs. Mac?' he asked and went into the bedroom.

'She's a joy to look after,' Renske went on. 'She doesn't make
any bones when she's in need. Sometimes, for example, she
doesn't have the energy to pass me the rollers for her hair. Since
August, she's gone down and down physically, but spiritually
she's grown tremendously.'

Henry came in, smiling, with a face like Cimabue's St. Francis.
What had the last five years been like? 'The most fruitful and
the happiest of our married life,' he replied. 'I've appreciated
Myra more than I ever did before and we've had to turn to God
so much that we've learnt a great deal more about Him and faith
and what life is all about.

'You know, I had the ambition to be a model husband of a
sick wife, and I cracked under the strain! One day, I spilled
water on her head and she expostulated. I said, "Oh, don't make
such a fuss, it's only a little." Afterwards, I felt awful. "Why
on earth are you making such a fuss?" she said. "All you have
to say is sorry, and it's all over!"

'She's so light of heart. She's a lifelong teetotaller but, when
she takes her egg-nog with brandy, she licks her lips and says
"Where's my hooch?" with such a twinkle in her eye. We've
got a buzzer system rigged up so she can call me any time. One
buzz means "Come"; two means "How are you doing"; and
three means "What the devil are you up to? – Go to bed!"

'She very happily spends the morning in prayer, and then
in the evening we sing hymns together, though she can't sing
for toffee. She always sings those hymns not for herself but for
the whole world.

'You really do feel the value of a day, and that's all anybody
has, come to think of it. She is astonishingly at peace. Our local
doctor just couldn't believe it. "Is she really always as peaceful
as that?" he asked.'

Later the same afternoon, I met Myra. Outside it was a typically
damp January day, and the fire in that low-beamed room gave
out a welcome glow.

Myra came in wearing a blue dressing-gown with a purple
scarf at her neck. She looked more beautiful than I had ever
known her, and entirely at ease. There was such a calm peace
in her eyes as I shall never forget: so open, so quiet, such warmth,

such purity in the smile. She glided in like a ministering angel, not a sick woman. Because of her total freedom, all my concern and fear evaporated. I felt that she had come to care for me, not I for her. 'We must draw the curtains,' she said and did it herself. Then she sat me in the most comfortable chair and gave me a cup of tea.

Did she have pain, I asked. 'No,' she replied, 'but I do have a lot of discomfort in a digestive way.' Henry reminded her gently that she had had a great deal of pain six weeks earlier, with very severe pains in the head. 'Oh yes,' she said smiling. 'What a marvellous gift it is to be free of pain.

'When I do have pain,' she went on, 'I have to turn to God in a child-like way. In extreme moments, I put out my hand, hoping Jesus will take it. Then I often go off to sleep. Part of it is a clear decision on my part to relax. It's a matter too, of leaning on "the Everlasting Arms". Yet, you know, I've always hated anything wrong with me physically and couldn't stand the sight of blood.

'God has just seemed to give me all I needed. Jesus can calm the storm in my mind just as He calmed the storm on the waters.'

How had it happened? 'I think it's all possible because I've had hard lessons of giving my will to Him. Going against my human feelings.' She chuckled. 'Giving Henry to God when I was sure he'd marry someone else. Not having children. To accept Newcastle instead of Edinburgh. That's been my basic training. It was a priceless preparation in learning to turn to God.

'When it came to saying "Happy New Year", I just couldn't do it. Tears came into my eyes and I felt a real surge of evil. I asked Jesus to cure me—"risen with healing in His wings", the line from the hymn, came into my mind. Within minutes we'd prayed, given it to God and I was at peace again. I saw how terrible it was to have an ungrateful heart after all God had done for me.

'I never had any intention of giving in to this thing—I decided by God's grace to fight it, and I still have a real sense of expectancy for as long as God wants me to live.

'It's been the richest part of my life because I've really learnt to put other people first. I trained as a secretary and always found it easy to get buried in my work, and I grew up with a great many hurts, so that I didn't have a natural love for people.

'I used to read that line from the hymn "Oh for a passionate passion for souls", and I knew that that had to grow in me. Now I'm free in my spirit to care for others, and plenty of time to do it, too. Thinking of others relaxes me more than anything. I wish I'd always made it a priority. I have leisure to really pray for different countries and all our friends around the world. I feel real passion and concern for what is happening in India and Pakistan. Physical suffering can open your heart to what other people and countries are going through. You have no time to think of yourself because your heart is so wide open.

'I'm a more outgoing person, and more happy and contented — it is deeply true and it surprises me. In hospital I had always with me the thought, "What can I give to the next person, the next nurse?" whatever I felt like physically.

'And whatever I've felt like early in the morning, I've always taken time with God and sought guidance for other people. Often, it's been very early. God always wakes me up early enough to give me enough time in quiet.'

Was what she felt a kind of resignation, I asked. 'Certainly not,' Myra said. 'I'm never bored, time never seems heavy. This has been a rich fulfilment, it's given me what I always needed. I asked God to heal me and He didn't. Then I discovered the cancer had reached my spine and I accepted it. This must be God's plan, I thought, though I didn't fully understand it.'

Had she ever been overwhelmed by bitterness or self-pity? 'Why waste energy on that?' she replied. 'I have a sense of so much suffering in the world and that it is given to me to live the answer.

'I'm not at all afraid of death because I really do trust God. Someone,' and she chuckled again, 'sent me a book about the After-Life, but I'm not really interested, I'd sooner live a day at a time! The rosy glow of heaven has never appealed to me! I just wish Henry was going with me, that is the passing temptation I have, to give me a human companion as I go. Death itself is no barrier, but the biggest crossing-out is the pain of parting from Henry.

'What I've found is a complete trust and peace in God, a sense that He's adequate for every need. I'm so completely ready to trust Him that I'm sure I'll find delight and joy when He calls me.'

As I said goodbye to Myra next day, we laughed and joked,

though both of us knew we would never see each other again.
'So many letters,' Myra wrote in her notebook two days later.
'How can we acknowledge them all? You want to tell everyone
how rich every new day is and our times with so many old and
new friends when I am able to have visitors. Facing the nearness
to Heaven honestly together, our eternal bonds and sense of
continuing battle and life of the Spirit together. The abounding
love of God in upholding strength, and provision and nearness
in every need.

'I am only left with a passionate passion for souls, which I
have always prayed for, and it is so fulfilling and satisfying. I
cannot do any reading or be active but I am never bored. Our
life in the lodge with Meili and any visitors is a merry one, as
God pours out His best gifts of the Spirit for us all. I am content
to live fully a day at a time and I feel I can trust God with the
even more abundant life ahead. The only strong sense I have is
that I will be able to keep an eye on Henry!'

She now had only a fortnight to live. Soon she was no longer
able to get up for tea, though she still fought to help her visitors
to discover the faith which she had found. Then there were days
when she wandered in her mind and said very little, and nights
of pain, though never of the intensity which her local doctor
had expected.

After one such night, she said to Henry, 'Tell everyone it's
all valid. I've been through the darkness and Jesus has been
through it all before. Now, with all the birds singing, it's like
Mary in the garden when Jesus met her.'

To a doctor friend she said, 'Tell everyone—if they'd only
have a quiet time every day of their lives, when they get where
I am everything would be hunky-dory.'

Three days before Myra died, Henry felt she had let him
go. 'She somehow knew the last night she was going to be *compos
mentis*,' he said, 'and she told me this was the night for a song
written for her by a friend.' The song began

> Jesus said 'Hello',
> I said 'Lord, I'm here and ready to go,
> Ready to walk that highway with You'.

and Henry sang it to her.

Then, Myra fell into a deep sleep and Henry had the clearest thought that Myra had said goodbye to him. 'She slept for two days,' he said, 'and her breathing became gentler and gentler until it stopped. It made me think of a little rowing-boat coming into a West Highland harbour and gliding ashore. It made Heaven seem so close.

'In death, she looked like Joan of Arc. We had both faced the worst and she had never sunk into depression or accepted defeat.' On the card which accompanied the flowers Henry put on her grave were the same words he had used when he asked her to marry him: 'With all my heart.'

'She is with Jesus now,' he said, 'and by her way of honesty and her love of Him, she has shown me the way to Him too. My part now is to love and serve Him. Every memory of her helps me to do that and, as I go that way, I find her by my side. It *is* eternal life.'

Since then, Henry has spent almost three years in Rhodesia and South Africa, fighting hard to change the attitudes of both white and black in an effort to avert a blood-bath, and has amply fulfilled Myra's thoughts that his most fruitful years lay ahead.

A few days before she died, Myra said to him, 'I'm not a saint and never will be. I'm only a little Cockney butcher's daughter. If God can do this for me, He can do it for anyone.'

Epilogue

THE IDEA OF telling these stories was not that they should serve as models for people in similar predicaments. They were written to illustrate both the ways of God with man and the amazing variety of ways by which men and women find Him.

Re-reading them, what strikes me most is how often God meets people when they are at the end of their tether, when they are all but lost, or when they can see nothing but darkness ahead.

This is not, I think, because God prefers us to be in terrible straits before He will show Himself to us. With many of us, these are the only circumstances when we are ready to turn to Him or, at least, open enough to receive Him. While we think we can handle life by ourselves, while we fancy we are in control, we prefer to remain, as we imagine, masters of our own destiny.

The fact is that, as we grow up, we allow a hard shell to develop around us, a shell made up of all the things which bind us to this world and its values – our ambition for our careers, our attachment to material objects and, most of all perhaps, our daily habits, our dishonesties, compromises and selfishness which, as they become standard practice, we acquire a vested interest in defending. As Baba Amte put it, 'The worst in me is very intimate with me.'

Somehow, if God is to have his way with us, that shell has to be cracked and broken, and cracking it is not a matter of persuading us to amend our agenda marginally to include some ritualised devotion or smattering of daily piety while leaving our basic motives untouched, but to help us surrender our whole selves to God, so to open ourselves to Him that we allow Him to penetrate to the core of our wills, where God and man most truly meet.

What is more, it is exactly when we are at our lowest, when

our defences of pride and self-confidence are down, that we are most likely to allow God to meet our *real* selves, not the superficial, artificially humble, prettified selves which we so frequently present to Him.

It really is amazing that so many of us expect to meet God without allowing Him to meet us, to require Him to show Himself or prove Himself to us like some redundant genie of the lamp who can be summoned up at any time to satisfy our curiosity. Human friendships don't work like that and neither do divine ones. You have to let God know the real you before you can know the real Him.

For many of those whose stories are told in this book, that involved facing the truth about themselves for the first time; facing the cost to others of their selfishness, their indulgence and even (in Les Dennison's case) their ideals.

Exactly the same thing happened to me when I began to find a faith, when I first reluctantly made the experiment of asking a God I did not even believe in to give me a real picture of myself when measured by Christ's standards.

At that time, I had no idea what I was living for. Life was just a series of *ad hoc* events which I rated according to the success or failure, pain or pleasure which they yielded. If anyone had asked me what was wrong with me or what effect I had on the world around me, I might have felt vaguely uneasy but I doubt if I could have been very specific.

In the silence, a flood of thoughts poured into my mind, illuminating my real nature for me for the first time. I saw that my whole life was built on a desire to get up the ladder as fast as I could; sensed the hurt I must have caused my parents by the snobbery with which I treated them after I had gone up to Oxford; and became aware of the way I exploited others for my own gratification. God also told me exactly what to do to begin to put these things right, just as he told Anna and Les Dennison and (as I believe) Walt what *they* must do.

People so often seem to think of repentance and restitution as some kind of evangelical formula, part of a ritual of being 'saved', or else a process by which you 'wipe the slate clean' and which then enables you to feel morally superior to others.

Nothing, of course, could be further from the truth. Readiness to restore for the past shows, first of all, that we are prepared to pay the price of becoming different. I shall not forget in a hurry driving home after my second painful interview with the tax-man after I had told him about my fraudulent returns. I asked God angrily what He meant by putting me through such unhappiness when I was being such a good boy. The reply, as it seemed to me, was short and very much to the point: 'You have to pay.'

It is interesting that none of the people in this book made excuses for themselves when it came to paying the price of starting afresh. None of them blamed a grim childhood or the mistakes of other people, as they might so easily have done. Whatever the cost — going to jail as in the case of John Armore or yielding up his inheritance like Baba Amte — they were prepared to face it.

But the second point about restitution, which Armore's story illustrates so well, is that each act of restoration for the past also sets our feet on a new road. It not only shatters our pride and helps break our will but also gives us experience of living by God's dictates instead of our own. It is a clear sign to God that we are ready to take the risk of letting Him set His priorities in our lives.

These stories suggest that we can best find God when we go to Him in total helplessness, with the simplicity and openness of little children, not reluctantly because our lives are so busy and *our* priorities so important, full of know-how, encrusted with layer upon layer of our own way of doing things, like a load of pre-cast concrete, implicitly telling God that 95 per cent of our lives are unchangeable but that, if He is interested in the other 5 per cent, He is welcome.

We have to offer Him an empty vessel and then be willing to let Him, in His own time and way, dismantle the structure of our old lives and help us build new ones. We have to be ready to wait patiently upon Him, to listen to Him as well as talk to Him, and to obey when He requires us to break the bonds which bind us to this world.

The message of these stories is that it is never too late and we are never too far gone; that simplicity, honesty and courage are the qualities we need to find God; and that God's new world is waiting for any and every one of us when we are willing.

Paul, echoing Isaiah, declares that 'Eye hath not seen, nor

ear heard, neither have entered into the heart of man, the things which God hath prepared for them that love Him.' That is the experience of the men and women in this book. It is my experience and I believe it can be everyone's experience.